THE NEW WARRIOR CASTE

HOW RECRUITING FAILED THE ALL-VOLUNTEER FORCE

SCOTT L. EFFLANDT

Copyright © 2025 by Scott Efflandt
All Rights Reserved
Austin, Texas

Language: English

Name: Scott L. Efflandt
Title: The New Warrior Caste:
How Recruiting Failed the All-Volunteer Force
ORCID ID: 0009-0007-5190-7488

Library of Congress Control Number: 2025922888

ISBN (hardcover): 979-8-9936087-0-9, (paperback): 979-8-9936087-1-6, (e-book): 979-8-9936087-2-3

BISAC CODES: SOC04000, SOC26030, HIS027110

Subjects: civil-military gap, political science, military history, sociology

Key words: civil-military relations, conscription, all-volunteer Force AVF, military gender roles, military racial composition, military veterans, military recruiting, military sociology, philosophy of technology, professions

Published by Undaunted Service

Cover: Wendi-Lu Art & Designs

❦ Formatted with Vellum

CONTENTS

Acknowledgments	vii
CHAPTER 1 *Introduction*	1
Research Question: Are There Systemic Causes of Poor Recruiting?	5
Democracy's Recruiting Problem	6
The U.S. Recruiting Problem	7
The New Warrior Caste Hypothesis	10
The AVF as a System Outcome	12
Methodology	17
Data and Analysis	29
Summary of Chapters	31
CHAPTER 2 *A Place for Virtue: The Role of Civic Duty in the All-Volunteer Force*	35
The American Philosophy of War	38
America's National Strategy and Its Military Strategy	46
The Emergence of the AVF	54
The All-Volunteer Force in Application	65
Conclusion	73
CHAPTER 3 *The Crooked Smile: Where the New Warrior Caste is From*	75
Foundational Scholarship on AVF Composition	79
Methods and Data	89
Analysis	89
Findings	95
Conclusion	99
CHAPTER 4 *The Residual Challenge: Race, Gender, and the Changed Demographics of the All-Volunteer Force*	102
Foundational Scholarship	105
Method and Data	127
Analysis	128
Findings	144
Conclusion	147

CHAPTER 5	150

Insular Oversight: The Military Profession, Government, and Their Role in Recruiting

Foundational Scholarship	152
Methodology for Understanding the Military Profession	158
Analysis of Post-1990 American Paradoxical Trinity	166
Findings	180
Conclusion	183
CHAPTER 6	186

Deceived by Success: How Technology Made Recruits a Commodity for the All-Volunteer Force

Foundational Scholarship	188
Method for Understanding Recruiting as a Technology	197
Analysis of Technology and Recruiting	199
Findings	207
Conclusion	209
CHAPTER 7	212

Conclusion

Findings	215
Implications	217
Recommendations	222
Glossary	227
Bibliography	231
Index	251

Dedication

Lest we forget, this book is dedicated to the sergeants—from many nations—with whom I served. As brothers and sisters in arms, they taught me the true moral definition of selfless service for a cause greater than oneself. Humanity and I are in their debt for the sacrifice they made, one that can never be fully acknowledged. In a small way, this book tells the story of the U.S. Army's sergeants. They came from all walks of life and from all parts of the country with a willingness to pay the ultimate sacrifice. The non-commissioned officer not only answered the call to defend the dignity of freedom and American ideals when they enlisted, but continues serving to build the next generation of officers and sergeants. Over the decades, they built America's armed forces and perpetuated the military as an honorable institution. Unfortunately, no single work can tell their whole story.

ACKNOWLEDGMENTS

A project such as this book, if done correctly, portrays complex and important material in a simple manner that is easily understood. I hope what follows fulfills this charter, and where successful, the result came from a team effort. Should one deem that a portion of this work falls short, the cause is one of my own making. I am indebted to the counseling and tutelage of three wise scholars, who provided me with great guidance and direction from which to begin this project. I am in debt to the mentorship and counsel of Drs. Jeffrey Shaw, Luigi Bradizza, and Brian Reed. For the support and mentorship before, during, and after this project, I am especially grateful to Dr. Morten Ender for career-long mentorship. Unselfishly, he offered wise counsel and advice when I needed it.

This book would not have been possible without unnamed and indispensable reviewers who provided invaluable feedback and those who also asked insightful questions when draft portions of the research were presented at the 2023 IUS-AF&S conference and then at West Point's AKD induction ceremony. Also, the book would not have been possible without the assistance of the dutiful civil servants who provided information and answered questions, because for no other reason other than it was their duty and the right thing to do. This work does not reflect the opinion of either the Department of Defense or the Department of the Army. The analysis, conclusions, and recommendations (as well as any errors) are solely those of the author.

Deserving special recognition is my wife, Wendi. As is the case with all my work, I am immensely thankful for her unselfish, intangible, and immeasurable support.

CHAPTER 1
INTRODUCTION

> *The paratroops did not mingle with the local population; they lived on their own, outside the town and its customs, like occupants from another planet. They answered no questions, refused the wine and sandwiches that people offered them. They broke the strike, they destroyed the bomb network, but even the best-informed journalist could not tell 'what was going on.'*
>
> –Jean Larteguy, *The Centurions*

Recruiting for America's All-Volunteer Force (AVF) in 2025 marked a substantial reversal after successive abysmal recruiting years starting in 2022. Both the outgoing and incoming administrations cited the turnaround in Army recruiting as a vindication of their respective policies. Departing Democrats credited the expanded initial entry training that allowed previously unqualified applicants to enlist as the cause.[1] At the same time, incoming Republicans hailed a surge of patriotism infused by the new president as the primary causal factor.[2] The success of recent recruiting has extinguished the unresolved debate in the U.S. regarding the future viability of the AVF. When the recent history of the AVF is considered, the recruiting success of 2025 stands as an exception, and of limited significance given the other indicators of the AVF's declining viability.

On September 30th, 2022—the conclusion of the fiscal year, the U.S. Army had failed to meet its recruiting requirement by 25%, falling short by roughly 15,000 new enlistments.[3] In a similar pattern, the Navy, Air Force, and Marine Corps barely made their targets.[4] While this is the largest manpower shortage to confront the services since the end of conscription in 1973, it is in keeping with the trendline of the last several years. In the 50-year history of the All-Volunteer Force (AVF), the Department of Defense (DOD) failed to achieve its accession targets for 26 years. The accession shortfall has occurred with increasing frequency, as 9 failed recruiting missions occurred in the last 10 years.[5] Internal DOD reports predict that the services will likely continue to experience this problem for the foreseeable future.[6] The

---

1. Lolita C. Baldor, "Army to Meet 2025 Recruiting Goals in Dramatic Turnaround, Denies 'Wokeness' Is Factor," News, PBS News, January 17, 2025, https://www.pbs.org/newshour/politics/army-to-meet-2025-recruiting-goals-in-dramatic-turnaround-denies-wokeness-is-factor.
2. Alexandra Koch, "US Army Recruiting Shatters Record After Trump Election Win," News, New York Post, February 5, 2025, https://www.foxnews.com/us/army-recruiting-shatters-records-after-president-trump-election-win-inauguration. See also Joe Saballa, "US Army Recruitment Surges to 15-Year High: Hegseth," The Defense Post, February 7, 2025, https://thedefensepost.com/2025/02/07/us-army-recruitment-surges/.
3. Lolita C. Baldor, "U.S. Army Misses Recruiting Goal; Other Services Squeak By," *U.S. News and World Report*, October 1, 2022, accessed October 13, 2022, https://www.usnews.com/news/politics/articles/2022-10-01/us-army-misses-recruiting-goal-other-services-squeak-by.
4. Courtney Kube and Molly Boigon, "Every Branch of the Military Is Struggling to Make Its 2022 Recruiting Goals," NBC News, June 27, 2022, accessed June 22, 2022, https://www.nbcnews.com/news/military/every-branch-us-military-struggling-meet-2022-recruiting-goals-officia-rcna35078.
5. United States Army Recruiting Command, "Army Recruiting 1974-2021," XLSX (Fort Eustis, VA: U.S. Army Training and Doctrine Command, January 15, 2022).
6. Office of People Analytics, "State of the Recruiting Market Joint Advertising, Market Research & Studies" (Pentagon, Washington DC: Department of Defense, June 2022), 5.

severity of the military's accession problem is obscured by the fact that in 2022, the DOD only needed to recruit 61% as many people as it did in 1973, from a national population that had increased by 84 million.[7] A variety of sources offer several reasons to explain the problem; prominent rationale includes a competitive job market, mistrust of the institution, declining propensity to enlist, and a declining number of qualified applicants.[8] Following a subsequent year of exceptionally poor recruiting results, Secretary of Defense Lloyd Austin stated that the recruiting problem was years in the making and would take time to correct.[9] The DOD's responses to this military manpower shortage are ongoing and follow traditional patterns while being aware that the Southeastern United States (U.S.) is overrepresented in accessions.[10]

See also, Office of People Analytics, "Official DOD Quality of Military Availability (QMA) Study (2022)," Official (Pentagon, Washington DC: Department of Defense, June 22, 2022), 6. See also Meghann Myers, "Army, Navy and Air Force Predict Recruiting Shortfalls This Year," *Military Times*, April 19, 2023, sec. Your Military, accessed August 3, 2023, https://www.militarytimes.com/news/your-military/2023/04/19/army-navy-and-air-force-predict-recruiting-shortfalls-this-year/ (accessed August 3, 2023).

7. Accession numbers from David Coleman, "U.S. Military Personnel 1954-2014: The Numbers," Research, July 24, 2014, https://historyinpieces.com/research/us-military-personnel-1954-2014, and Office of the Secretary of Defense, "Accession Demographics of Active Component Services in the DOD from 1990-2022," XLSX, FOIA Request (Washington, DC: Department of Defense, May 24, 2023). Population figures from United States Census Bureau, "1990 State Population Estimates: Annual Time Series," ASCI (Washington, DC: United States Department of Commerce, December 29, 1999), https://www2.census.gov/programs-surveys/popest/tables/1990-2000/state/totals/st-99-03.txt, and United States Census Bureau, "2020-2022 State Population Totals and Components of Change," XLSX (Washington, DC: United States Department of Commerce, December 15, 2022), https://www.census.gov/data/datasets/time-series/demo/popest/2020s-state-total.html#v2022.

8. Lolita Baldor, "Army Sees Safety, Not 'Wokeness,' as Top Recruiting Obstacle," *Army Times*, February 12, 2023, sec. Your Army, https://www.armytimes.com/news/your-army/2023/02/12/army-sees-safety-not-wokeness-as-top-recruiting-obstacle/, (accessed February 15, 2023).

9. Jim Garamone, "After Tough Year, Military Recruiting Is Looking Up," U.S. Department of Defense, *DOD News*, December 22, 2023, accessed January 09, 2024, https://www.defense.gov/News/News-Stories/Article/Article/3625464/after-tough-year-military-recruiting-is-looking-up/https%3A%2F%2Fwww.defense.gov%2FNews%2FNews-Stories%2FArticle%2FArticle%2F3625464%2Fafter-tough-year-military-recruiting-is-looking-up%2F.

10. CFR Editors, "Demographics of the U.S. Military," *Council on Foreign Relations, Backgrounder*, July 13, 2020, https://www.cfr.org/backgrounder/demographics-us-military. See also Chuck DeVore, "States That Defend Us—Where Do Our Military Volunteers Call

Concurrently, others argue that the continued recruiting problem is another indicator of a broader civil-military divide in America.[11] Before the U.S. military's recruiting crisis in 2022, the limitation of America's volunteer force was already identified in 21st-century combat. The Global Wars on Terrorism (GWOT), beginning in 2001, exposed several problems with the AVF, including an insufficient volume of volunteers to meet personnel requirements during wartime.[12] Not being discussed publicly at the highest political level is whether failed recruiting in 2022 and during the GWOT indicate a more significant systemic problem with the AVF that threatens national security.

In the spring of 2023, the Congressional Committees of Jurisdiction convened their annual "Posture Hearings" as an oversight function to inform the annual National Defense Authorization Act (NDAA) and Defense Appropriations Act (DAA). Understandably, recruiting and personnel requirements were discussed, along with modernization, equipping, and training costs. The Army stated it sought to resolve the recruiting problem with: a) an even larger recruiting goal for 2023, b) increased enlistment bonuses, c) retaining a greater number of currently serving Soldiers, and d) increasing its marketing budget.[13] Congress accepted this testimony with little elaboration and then, in

---

Home?," *Forbes*, February 20, 2020, https://www.forbes.com/sites/chuckdevore/2020/02/19/states-that-defend-uswhere-do-our-military-volunteers-call-home/ (accessed November 02, 2022).

11. Ethan Brown, "The Ghost of GWOT Haunting the Military Recruiting Crisis" (West Point, NY: Modern War Institute, December 28, 2023), https://mwi.westpoint.edu/the-ghost-of-gwot-haunting-the-military-recruiting-crisis/.

12. Ulrich, "The Civil-Military Gap," 288, 294. See also Taylor, *The Advent of the All-Volunteer Force*, 88. See also Beth Bailey, *America's Army: Making the All-Volunteer Force*, 1st edition (Cambridge, MA: Belknap Press: An Imprint of Harvard University Press, 2009), 259. See also Phillip Carter et al., "AVF 4.0: The Future of the All-Volunteer Force" (Washington, DC: Center for a New American Security, March 28, 2017), https://www.cnas.org/publications/reports/avf-4-0-the-future-of-the-all-volunteer-force (accessed April 6th, 2023). See also Rostker, *I Want You!*, 691. See also Taylor, *Military Service and American Democracy*, 180.

13. Davis Winkie, "Army Doubles Down on Retention for Fiscal 2023 amid Recruiting Woes," *Army Times*, January 18, 2023, accessed January 19, 2023, https://www.armytimes.com/news/your-army/2023/01/18/army-doubles-down-on-retention-for-fiscal-2023-amid-recruiting-woes/.

the forthcoming NDAA, reduced the Army active force personnel authorizations (referenced as "end-strength") from 485,000 to 452,000, along with reductions in the Army National Guard and Reserve end-strength.[14] Despite a revanchist Russia and an increasingly aggressive China, Iran, and North Korea, the hearing did not address whether this size of the Army was sufficient to sustain ongoing operational requirements or anticipated war plans.

RESEARCH QUESTION: ARE THERE SYSTEMIC CAUSES OF POOR RECRUITING?

When the accession problem of 2022 is placed within the context of an increasingly reoccurring accession shortfall for a declining recruit requirement, then a broader question is called for. Are there significant systemic problems with the AVF causing the DOD's worsening recruiting problem? The supporting analysis establishes two founding conditions of the AVF. First, republicanism in matters relating to U.S. military service has consistently been a national civic virtue. The second assumption specifies the critical role of patriotism, the size of the force, and the force structure (active and reserve) necessary to enable republicanism. If analysis answers the question in the affirmative, then even a subsequent successful recruiting year (i.e., in 2025) would only represent a short-term obscuration of a problem destined to return as worse. While the AVF model was effective in the 1980s, it may no longer be "fit for purpose." Without considering whether the AVF model remains a viable military system, the U.S. risks repetitive recruiting insufficiency or discarding the volunteer force model unnecessarily—either error risks reduction in military capacity and legitimacy.

---

14. Davis Winkie, "Can the Army Fill Its Ranks?," *Military Times*, December 26, 2022, https://www.militarytimes.com/news/your-army/2022/12/26/can-the-army-fill-its-ranks/.

DEMOCRACY'S RECRUITING PROBLEM

Today, the DOD regularly has insufficient volunteers to meet its personnel requirements. With the approval of civilian oversight, the DOD is pursuing youth to join with the employment of the recruiting methods that have been refined over the 50-year history of the All-Volunteer Force (AVF). For example, the Army and Navy—the two largest service branches—have stated they plan to address recruiting shortfalls with increased recruiting resources and changed engagement methods to find those eligible and predisposed to serve and then entice qualified youth to enlist with a variety of incentives.[15] While these recruiting methods have again enabled sufficient accessions in 2025—when considered in the context of significantly reduced requirements via smaller service end-strength—these methods have become increasingly less successful and may no longer be adequate to meet the personnel requirements for military operations and national defense. Because this pattern of failing volunteer accessions is not confined to the U.S., it portends a problem for modern Western democracies.

In Europe, when Russia resumed its 2014 invasion of Ukraine in February of 2022, military personnel shortages went from a philosophical debate over civil liberties to an existential problem. Compared to America, Europe's problems with adequate military accessions developed more slowly. At the Cold War in 1990, 27 of 28 European countries (all but the U.K.) still retained conscription. Soon after, political pressure to reappropriate monies from the military to other social programs grew, and nations increasingly transformed to smaller, volunteer militaries—often focused on peacekeeping.[16] As this trend continued, the problem of securing an adequate number of volunteers increased. In Europe, the explanations for poor recruiting are just as far-ranging and inconsistent in their application as those proposed in

---

15. Diana Correll, "Navy Misses Active Duty, Reserve Recruiting Goals for 2023," *Navy Times*, October 10, 2023, sec. Your Navy, https://www.navytimes.com/news/your-navy/2023/10/10/navy-misses-active-duty-reserve-recruiting-goals-for-2023/.
16. Christopher Jehn and Zachary Selden, "The End of Conscription in Europe?: Contemporary Economic Policy," *Contemporary Economic Policy* 20, no. 2 (April 2002): 93-100, https://doi.org/10.1093/cep/20.2.93, 93-95.

the U.S.[17] Concerned about the possibility of further Russian aggression and an inability to entice a sufficient number of volunteers to meet readiness requirements, European countries—unencumbered by the cultural resentment of the 1960-70s Vietnam draft that is found in the U.S.—have begun discussing a return to conscription, or have reinstated it.[18] Since the low point of 2015, the number of Council of Europe countries with military conscription has risen to 18 of 46.[19] Additionally, other countries such as Germany and the United Kingdom are in the midst of public debates on whether they, too, should depart from their volunteer force design and reinstate conscription.[20] The changing geopolitical nature of Europe at the end of the 20th century precludes a precise statistical conclusion about military accessions, as the number of countries present changed significantly during this time. However, what is qualitatively not in dispute is that European democracies, like the U.S., have increasing difficulty securing sufficient volunteers to meet their military personnel requirements in the absence of conscription. Understanding the recruiting problem of America's volunteer army, the largest of any Western democracy, would provide a starting point for understanding this transnational cultural trend.

THE U.S. RECRUITING PROBLEM

The literature on the AVF's 2025 recruiting success and 2022 recruiting

---

17. Andrew Askew, "Conscription Is Resurging across Europe.," *Euronews*, September 1, 2023, accessed May 5, 2024, https://www.euronews.com/2023/09/01/conscription-is-seeing-a-revival-across-europe-is-that-a-good-thing.
18. "Denmark to Start Conscripting Women for Military Service," *BBC*, March 13, 2024, sec. World-Europe, 68557038, accessed May 8, 2024, https://www.bbc.com/news/world-europe-68557038.
19. Derek Brett et al., "Conscientious Objection to Military Service in Europe 2020," Annual Report (Brussels, Belgium: European Bureau for Conscientious Objection, February 15, 2021), https://wri-irg.org/sites/default/files/public_files/2021-02/2021-02-15-ebco_annual_report_2020.pdf.
20. Richard Connor, "Germany Outlines Plans for 'new' Model of Military Service," *DW News*, June 12, 2024, accessed June 17, 2024, https://link.defensenews.com/click/35700628.40142/. See also Leo Sands, "U.K. Conservatives Want Mandatory National Service. Gen Z Is Cringing.," *Washington Post*, May 27, 2024, accessed May 27, 2024, https://www.washingtonpost.com/world/2024/05/.

problem is ample; less robust is longitudinal scholarship on recruiting and whether the resulting AVF composition burdens civil-military relations. In summary, the scholarly explanations for recent recruiting problems point out differences between today and 1973; these fall into three general categories.

First, there is a low state of personal readiness among America's youth. Nowadays, rampant obesity, as well as physical and mental illness, are at unprecedented levels.[21] As part of this, individual lifestyle choices have reduced the pool of qualified youth. Instances of drug use, criminal behavior, poor education, and poor test scores have further narrowed the pool of eligible youth.[22] The aggregate effect of these factors is that only 23% of those age 18-35 are eligible to serve in the Army under the current requirements.[23]

Second, youth today lack familiarity with the military and base their perception on thirdhand sources such as traditional or social media. This makes their self-actualization as a servicemember difficult. A survey commissioned by the Department of the Army (DA) found 13 statistically significant reasons for youth not seeing the Army as relevant to them, citing concerns such as personal safety, mistrust of civilian leadership, and becoming a socially oversensitive institution.[24] These reasons were summarized succinctly by the Army in testimony to the House and Senate Armed Services Committees (HASC and SASC, respectively) as a declining number of youths are qualified to serve in the military, and this dwindling candidate pool has a declining propensity to serve.[25] While the military remains a respected institution, actual personal service in the institution suffers from declining

---

21. Erin Tompkins, "Obesity in the United States and Effects on Military Recruiting," Government, In Focus (Washington, DC: Congressional Research Service, December 22, 2020), https://crsreports.congress.gov/product/pdf/IF/IF11708, 1-3. See also Office of People Analytics, "Official DOD Quality," 3.
22. Office of People Analytics, "Official DOD Quality," 3.
23. Office of People Analytics, "State of the Recruiting Market" 4.
24. Baldor, "Safety, Not 'Wokeness.'"
25. Office of People Analytics, "State of the Recruiting Market," 2.

social prestige.[26] This enables the third reason found in the literature for poor recruiting.

There is a decline in the endorsement of the military institution by other youth influencers, such as coaches and guidance counselors. As a result, recruiters are increasingly less welcome or invited to speak at events.[27] The reduction of structured engagements between recruiters and youth at schools and public events is made worse by the youth's lack of first-hand familiarity with the military. Less than 1.0% of the population over age 18 has served in the armed forces.[28] Among current servicemembers, 80% have a relative who served, and 20-30% have a parent who served.[29] Since 2019, current servicemembers are increasingly less likely to recommend pursuing military service to their children.[30] Not surprisingly, the presence of veterans in the potential enlistee's community is statistically the strongest predictor of recruiting success.[31] The increasingly familial composition of the AVF, with the highest rate of professional inheritance since its inception, has

---

26. David L. Leal, "American Public Opinion toward the Military: Differences by Race, Gender, and Class?," *Armed Forces & Society* 32, no. 1 (October 1, 2005): 123–38, https://doi.org/10.1177/0095327X05278168, 123-124.
27. Phillip Walter Wellman, "Perception of 'Wokeness' Isn't Major Driver of Recruitment Woes, Army Former Enlisted Leader Says," *Stars and Stripes*, June 23, 2023, accessed June 26, 2023, https://www.stripes.com/branches/army/2023-06-23/sergeant-major-army-unawareness-recruitment-10526444.html.
28. Marybeth P. Ulrich, "The Civil-Military Gap," in *The All-Volunteer Force: Fifty Years of Service*, ed. William A. Taylor (Lawrence, Kansas: University Press of Kansas, 2023), 279–302," 288.
29. Rosa Brooks, "Civil-Military Paradoxes," in *Warriors and Citizens: American Views of Our Military*, ed. Jim Mattis and Kori N. Schake (Stanford, California: Hoover Institution Press, 2016), 23.
30. David W. Barno and Nora Benshal, "Addressing the U.S. Military Recruiting Crisis," War on the Rocks, March 10, 2023, https://warontherocks.com/2023/03/addressing-the-u-s-military-recruiting-crisis/.
31. Matthew S. Goldberg et al., "Geographic Diversity in Military Recruiting" (Alexandria, VA: Institute for Defense Analyses, November 2018), https://apps.dtic.mil/sti/pdfs/AD1122506.pdf, v. See also Meredith Kleykamp, Daniel Schwam, and Gilad Wenig, "What Americans Think About Veterans and Military Service: Findings from a Nationally Representative Survey," Research Reports (Santa Monica, CA: RAND Corporation2023, 2023), https://doi.org/10.7249/RRA1363-7, 20. See also Peter D. Feaver, *Thanks for Your Service: The Causes and Consequences of Public Confidence in the US Military* (New York, NY: Oxford University Press, 2023), 2, 187.

led some to consider it a warrior caste.[32] As Amy Schafer explains, "The warrior caste contributes to the familiarity gap between civilians and the military, posing a fundamental challenge to a functioning democracy by narrowing society's representation within the force."[33] Beyond being a family business, little else is understood about the warrior caste. Questions such as why the warrior caste arose, and to what degree it skews recruiting are not understood.

THE NEW WARRIOR CASTE HYPOTHESIS

The advent of the AVF in 1973 returned America's military to its historical pattern of volunteer service under conditions without precedent, namely as a superpower at the dawn of a new technological era. In the subsequent 50 years, the military has become significantly smaller and busier, and struggles with a fractured policy for the reserve force. In response, the AVF has adapted and changed, but is now increasingly struggling to recruit sufficient volunteers. The AVF's expanding density of generational members and its successful use of technology to improve lethality and management have unintentionally allowed it to become more professional and distant from government and society. What is not known is why the lack of representativeness, which strains civil-military relations, has gone unaddressed for so long, or how these patterns affect the AVF's recruiting and long-term viability.

This book argues that the DOD's recurring recruiting problems are a by-product of a more significant problem with the AVF. The cumulative effects of the AVF's 50-year market-driven approach to recruiting have allowed three social changes—a decline in republicanism as a civic virtue, declining oversight, and an expanded role of technology—to result in a new warrior caste not representative of the society it serves and recruits from. This systemic condition is not only problem-

---

32. Amy Schafer, "Generations of War: The Rise of the Warrior Caste & the All-Volunteer Force" (Washington, DC: Center for a New American Security, 2017), https://www.jstor.org/stable/resrep06443, 7. See also Mark Thompson, "An Army Apart: The Widening Military-Civilian Gap," *TIME Magazine*, October 23, 2011, https://nation.time.com/2011/11/10/an-army-apart-the-widening-military-civilian-gap/, Time.com.
33. Schafer, "Generations of War," 11.

atic for recruiting, but also for the foundational civic virtue (republican) in American society. Additionally, the new warrior caste strains civil-military relations by creating unequal citizen efficacy—or polarization—on U.S. military matters. This new warrior caste, which stands separate from society by family history and other conditions, stands in stark contradiction to the principles of democracies in general and to those of America in particular.

Some might counter that this hypothesis is unwarranted because the AVF is a value proposition in an exchange relationship, rather than a social system. This logic holds that the AVF was founded on market principles and that any problem in recruiting reflects inadequate compensation for an individual's service. In short, the solution to poor accessions is to offer potential recruits better pay and allowances. The following will explain why such a purely rational approach is in error. As a start point, a democratic military tradition—where a citizen's military service is considered both virtuous and necessary duty—was a social condition that was an essential assumption of the AVF at its inception.[34] Beyond this, accepting such narrow economic argument misses the larger democratic issue—whether a volunteer force as currently constructed remains a suitable military personnel system for today's threats. Today, the Department of Defense's budget is the largest single discretionary expenditure of the Federal Government, placing it at continued risk of reduction in the face of other competing Federal fiscal requirements. Within the Marine Corps' and Army's budgets, personnel costs are the largest single activity of their respective service (and a significant portion of the Air Force and Navy's budget)—leaving little room for large pay and allowance increases to make military service more economically attractive to youth. In 2023, the Army requested a budget of $177.5 billion (B), of which it allocated $69.1B (38.5%) for personnel costs. To put this in perspective, this represents an amount almost equal to the Army's total operations and maintenance costs of $69.7B (39.2%) and is greater than the Army's

---

34. "Report of the President's Commission on an All-Volunteer Armed Force" (Washington, DC, February 1970), Nixon Foundation, https://www.nixonfoundation.org/wp-content/uploads/2012/01/The-Report-Of-The-Presidents-Commission-On-An-All-Volunteer-Armed-Force.pdf, 6.

personnel budgets in both fiscal year (FY) 2021 and 2022—when the Army had more personnel.[35] As recruiting gets more challenging, there is less money available to entice potential recruits.

THE AVF AS A SYSTEM OUTCOME

Historically, America has predominantly relied on volunteers to fulfill its military manpower requirements, but has also used conscription during peace and wartime. For many, when confronted with an argument that the AVF lacks long-term viability, a typical heuristic response is a call for conscription as the only alternative.[36] Framing the choices as dichotomous is unwarranted. Historically, nation-states have employed eight types of military organizations—the standing volunteer force and conscription being just two forms—based on the threat, politics, social sentiment, and national ethics of the time.[37] The variable nature of these factors and their effect on the military result in a recursive social system.

Over the AVF's 50-year history, social culture, warfare, and politics have changed, causing it to evolve and change as well. Typically, the change is patterned by establishing blocks of time that are related to significant events. Carter provides such a rubric by defining four distinct periods of the AVF, labeled using popular vernacular as *AVF 1.0* through *AVF 4.0*.[38] As a starting point, *AVF 1.0* began in 1973 based on the "Report of the President's Commission to an All-Volunteer Armed Force" (the Gates Report), which specified three central assumptions for its findings. First, military service is informed by a sense of duty and patriotism. Second, individual liberty was the para-

---

35. Gabe Camarillo, "Army FY 23 Budget Overview" (Under Secretary of the Army Budget Briefing, Washington, DC, March 28, 2022), https://www.asafm.army.mil/Portals/72/Documents/BudgetMaterial/2023/pbr/Army%20FY%202023%20Budget%20Overview.pdf, (accessed March 7, 2023). See also Assistant Secretary of the Army (Financial Management and Comptroller, "FY 2023 President's Budget Highlights" (Washington, DC: Department of the Army, April 2022), (accessed March 7, 2023).
36. Louis G. Yuengert, "America's All-Volunteer Force: A Success?," *Parameters* 45, no. 4 (December 1, 2015): 53–64, https://doi.org/10.55540/0031-1723.2986, 64.
37. Eliot A. Cohen, *Citizens and Soldiers: The Dilemmas of Military Service*, 1st Edition, Cornell Studies in Security Affairs (Ithaca, NY: Cornell University Press, 1985), 15, 35-36.
38. Phillip Carter et al., "AVF 4.0."

mount American value. Third, this value was best protected by free market principles.[39] As a hedge, the Commission acknowledged that the proposed volunteer force was intended as a peacetime formation that would require both a ready and a strategic reserve (to include a ready Selective Service System)—that in the event of war, the President could request that Congress activate it for mobilization.[40] The Gates Report explicitly detailed that a volunteer force required proportional participation by Blacks as an imperative for obtaining necessary personnel and maintaining social legitimacy.[41]

Objections to the Gates Report volunteer force recommendation centered on risks to civil-military relations from: a) a loss of the republican virtue in society—where each citizen accepts a personal duty to the state; and b) that it would not represent American society, in terms of economic status, education, geography—and especially race.[42] The subsequent Presidential decision to enact the AVF in 1973 did not validate the Gates Report assumptions. The AVF immediately struggled with severe recruiting shortfall and then lingering accession problems so severe that in the spring of 1980, Chief of Staff of the Army (CSA) General (GEN) Myer publicly stated that America had a "hollow Army."[43]

The failed shift from conscription to the AVF was countered by the services' drastically changed recruiting methods that resulted in an explosion of opportunity for women, propelled by Congress's passing of the Equal Rights Amendment in March 1972.[44] This change was part of a larger social change, that David Segal argues as, "the single greatest institutional reconfiguration in industrial societies during the

---

39. "Commission on an All-Volunteer Armed Force," 6, 49.
40. Rostker, I Want You!, 79-81. See also Lawrence B. Wilkerson, "Efficiency," in The All-Volunteer Force: Fifty Years of Service, ed. William A. Taylor (Lawrence, Kansas: University Press of Kansas, 2023), 183. See also Bailey, America's Army, 227.
41. "Commission on an All-Volunteer Armed Force," 143.
42. William A. Taylor, The Advent of the All-Volunteer Force, 1st edition (New York, NY: Routledge, 2023), 59-63.
43. Bailey, America's Army, 172-173.
44. Wilbur J. Scott, Karin Modesto De Angelis, and David R. Segal, Military Sociology: A Guided Introduction (New York, NY: Routledge, 2022), 109. Because of insufficient State ratification following the Congressional ratification, the proposed 14th Amendment failed to become part of the U.S. Constitution.

past century has been the advent of the welfare state. In this way, the government assumes responsibility for guaranteeing its citizens certain minimum standards of living in terms of income, maintenance of health and nutrition, education, and housing."[45] With President Johnson's "Great Society," the military, as a government function that employed and trained millions, became a deliberate extension of the welfare state. The results of the Project 100,000 experiment, held in 1967, reverberated in discussions of the composition of the AVF and its role as an institution.[46] As David Segul explains, "military service comes to be viewed, not as an obligation of citizenship, but as a right of citizenship—the right to a job."[47] The initial integration of women and African Americans into the military was primarily driven by necessity, but the subsequent expansion of their roles (and later acceptance of homosexuals) reflected the government's desire to institutionalize social values.[48] In response to changed social perceptions and the establishment of the All-Volunteer Force, the recruiting enterprise marketed the Army to both groups as a melting pot of multiculturalism and a path to the middle class.[49] By the 1990s, the Army was comfortable portraying itself in recruiting advertising as providing for the social good, with its responsibilities to secure the nation portrayed as a muted supporting argument.[50]

By 1991, *AVF 2.0* began, having changed its recruiting methods to meet requirements and vanquished its Vietnam image with a clear

---

45. David R. Segal, *Recruiting for Uncle Sam: Citizenship and Military Manpower Policy*, 1st edition (Lawrence, KS: University Press of Kansas, 1989), 77.
46. Project 100,000 was an early effort of such deliberate engineering. It allowed for "deprived" young men who were otherwise unqualified military applicants to receive a waiver to the enlistment standards and special training to join the military. See Ambrose and Ambrose, Jr., *The Military and American Society*, 168. See also Bailey, *America's Army*, 107. See also Griffin, Jr, and Mountcastle, *The U.S. Army's Transition*, 186.
47. Segal, *Recruiting for Uncle Sam*, 95.
48. Segal, *Recruiting for Uncle Sam*, 9-11, 107-124. See also Ronald R. Krebs, *Fighting for Rights: Military Service and the Politics of Citizenship*, 1st edition (Ithaca, N.Y: Cornell University Press, 2006), 185-187. See also Taylor, *Military Service*, 165-167. See also Bailey, *America's Army*, 136-154.
49. Saucier, "Mobilizing the Imagination: Army Advertising and the Politics of Culture in Post-Vietnam America" (Rochester, New York, University of Rochester, 2010), pg, 16-31, 150-164.
50. Bailey, *America's Army*, 200-201.

victory in Kuwait. This new AVF version was marked by a pivotal shift in force structure design.[51] The fall of the Soviet empire led to political cries for a peace dividend derived from reduced military expenditures. By fiat, the military was downsized to half of its 1973 strength.[52] During *AVF 2.0,* the employment of technologically advanced weapons moved to the forefront, where the military profession continued to substitute advanced technology for a reduced number of uniformed service members.[53] Debates on force structure and size were inherently intertwined with the military theorists' above-referenced debate on the significance of a "Revolution in Military Affairs."[54] This technological shift, that unintentionally left second-order effects unobserved, rendered obsolete the role of the reserves as envisioned in 1973.[55]

Twenty years later, *AVF 3.0* resulted from the military response to the September 11, 2001, attacks. The AVF adapted to the wars in Iraq and Afghanistan, as an even smaller military had to fight unanticipated counterinsurgencies, integrate overtaxed reservists in an unplanned manner, and rely heavily on contractors.[56] The disarray of the AVF's Total Force Policy, which specifies the size and role of the two reserve forces (i.e., National Guard and Reserves) in relation to the

---

51. Moskos and Burk, "The Postmodern Military," 163–174. See also Segal, *Recruiting for Uncle Sam*, 5, 14.
52. David Coleman, "U.S. Military Personnel 1954-2014: The Numbers," Research, July 24, 2014, accessed March 7, 2023, https://historyinpieces.com/research/us-military-personnel-1954-2014.
53. Segal, *Recruiting for Uncle Sam*, 5. See also Titus Firmin, "Socioeconomics," in *The All-Volunteer Force: Fifty Years of Service*, ed. William A. Taylor (Lawrence, Kansas: University Press of Kansas, 2023), 144-154.
54. Brian Downing, *The Military Revolution and Political Change* (Princeton University Press, 1992), 11.
55. Bailey, *America's Army*, 31.
56. Jeffrey E. Philips, "Reserve Components," in *The All-Volunteer Force: Fifty Years of Service*, ed. William A. Taylor (Lawrence, Kansas: University Press of Kansas, 2023), 215. See also David Isenburg, "A Government in Search of Cover: Private Military Companies in Iraq," in *From Mercenaries to Market: The Rise and Regulation of Private Military Companies*, ed. Simon Chesterman and Chia Lehnardt, 1st edition (Oxford; New York: Oxford University Press, 2007), 91. See also "Department of Defense Personnel Reform and Strengthening the All-Volunteer Force" (Washington, DC: U.S. Government Publishing Office, December 2, 2015), https://www.govinfo.gov/content/pkg/CHRG-114shrg20957/pdf/CHRG-114shrg20957.pdf, 33-38.

active component, became painfully apparent during the wars in Iraq and Afghanistan. This condition was due in part to the politically sensitive nature of addressing needed changes and the DOD's neglect of it since the 1990s—when the role of reserves devolved into ambiguity.[57] Although highly technically and tactically competent, in the absence of the individual-ready reserve and the stand-by reserve being federalized, the military struggled to expand with retention and recruiting in sufficient numbers to meet wartime requirements. As a result, personal compensation for volunteers soared.[58]

As the wars in Iraq and Afghanistan wound down, the need to address these problems marked the proposed move to *AVF 4.0*, with Secretary of Defense Carter calling for strategic concepts on which to build the "Force of the Future." [59] This conversion is ongoing today; what *AVF 4.0* will look like and how it operates remains to be determined, but it is intended to address several criticisms of the AVF that emerged from the long wars. Today the AVF faces criticism for: a) the underrepresentation of minorities and women in many specialties, and their limited advancement to senior leadership positions, b) the Total Force being misaligned with national policy while the active-reserves overtasked and individual reserves are ineffective, c) the Active Component (AC) was too small and expensive—necessitating heavy reliance on incentives and use of contractors for combat operations, d) insufficient volunteers, an absence of citizen obligation to serve, e) inconsistent recruit quality, too small of a talent pool in civilian society, f) promoting military adventurism by political leaders.[60]

Any change from the current *AVF 3.0* to create *AVF 4.0* to address

---

57. Government Accountability Office, "Military Personnel: Reporting Additional Servicemember Demographics Could Enhance Congressional Oversight," Report to Congressional Requesters (Washington, DC: U.S. Government, September 2005), https://www.gao.gov/assets/gao-05-952.pdf, 19.
58. David Kieran, "The Patriot Penalty: National Guard and Reserve Troops, Neoliberalism, and Manufactured Precarity in the Era of Perpetual Conflict," in *Service Denied: Marginalized Veterans in Modern American History*, by John M. Kinder and Jason A. Higgins, (Amherst, MA: University of Massachusetts Press, 2022), 181–202, https://muse.jhu.edu/book/102909/, 182. See also Bailey, *America's Army*, 252.
59. Phillip Carter et al., "AVF 4.0."
60. Ulrich, "The Civil-Military Gap," 288, 294. See also William A. Taylor, *The Advent of the All-Volunteer Force*, 1st edition (New York, NY: Routledge, 2023), 88. See also Bailey,

problems with accessions will also have to respond to specific external changes. First, there has been a decline in the endorsement of military institutions by those most influential to youth.[61] Second, recruiters have a harder time gaining access to contact young people, whether in schools or at public events.[62] Third, current servicemembers are increasingly less likely to recommend the Armed Forces to their children.[63] Fourth, while the AVF has become increasingly homogeneous as "the family business," larger society has become more fractional. For example, Adrian Lewis argues that "the people" in America are no longer a single group but highly fractionalized into tribes where each, as a component of society, pursues their own relationship with the other two parts of Clausewitz's Trinity—the military and the state.[64] The net effect of these changing social conditions is that the military has become increasingly isolated from society and is viewed as "a warrior caste" while continuing to be held in contempt by political elites.[65]

METHODOLOGY

The 50-year history of the AVF shows its ability to adapt in response to changes in its environment. During the previous 50 years, the AVF has repeatedly confronted accession problems that began at its inception in 1973. However, in the +30 years after 1990, these types of actions have not been able to arrest the general decline in accessions. Most recently, as summarized above, the DOD has identified current social environ-

---

America's Army, 259. See also Carter et al., "AVF 4.0." See also Rostker, *I Want You!*, 691. See also Taylor, *Military Service and American Democracy*, 180.
61. Barno and Benshal, "Addressing the U.S. Military."
62. Wellman, "Perception of 'Wokeness.'"
63. Barno and Benshal, "Addressing the Recruiting Crisis." See also Brooks, "Civil Military Paradoxes," 23.
64. Adrian Lewis, "Military Culture," in *The All-Volunteer Force: Fifty Years of Service*, ed. William A. Taylor (Lawrence, Kansas: University Press of Kansas, 2023), 234.
65. Lionel Beehner and Daniel Maurer, "Introduction," in *Reconsidering American Civil-Military Relations: The Military, Society, Politics, and Modern War*, ed. Lionel Beehner, Risa Brooks, and Daniel Maurer (New York: Oxford University Press, 2020), 2. See also, Andrew J. Bacevich, "Tradition Abandoned: America's Military in a New Era," *National Interest*, no. 48 (July 15, 1997): 45.

mental factors that affect recruiting (i.e., low unemployment, declining propensity), while larger explanatory social changes remain missing from the discourse. This is a problematic approach to declining accessions because the U.S. military, in addition to comprising an armed force, is also an American institution. As a result, it functions in and adapts to a complex network of social structures and connections. Military accessions represent the robustness of the larger social-structural network nested within a broader pattern of civil-military relations. In the absence of a robust network that provides required accessions, the resulting "disassociation from the military on the part of large segments of society weakens society's ability to make informed judgments about military issues and influence military decision-making."[66] Thus, understanding the AVF's problems with accessions requires expanding the analysis paradigm beyond labor market factors (i.e., unemployment and wages) and instead consider the AVF as the product of a dynamic social system.

The end of mass armies and the emergence of the U.S. as a single global superpower have exacerbated the inherent tensions of American civil-military relations to create a new divide.[67] Despite the subsequent 30 years of scholarship on civil-military relations, little has been identified regarding who volunteers and whether the associated trend lines improve or detract from civil-military relations.[68] Beth Bailey eloquently identifies the return of the historical tension associated with the AVF's accessions in current civil-military relations.

> The debate about race, class, and equity, however, though legitimate and well-grounded in history, obscures a more significant question. Is it just or fair for a small number of Americans to bear the heavy burden of military defense, while the rest of the nation is asked no sacrifice? As

---

66. John Allen Williams, Stephen J. Cimbala, and Sam C. Sarkesian, *US National Security: Policymakers, Processes, and Politics*, 6th edition (Boulder: Lynne Rienner Publishers, Inc., 2022), 309.
67. Eliot A. Cohen, "Why the Gap Matters," *The National Interest*, no. No. 61 (Fall 2000), 41.
68. Donald S. Inbody and Patricia M. Shields, "Perspectives on the Afghanistan War: Commentaries on a Misadventure," *Armed Forces and Society* 49, no. 4 (October 2023): 883–92, https://doi.org/10.1177/0095327X231155220, 886.

a vast majority of Americans remain untouched by war, not even subject to the shared risk of the draft, or the obligation of service, the lives of others—those who volunteer—are disrupted or destroyed.[69]

The existing literature, research, and scholarship that frame the topic of military accessions for the AVF as part of the larger network of civil-military relations is summarized and organized here into three categories. The first category comprises the historical role of republicanism in military accessions within the U.S. The second category of scholarship identifies the responsibilities and role of accession oversight as part of effective civil-military relations. The third category examines how the expanded role of technology has affected the military, including accessions, in ways unanticipated when the AVF was created.

Role of [r]epublicanism in AVF Accessions

In America, the oversight of declaring war and raising an army follows the tradition of the ancient Greek democracies, as documented in Thucydides—it is a public and governmental affair.[70] According to Prussian philosopher Carl von Clausewitz, this republican virtue (small "r") existed as both a personal condition, and as a social resource available to the state in pursuit of its martial affairs. This duality emerged with Bonaparte and, in doing so, changed the character of the state and of war.

At the Constitutional Congress of 1787, the framers—while rejecting the direct participation of the Greeks and the monarchies of Europe—reflected upon the republic's core philosophies regarding liberty and America's victory over the British to determine how best to organize a national defense. Regarding the formation of an army, Andrew Bacevich summarizes the history and debate, "The imperatives of responsible citizenship and a lively concern for the preserva-

---

69. Bailey, *America's Army*, 259.
70. Thucydides, *The Landmark Thucydides: A Comprehensive Guide to the Peloponnesian War*, ed. Robert B. Strassler, trans. Richard Crawley, 1st ed. (Free Press, 1998), 39-126.

tion of liberty demanded reliance on a citizens' army. . . . In a republic of virtue, citizens rely upon themselves for collective defense."[71] This framework remains today, enduring temporal challenges with the imposition of compulsory military service (conscription/draft) on four occasions: the American Revolution, World War I, World War II, and the Korean War to the end of the Vietnam War.[72] The constitutional authority of conscription has been affirmed by Federal courts four times—known collectively as *Selective Draft Law Cases*—in response to challenges coming each time the draft was reinstated.[73]

Post-Vietnam, much of the debate over military service as an essential civic duty was an intra-Republican (big "R") debate over the notion of citizenship and its belief in the primacy of individual liberty.[74] The large number of veterans from WW II and Korea, as well as a host of women auxiliaries (e.g., WAVES, WAC, CDC) from these wars, provided widespread familiarity with the military among the civilian populace.[75] In 1973 civil-military relations regarding compulsory military service were strained for three reasons: a) a large number of draft-eligible males (age 18-35) exceeded the military's demand, making selective service seem increasingly like an unfair tax; b) the Vietnam War was hugely unpopular; c) a long-standing liberal argument against compulsory service gained prominence.[76] While these provided the political impetus for President Nixon to end the draft, the

---

71. Andrew J. Bacevich, "Who Will Serve?," *Wilson Quarterly* 22, no. 3 (Summer 1998): 5, https://web-s-ebscohost-com.ez-salve.idm.oclc.org/ehost/detail/detail?vid=9&sid=e39e8a18-7d6c-457c-a2ba-4d530f7c8696%40redis&bdata=JnNpdGU9ZWhvc3Qtb Gl2ZQ%3d%3d#AN=2887466&db=lfh.
72. Bacevich, "Who Will Serve?," 3-6.
73. Leon Friedman, "Conscription and the Constitution: The Original Understanding," *Michigan Law Review* 67 (1969): 1493–1552, https://scholarlycommons.law.hofstra.edu/faculty_scholarship/19, 1548-1549.
74. John Worsencroft, "The Wrong Man in Uniform: Antidraft Republicans and the Ideological Origins of the All-Volunteer Force, 1966-73," in *Service Denied: Marginalized Veterans in Modern American History*, by John M. Kinder and Jason A. Higgins, Veterans (Amherst, MA: University of Massachusetts Press, 2022), 159–78, https://muse.jhu.edu/book/102909/, 176.
75. "Commission on an All-Volunteer Armed Force," 152.
76. Bernard D. Rostker, *I Want You!: The Evolution of the All-Volunteer Force*, 1st ed. (Santa Monica, CA: RAND Corporation, 2006), 2.

majority of Americans, in principle, still supported the draft at the time of his election.[77]

While the reforms and success of the AVF restored the image of the military institution, the change did not correspond with an increased demonstration of republicanism. The military's success in the first Iraq war in 1991 vindicated it from the legacy of Vietnam and saw the emergence of "vicarious sacrifice" as a form of civic duty.[78] In the post-Cold War period—marked by an increase in peace-keeping missions and combat operations in the Middle East—enlistment did not appear as a compelling duty since the military missions appeared at worst, frivolous, and, at best, not truly of vital national interest.[79] Duty and sacrifice to the state were becoming redefined, per Charlie Moskos and James Burk: "The practice of citizenship had been turned into a mere 'simulation,' a sign with no reference."[80] In this manner, a citizen's giving to the troops—via personal offering or support for public recognition—has come to legitimize one's patriotism as adequate republican behavior.[81] Following the 9/11 attacks on the U.S., the AVF achieved initial success with the Afghanistan and Iraq invasions and enjoyed widespread societal support for the military profession, the institution, and its servicemembers. However, the concept of citizenship and military service did not revert to their pre-1991 meaning. As David Fitzgerald explained, "Aside from these acts of gratitude and occasional crises, the general public is free to ignore these unending wars. Despite good intentions, they [the acts] have not served in any mean-

---

77. John M. Kinder and Jason A. Higgins, *Service Denied: Marginalized Veterans in Modern American History* (Amherst, MA: University of Massachusetts Press, 2022), 163.
78. David Fitzgerald, David Ryan, and John M. Thompson, *Not Even Past: How the United States Ends Wars* (New York, NY: Berghahn, 2020), 108.
79. James Burk, "Thinking Through the End of the Cold War," in *The Adaptive Military: Armed Forces in a Turbulent World*, ed. James Burk, 2nd ed. (New Brunswick, NJ: Transaction Publishers, 1998), 38–45. See also Barno and Benshal, "Addressing the U.S. Military."
80. Charles C. Moskos and James Burk, "The Postmodern Military," in *The Adaptive Military: Armed Forces in a Turbulent World*, ed. James Burk, 2nd ed. (New Brunswick, NJ: Transaction Publishers, 1998), 14–31, 167.
81. Fitzgerald, Ryan, and Thompson, *Not Even Past*, 242-243. See also Kleykamp, Schwam, and Wenig, "What Americans Think," 17.

ingful way to close the gap between the all-volunteer force and the society that it serves."[82]

Oversight of the AVF System

The social contract that enables the military is subsumed under the label of *civil-military relations*; in the U.S., the government represents the former, and the senior generals the latter. Through this process, consensus is established on performance, authority, and resources—the most important of which is civilian personnel for military service. In this way, both parties share the responsibility for accessions. The following literature summary of the military profession and government oversight provides a framework for understanding their role and behavior regarding AVF accessions.

Role of the Military Profession in Accessions

In modern times, there exists an expectation that a military profession is the steward of the force and represents it in civil-military relations according to accepted normative behavior. Sociologists generally define a profession as an occupation that is of service or demand to the larger society based upon its mastery of specialized knowledge. It is perpetuated by using this knowledge to train new members and as a benchmark for regulating members' behavior. The fulfillment of these functions garners the profession's social credentials and unique authority.[83] In this way, the profession would publicly represent the military's condition compared to societal expectations. The challenge for Western states is to have a military profession that remains subservient to civilian oversight, even when political decisions are contrary to the profession's best military advice.[84] To understand how accession problems indicate a systemic problem with the AVF requires an understanding of the military profession's behavior in civil-military

---

82. Fitzgerald, Ryan, and Thompson, *Not Even Past*, 246.
83. Williams, Cimbala, and Sarkesian, *US National Security*, 204. See also Allan G. Johnson, The Blackwell Dictionary of Sociology: A User's Guide to Sociological Language, 1st Edition. (Cambridge, MA: Wiley-Blackwell, 1995), 216-217.
84. Peter D. Feaver, *Armed Servants: Agency, Oversight, and Civil-Military Relations*, Revised edition (Cambridge, MA: Harvard University Press, 2005), 6.

relations. Scholarship to date has four prominent models that argue why and how a military profession should act within a modern democracy.

Since World War II, the foundational models for the military profession have been anchored on variations of *objective* or *subjective* control of the military. Samuel Huntington argued that the best way to foster a military profession and protect civil-military relations was through *objective* control of the military. The required apolitical nature of the military profession was to be achieved through focused education on martial arts and inculcation of the military ethic to serve the state in a non-partisan fashion.[85] A functional approach to the military profession, particularly Huntington's *objective* control, features prominently in the Professional Military Education (PME) of the U.S. military.[86] In this model the profession could be expected to embrace autonomy in military recruiting. In contrast, Morris Janowitz offered that the emergence and proliferation of technology in general, and nuclear weapons in particular, required a constabulary force where the military professional officer "is *subject* [italics added] to civilian control, not only because of the rule of law and tradition but also because of self-imposed professional standards and meaningful integration with civilian values."[87] Under this model the resulting recruiting could be expected to show greater variance and diversity in accessions.

In more recent scholarship, Peter Feaver retains a Huntington-like functional professional approach to military professions but argues for Agency Theory as a new paradigm of civil-military relations. He explains that typically, in civil-military affairs, there is an agreement between political leadership (the principal) and the military (the agent)

---

85. Samuel P. Huntington, *The Soldier and the State: The Theory and Politics of Civil-Military Relations* (Cambridge, MA: Belknap Press, 1957), 80-87.
86. Lionel Beehner, Risa Brooks, and Daniel Maurer, eds., *Reconsidering American Civil-Military Relations: The Military, Society, Politics, and Modern War*, "Introduction" (New York: Oxford University Press, 2020), 6. For a detailed examination of PME, see Don Snider and Lloyd Matthews, *The Future of the Army Profession*, Revised and Expanded Second Edition, 2nd ed. (Boston, MA: McGraw Hill-Education, 2005). See also Finney and Mayfield, *Redefining the Modern Military*, 4.
87. Morris Janowitz, *The Professional Soldier: A Social and Political Portrait*, Reissue edition (New York: Free Press, 2017), 421.

on the desired ends but not the means—which is left to the judgment of the profession. When the political principal's ends are not of importance to the military agent, the military profession "shirks" its duty by knowingly pursuing the desired ends in a sub-optimal manner in one of three ways; inflated costs, making an end run (e.g., press leaks), or bureaucratic foot-dragging.[88] In this manner, the military profession—while endorsing civilian supremacy—willfully underperforms select tasks assigned by the government, which risks creating adverse outsized consequences such as a loss of trust from the public.[89] In this functional model the military professional would "shirk" engaging on systemic AVF problems, as such accessions, because the topic was "unimportant" to civilian leadership.

In contrast to these functional approaches to professions, where entry into the profession is fixed and clearly defined, Andrew Abbott argued for a systems approach with more open entry. In this way, professions operate in a dynamic and competitive environment where they will adapt or perish based on their work performance and ability to fulfill societal demands.[90] The emergence of new technologies presents a challenge to existing professional jurisdictions. According to Abbott, "the major shift in the legitimization of professions [in the last quarter of the 20th century] has thus been a shift from a reliance on social origins and character values to a reliance on scientization or rationalization of technique and the efficiency of service."[91] Such technological change can lead to the emergence of a new profession or be inculcated by an existing profession by changing how it works or the services it provides.[92] The resulting adaptation redefines the professions' jurisdictions within the larger system.[93]

The AVF's recent combat operations have demonstrated the dynamic nature of the military profession. During America's long wars

---

88. Feaver, *Armed Servants*, 62-65, 100-105
89. Mackubin Thomas Owens, "What Military Officers Need to Know About Civil-Military Relations," *Naval War College Review* 65, no. 2 (Spring 2012): 68.
90. Andrew Abbott, *The System of Professions: An Essay on the Division of Expert Labor* (Chicago, IL: University of Chicago Press, 1988), 16.
91. Abbott, *The System of Professions*, 195.
92. Abbott, *The System of Profession*, 225-227.
93. Abbott, *The System of Profession*, 267-279.

in Iraq and Afghanistan, the AVF proved insufficient; it was undersized and struggled to meet recruiting requirements at the height of the fighting in 2006. As a means of compensation for inadequate force structure, the use of contractors in the two war zones expanded at an unprecedented rate and scale.[94] In a break with tradition, war zone contractors now included a large number of Private Military Security Companies (PMSCs) that had the authority to employ lethal force on behalf of the State, an activity previously restricted to law enforcement and military professionals.[95] PMSCs operated with the acceptance of the government that: a) exempted their participation from counting against the military force manning levels, and b) sanctioned and paid for their involvement as a near-term solution to personnel shortages without addressing AVF's structural issues. Because these reasons almost compel the use of PMSCs, some argue that the jurisdiction and authority of the military profession are eroding and as a result, the military profession has less leverage with the government to address systemic AVF problems, such as accessions.[96]

Role of the Government in Accessions

Historically, the role of the Executive Branch and Congress in supporting the military was easily identified by the government's systems and initiatives to secure the necessary military force structure to protect American interests. During the draft, the government exercised its civil-military obligations for accessions through the Selective Service System (SSS), an organization outside of the DOD that had local representation in every American county.[97] The government also fulfilled its obligation indirectly. For example, in World War II, the U.S. faced significant manpower shortages from the high number of young men disqualified health problems from chronic childhood malnutrition

---

94. Taylor, *Military Service*, 173.
95. Christopher Spearin, *Private Military and Security Companies and States: Force Divided*, 1st ed. 2017 edition (New York, NY: Palgrave Macmillan, 2017), 3-15.
96. Scott L. Efflandt, "Military Professionalism & Private Military Contractors," *Parameters: U.S. Army War College* 44, no. 2 (Summer 2014): 49–60, https://doi.org/10.55540/0031-1723.2884, 59.
97. William A. Taylor, *Military Service and American Democracy: From World War II to the Iraq and Afghanistan Wars*, Illustrated edition (Lawrence, KS: University Press of Kansas, 2020), 7.

(e.g., rickets). In response to this problem, Congress passed, and President Truman signed into law the National School Lunch Act of 1946 as a matter of national security. It endures today as one of the largest public assistance programs.[98] Other examples of the government directly engaging society regarding the need for military service occurred when Congressmen and Senators made public speeches to colleagues and constituents from the floor of their respective chambers about the need to support the AVF in 1973.[99] Similarly, Congressmen and Senators contacted private companies to spur forward quality-of-life reforms deemed essential to implementing the AVF.[100] However, as Marybeth Ulrich concludes—since the 1980s, the aggregate governmental oversight of military operations and national security affairs has declined.[101] As a result, problems with military accessions go without public notice until they cannot be ignored—as happened with the recruiting shortfall of 2022.

Technology and Recruiting for the AVF

The transition from a conscripted to a volunteer force in 1973 occurred concurrently with the dawn of the computer age.[102] While these technological advantages were understood to offer vast potential, their eventual role, and second-order effects were unknown at the time. In 1972, as the Army prepared to transition to the AVF, it had two essential tasks. First, it had to incentivize enough young Americans to serve to meet national security requirements. Second, it had to reform its public image to close the divide.[103] By leveraging technology for cutting-edge weapons and marketing their utility on the battlefield, the

---

98. Gordon W Gunderson, "The National School Lunch Program: Background and Development" (Washington, DC: Department of Agriculture, 1971), https://www.fns.usda.gov/nslp/program-history, 17.
99. Robert K. Griffin, Jr, and John W. Mountcastle, *The U.S. Army's Transition to the All-Volunteer Force*, 1968-1974 (London, England: Military Bookshop Company, 2011), 229-230.
100. Griffin and Mountcastle, *The U.S. Army's Transition*, 168.
101. Ulrich, "The Civil-Military Gap," 294.
102. Manuel Castells, *The Rise of the Network Society (The Information Age: Economy, Society and Culture)*, 2nd ed., vol. 1 (Oxford, UK: Blackwell Publishers, Inc., 2000), 30.
103. Bailey, *America's Army*, 37.

Army had burnished the Vietnam image and rose to become one of America's most trusted institutions.[104] By the end of Desert Storm in 1991, having enacted extensive internal restructuring and significant quality-of-life improvements, the Army found itself with surplus manpower.[105] The subsequent collapse of the Soviet Union in 1991 and the absence of any other formidable foe created the political conditions to justify a much smaller but technologically enabled military.[106] Modern technology has made the U.S. and other militaries more lethal and thus enabled them to function with fewer people.[107] There is little question that technology continues to be an exogenous factor that shapes the military directly by its integration on the battlefield and indirectly by providing the mechanism for the military profession to manage the force.[108]

Regarding military recruiting, the literature references technology in two areas. First, in recognition that civic virtue alone would not compel sufficient enlistments, the military profession has learned the necessity of applying technology to the marketing of the AVF to meet accession requirements.[109] This result was a broader pool of applicants, which in turn exposed the second and third aspects of technology's effect on recruiting for the AVF. As a second-order effect, the success of technology in recruiting brought to the forefront an almost perennial tension over the minimum aptitude standards required for enlistment.[110] Lowering cognitive enlistment standards enlarges the applicant pool, and subsequently provides the disadvantaged post-military opportunities by virtue of exposure to military technology. At the same time, training and retaining those with low scores to use technologically advanced weapons is more difficult and costly.[111] Scholars argue

---

104. Saucier, "Mobilizing the Imagination," 195.
105. Rostker, *I Want You!*, 230-245.
106. Burk, "Thinking Through the End," 27.
107. Alex Roland, *War and Technology: A Very Short Introduction*, Illustrated edition (New York, NY: Oxford University Press, 2016), 108-114.
108. Nathan Finney and Tyrell Mayfield, eds., *Redefining the Modern Military: The Intersection of Profession and Ethics* (Annapolis, MD: Naval Institute Press, 2021), 224.
109. Bailey, *America's Army*, 175.
110. Stephen E. Ambrose and James Alden Barber, Jr., eds., *The Military and American Society - Essays and Readings*, 1st edition (New York, NY: Free Press, 1973), 168.
111. Rostker, *I Want You!*, 271, 509.

that technology, operating at an increasingly higher order of magnitude and abstraction, poses a risk to the U.S. military because the military struggles to find a sufficient volume of personnel with sufficient talent to implement the technology employed by the AVF.[112] As a point of comparison, because of the threat from, and demands of technology, Israel continues to use conscription to ensure it secures sufficient personnel with the requisite skills for the Israeli Defense Force.[113]

Third, while technological adaptation and integration are a must for the U.S. military to remain dominant, scholars warn that without deliberate stewardship, the extensive array of technologies employed by the U.S. military in peacetime and war—for the functions associated with command, control, and management—risks turning military service from a noble calling into a bureaucracy, where the members' commitment is defined by occupational responsibilities rather than a civic duty of service to the state.[114] In this manner, technology is seen as having greatly reduced the risk of bodily injury or the need for personal courage by military members, making such service simply another form of labor.[115] Should this phenomenon become commonly accepted, it can lead a society to see the military not as a profession but as a plug-and-play activity that can be easily expanded or replaced with civilian counterparts in times of need.[116]

In summary, the above references and literature provide three ways

---

112. Editorial Board, "Opinion | A Big Navy Is Vital. A More Lethal One Would Be Even Better.," *Washington Post*, January 4, 2024, accessed January 4, 2024, https://www.washingtonpost.com/opinions/2024/01/04/navy-houthis-ships-shipyards-sailors/.
113. Eyal Ben-Ari, Eitan Shamir, and Elisheva Rosman, "Neither Conscript Army nor an All-Volunteer Force: Emerging Recruiting Models," Armed Forces and Society 49, no. 1 (January 2023): 138–59, https://journals.sagepub.com/doi/10.1177/0095327X211048216.
114. Don Snider, Once Again, the Challenge to the U.S. Army During a Defense Reduction: To Remain a Military Profession, Enlarged Edition (Carlisle, PA: Strategic Studies Institute, 2013), https://a.co/d/gKNiiEp, (accessed May 21, 2023), vii, 4.
115. Morris Janowitz, *On Social Organization and Social Control*, ed. James Burk, 1st edition (Chicago: University of Chicago Press, 1991), 105-107.
116. Charles C. Moskos, John Allen Williams, and David R. Segal, eds., *The Postmodern Military: Armed Forces after the Cold War*, 1st edition (New York, NY: Oxford University Press, 1999), 3. See also Remi Hajjar and Morten Ender, "The McDonaldization in the U.S. Army: A Threat to the Profession," in *The Future of the Army Profession*, by Don Snider and Lloyd J. Matthews, 2nd Edition (Boston, MA: McGraw-Hill Education, 2005), 521.

to understand how the AVF functions as a system. First, a broad sense of republicanism as a civic duty was the foundation upon which additive economic incentives were to entice AVF participation. Second, oversight responsibility of the AVF system is shared between the government and the military profession as part of effective civil-military relations. Third, technology has both enabled greater military lethality and the marketing of military service as an economic choice. An analysis of AVF accessions over time and the related behavior of these three variables explains how the AVF has devolved into a new warrior caste.

DATA AND ANALYSIS

While other scholars have identified that military accession characteristics vary across the U.S., such work has been episodic and has not considered the causes or consequences. This research builds upon previous exploratory works to systematically evaluate U.S. military accessions over time and then consider how the identified patterns inform the current recruiting problem, civil-military relations, and the continued viability of the AVF. To test the new warrior caste recruiting hypothesis, the analysis will use a combination of qualitative and quantitative methods in an interdisciplinary manner that includes scholarship in philosophy, political science, and sociology. The application of Grounded Theory is well-suited to this exploratory examination of the relationship between technology, accessions, and civil-military relations. It is an extension of C. Wright Mills' "Sociological Imagination." In this way, information from various sources—such as statistical, experiential, ethnographic, and historiographies are, "theoretically coded" to provide an argument for improved understanding.[117]

The philosophy of Carl von Clausewitz provides the conceptual framework for organizing the web of relationships that comprise civil-military relations. Clausewitz explains that a state's capacity for war

---

117. Antony Bryant and Kathy Charmaz, eds., *The SAGE Handbook of Current Developments in Grounded Theory*, Second edition (Thousand Oaks, CA: SAGE Publications Ltd, 2019), 114-126.

results from the relationships (vertices) within a "Paradoxical Trinity."[118] In contemporary scholarship, these three forces are interpreted and represented as: a) the people, b) the commander and military, and c) the government and its policies.[119] When applied to the United States, this model is often further refined by noting that the government comprises the Executive Branch and Congress.[120] Similarly, here, "the commander" is expanded to include the chain of command and their staff as members of the military profession.

With Clausewitz as a framework to understand the significant relationships of civil-military relations that define the AVF, the New Warrior Caste hypothesis is tested with official records from Congress, DOD, DA, and the U.S. Army Recruiting Command (USAREC) and other national-level data collections. The analysis compares the accession/recruiting history of the Army enlisted personnel from 1990-2022 using information and data obtained through the Freedom of Information Act: request 23-F-0896 to the Office of the Secretary of Defense in 2023, and request 24-0200 to the U.S. Army Recruiting Command in 2024. The Army is used as an exemplar of the DOD in this analysis of military recruiting and accessions. This approach is appropriate for several reasons. First, the Army is the service with the largest personnel requirement, is most indicative of the recruiting environment for the DOD writ large, and was the service of greatest concern when the AVF was founded. Second, using the Army as the exemplar in this exploratory work testing the New Warrior Caste hypothesis reduces the number of exogenous variables (i.e., service cultural peculiarities) that need clarification. Third, an Army-centric approach is

---

118. Carl von Clausewitz, *On War*, trans. Michael Eliot Howard and Peter Paret, Reprint (Princeton, NJ: Princeton University Press, 1984), 84.
119. For examples, see James M. Dubik and Martin USA Dempsey, *Just War Reconsidered: Strategy, Ethics, and Theory*, Kindle (Lexington, Kentucky: The University Press of Kentucky, 2016)., location 1656. See also Cohen, Citizens and Soldiers, 22.
120. Marybeth P. Ulrich, "Civil-Military Relations Norms and Democracy: What Every Citizen Should Know," in *Reconsidering American Civil-Military Relations: The Military, Society, Politics, and Modern War*, ed. Lionel Beehner, Risa Brooks, and Daniel Maurer (New York: Oxford University Press, 2020), 44. See also William E. Rapp, "Crisis in the Civil-Military Triangle?," in *Reconsidering American Civil-Military Relations: The Military, Society, Politics, and Modern War*, ed. Lionel Beehner, Risa Brooks, and Daniel Maurer (New York: Oxford University Press, 2020), 192. See also Feaver, *Armed Servants*, 96-98.

robust and congruent with other scholarship that has found little statistical difference when comparing Army service personnel characteristics to the aggregate DOD coefficients.[121] With the analysis having quantified the presence of a new warrior caste—what happened, the philosophies of technology and professions are used to frame the analysis of how this happened.

SUMMARY OF CHAPTERS

To explain that the DOD's recruiting problems indicate a systemic problem with the AVF, this book expands the overview in Chapter 1. Part one, comprised of chapters 2-4, explains how the AVF system was intended to operate and then quantifies the system drift that created recruiting dysfunction and a new warrior caste. Part two, comprised of Chapters 5 and 6, considers other aspects of the AVF system. Specifically, these chapters consider why the system failed to adapt and why the rate of adaptation is declining more rapidly as time passes.

Chapter 2—*A Place for Virtue: The Role of Civic Duty in the All-Volunteer Force*. The military's legitimacy as an institution and its effectiveness as an armed force require broad national support to secure recruits. To understand this complex relationship as a system, Clausewitz's theory is applied to the AVF as a research framework to understand how it was intended to function. With this framework, the chapter argues that while an economic rationale demonstrated the feasibility of an AVF, the founding analysis also required republicanism as a civic virtue. The following analysis of the Gates Report identifies two founding conditions of the AVF regarding accessions. First, republicanism in matters relating to U.S. military service has consistently been and was assumed to remain a national civic virtue when the AVF was enacted. Second, the AVF, as conceived, required a minimum force size that was spread between the active and reserve components to enable America's civic virtue of republicanism and,

---

121. Andrea Asoni et al., "A Mercenary Army of the Poor? Technological Change and the Demographic Composition of the Post-9/11 U.S. Military," *Journal of Strategic Studies* 45, no. 4 (August 2022): 568–614, https://doi.org/10.1080/01402390.2019.1692660, 604.

provide a representative force. Initially, the AVF system adapted as these two foundational conditions changed, but accession problems of late call into question whether adequate adaptation can continue without purposeful action.

Chapter 3—*The Crooked Smile: Where the Warrior Caste is From*. The preceding chapter established the necessity of a high level of republicanism in society to have a viable volunteer force, and if it is to be seen as legitimate, it must represent American society. Is the AVF in compliance with these conditions, and if not, why are the DOD's recruiting efforts ineffective? In response to this question, this chapter argues that military recruiting suffers from a destructive cycle driven by market efficiency, resulting in a New Warrior Caste that is isolated from society in part by its lack of geographic representativeness. As this imbalanced condition increased over time, it caused a corresponding uneven geographic reduction in republicanism (where citizens participate in military service as a civic duty), further fueling nonrepresentative accessions. The net effect is twofold. First, AVF recruiting becomes increasingly difficult as it draws from an ever-smaller footprint. Second, AVF accessions based on cost-efficiency (i.e., easiest/cheapest to recruit) come at the expense of the long-term social system effectiveness derived from a representative military that increases citizen efficacy in civil-military relations. The chapter's analysis identifies that the Army's accessions from 1990 to 2022 declined in geographic representation and, in doing so, concentrated veterans in select parts of the country.

Chapter 4—*The Residual Challenge: Race, Gender, and the Changed Demographics of the All-Volunteer Force*. Having established that the AVF recruiting problem results in part from an increasingly less geographically representative of America and is overrepresented by veterans' children, the follow-on question is whether the New Warrior Caste violates other foundational conditions of the AVF. If it does not, how have the deviation(s) changed over time? This chapter argues that the New Warrior Caste is further separated from society by accessions that underrepresented Blacks and females. Despite the importance the Gates Commission placed on increasing the participation of Blacks and women in the AVF, the analysis of the Army's accessions between 1990 and 2022 finds that Black and female representation worsened. Additionally, the effects of market-based recruiting are again demonstrated as Black and female accessions by 2022 had become concentrated in the same geographic region despite their distinct geographic origins in 1990. The exception is the education level of recruits—a characteristic consistent with government engagement and intention—which saw little change.

Chapter 5—*Insular Oversight: The Military Profession, Government, and Their Role in Recruiting*. The preceding chapters demonstrate that the AVF was intended to be geographically and racially representative, but it is not today. At the same time, despite increasing opportunities for women in society and the military, the AVF's progress toward gender integration has stalled. Given that the emergence of the New Warrior Caste took over 30 years, there was ample time to reverse, or at least halt, this trend. Why have AVF accession methods been allowed to perpetuate and create a New Warrior Caste? This chapter argues that in the absence of engaged political oversight, a condition required for a balanced American Paradoxical Trinity, the military profession cannot manage the adverse and second-order effects of the AVF market-based recruiting enterprise. The qualitative analysis uses the above four military profession models to model how and under what conditions the military profession responds to meet the accession requirement in a manner that makes subsequent recruiting less representative and difficult.

Chapter 6—*Deceived by Success: How Technology Made Recruits a Commodity for the All-Volunteer Force*. The AVF's recruiting trendline shows that the drift towards a New Warrior Caste occurred over time, with increasing acceleration. Ineffective political and military stewardship explains why the AVF system failed to adapt, but not the nonlinear rate of change. This chapter argues that the computer/technology revolution of the 1980s changed the process of military accessions in ways the Gates Commission had not foreseen when it advocated for an increased recruiting enterprise for the AVF. The analysis shows that military recruiting has become a technology that, in the current system, measures success by the volume of accessions without regard to the foundational conditions deemed necessary for an all-volunteer force. Technology, when considered as a social phenomenon, explains that the initial success of marketing technology resulted in a societal shift to "supporting the troops" as sufficient fulfillment of the traditional republican virtue of actual shared service.

Chapter 7—*Conclusion*. As a book summary, this chapter integrates the findings from the preceding chapters and identifies some of their implications. It offers potential recommendations for consideration to address the identified problems. It closes with possible directions for further scholarship, not the least of which is whether this condition of non-representative accessions has hampered the militaries of other democracies.

CHAPTER 2
A PLACE FOR VIRTUE: THE ROLE OF CIVIC DUTY IN THE ALL-VOLUNTEER FORCE

> *Citizenship is an attitude, a state of mind, an emotional conviction that the whole is greater than the part . . . that the part should be humbly proud to sacrifice his self that the whole may live.*
>
> –Jean V. Dubois (philosophy teacher), *Starship Troopers*

AS AN UNWANTED EXCLAMATION POINT TO THE RECRUITING SHORTFALLS that befell the All-Volunteer Force (AVF) on its 50th anniversary in 2022, the Department of Defense (DOD) announced that the poor recruiting trend was perpetuated for fiscal year 2023.[1] Featured prominently in

---

1. The exceptions to DOD FY 23 recruiting shortfalls are the USMC and the very small Space Force, which met their recruiting goals. Dave Philipps, "U.S. Army, Navy, and Air Force Struggle for Recruits. The Marines Have Plenty," The New York Times, October 17, 2023, sec. U.S., https://www.nytimes.com/2023/10/17/us/marines-army-recruits.html. See also Thomas Novelly et al., "Big Bonuses, Relaxed Policies, New Slogan: None of It Saved the Military from a Recruiting Crisis in 2023 | Military.Com," Military Times, October 17, 2023, https://www.military.com/daily-news/2023/10/13/big-bonuses-relaxed-policies-new-slogan-none-of-it-saved-military-recruiting-crisis-2023.html?utm_

the announcements was the Army—the fulcrum of the AVF and most susceptible to changes in the recruiting environment—who nuanced its numbers in a separate press release. The Army announced that in fiscal year (FY) 2023, it had achieved its personnel target with 55,000 accessions and historically high retention of current Soldiers but acknowledged it fell short by 10,000 of its goal of 65,000 non-prior service (NPS) accessions. As a warning to future potential recruiting problems, the Army revealed that it had only 4,600 recruits under contract for induction next year under the Delayed Entry Program (DEP). Acknowledging that recruiting challenges are likely to perpetuate, the Secretary of the Army disclosed further force structure cuts.[2] In an accompanying press release, the Army announced five recruiting-related changes that included increased use of analytical technology and expansion of the U.S. Army Recruiting Command (USAREC) to a 3-star command.[3] Not mentioned in the press release was that the Army's "recruiting success" was also enabled by an accession requirement lower than 2022—a consequence of Congressionally directed end-strength reductions based on 2022's failed recruiting. Thus, recent problems with recruiting for the AVF are not an outlier. For national security reasons and civil-military relations, the causes of this recruiting crisis require identification and discussion.

After 50 years of an AVF, the debate on its future effectiveness is ongoing; there are concerns that the current system does not adequately resource military personnel requirements. Pundits point out that the recruiting problem exists even though wages for first-term enlistees are more competitive this decade than at any time in the past.

---

campaign=dfn-ebb&utm_medium=email&utm_source=sailthru&SToverlay=2002c2d9-c344-4bbb-8610-e5794efcfa7d.

2. Ashley Roque, "Army's Wormuth: Congress Will Soon Hear Plans to Revamp Force Structure, Trim SOF," Breaking Defense (blog), October 3, 2023, https://breakingdefense.sites.breakingmedia.com/2023/10/armys-wormuth-congress-will-soon-hear-plans-to-revamp-force-structure-trim-sof/, (accessed 04 Oct 23). See also Davis Winkie, "Exclusive: Army Secretary Talks Force Structure Cuts, SOF 'Reform,'" Army Times, June 28, 2023, sec. Your Army, https://www.armytimes.com/news/your-army/2023/06/28/exclusive-army-secretary-talks-force-structure-cuts-sof-reform/.

3. "Army Announces Transformation of Its Recruiting Enterprise" (U.S. Army Public Affairs, October 3, 2023), https://www.army.mil/article/270458/army_announces_transformation_of_its_recruiting_enterprise, (accessed 03 Oct 2023).

The Congressional Budget Office pegged military compensation at the height of the Iraq and Afghanistan wars at the 70th percentile of civilian wages.[4] Some argue that Milton Friedman's economic analysis, upon which the AVF was based, lacks contemporary validity.[5] Notable scholar of civil-military relations, Peter Feaver, offers that the success of the AVF to date owes more to the vigilance of scholars and military professionals than to its structural design and procedures. Because of this, there is a renewed need for a critical examination of America's current civil-military problems, which includes accessions.[6] The calls for America to return to the draft are premature as they assume that the draft is the only alternative to the AVF and that the AVF is flawed beyond adaptation. Arguments for a return to conscription fail to consider whether the AVF is being operated as intended and whether conscription is appropriate for America in the 21st century with its technology-driven economy and battlefield. Before calling for a return to conscription, it is better to ask whether the AVF's is functioning as intended. If not, what were the causes of the change that rendered the AVF ineffective? Answering these preliminary questions requires an understanding of AVF's history and the factors that shaped its design and subsequent adaptations.

This chapter argues that while an economic rationale demonstrated the feasibility of an AVF, the founding analysis also required republicanism as a civic virtue. The following analysis of the Gates Report identifies two founding conditions of the AVF regarding accessions. First, republicanism in matters relating to U.S. military service has consistently been and was assumed to remain a national civic virtue when the AVF was enacted. Second, the AVF, as conceived, required a

---

4. Brenda S. Farrell, "Military Personnel: Military and Civilian Pay Comparisons Present Challenges and Are One of Many Tools in Assessing Compensation," GAO Reports, no. GAO-10-561R Military Compensation (4/1/2010 2010): 16.
5. For example, see Michael Mai, "The All-Volunteer Army at 50 – Does Milton Friedman's Case Still Make Sense?" Real Clear Defense, July 1, 2023, https://www.realcleardefense.com/articles/2023/07/01/the_all-volunteer_army_at_50__does_milton_friedmans_case_still_make_sense_963429.html.
6. Peter D. Feaver, "Foreword," in *Reconsidering American Civil-Military Relations: The Military, Society, Politics, and Modern War*, ed. Lionel Beehner, Risa Brooks, and Daniel Maurer (New York: Oxford University Press, 2020), vii–x.

minimum force size that was spread between the active and reserve components to enable America's civic virtue of republicanism and provide a representative force. The hypothesis is supported by applying Clausewitz's "Paradoxical Trinity" to define the American philosophy of war (expressed as America's Paradoxical Trinity) and how this created the AVF as a social system. The chapter concludes with a summary of the findings and a conclusion with recommendations for future research.

THE AMERICAN PHILOSOPHY OF WAR

With the introduction of mass mobilization, the general staff, and operational maneuver (vice a traditional linear movement to battle), the Napoleonic wars proved a watershed period for Western civilization. The sum result was that conflict between states changed to become more than a computation of each party's "coefficient of forces" (a term of art for the kinetic capacity of an army), where the biggest force most often won. To explain this revolution in military affairs, Clausewitz wrote *On War*, which was published in 1832. Since then, its philosophy and explanation of a state's capacity to wage war have withstood the test of time and competing scholarship to remain a prominent paradigm for civil-military analysis. Two of his constructs are particularly applicable for understanding the current state of recruiting for the AVF: the Paradoxical Trinity and republicanism.

America's Paradoxical Trinity

The Department of Defense (DOD) is both an instrument of violence—under the direction of the Government—and an institution (as are each of its five subordinate services: Army, Navy, Air Force, Marines, and Space Force) within American society. In this capacity, the DOD's actions on and off the battlefield reverberate with society and government in a reciprocal relationship. Clausewitz codified this military dualism in early modern times with his theory of war as an extension of state policy. Conflict before the advent of the modern nation-state was relegated to the actions of "savage people," whereas modern war was a "total phenomenon" comprised of the variable relationship between three tendencies of a "Paradoxical Trinity." He described these forces as: a) primordial violence, hatred, and enmity; b) the free spirit found within chance and probability; and c) subordination as an instrument of policy and subject to reason. From these metaphysical tendencies, Clausewitz contextualized them for modern (18th century) application by saying that the three aspects are most often expressed as: a) the people, b) the commander and his army, and c) the government (see Figure 1).[7] This paradigm and its accompanying philosophy proved instrumental in the understanding of a state's capacity to wage war, which includes the ability to raise an army, and as such has remained foundational in ongoing scholarship regarding civil-military relations.

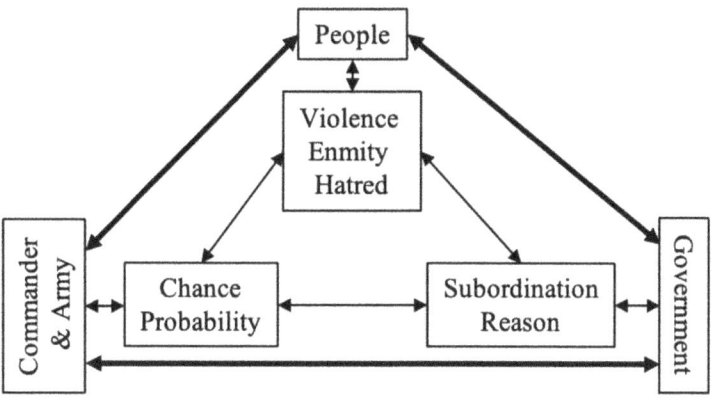

Figure 1. Clausewitz's Paradoxical Trinity

Since military accessions comprise young people from society under the government's authority, the modified Paradoxical Trinity is useful for examining recruiting for the AVF. This American Trinity is defined as: a) the government, comprised of the executive and legislative branch; b) society, with all the social characteristics of its people; and c) the military—represented as DOD or any of the four services—under the stewardship of the military profession for the active and

---

7. Clausewitz, *On War*, 89.

reserve forces (see Figure 2). The trinity can be considered a system that seeks balanced, robust, and productive (harmonizing) relationships between these three actors. Military accessions are an output of this system and an indicator of its health. The relationship between the military and society (*m-s* vertex) results from society providing recruits and the military returning veterans to society. The government-military relationship (*g-m* vertex) exists as the former provides resources and authority for recruiting (and other duties) and the standards for induction. At the same time, the latter accepts and responds to civilian control. The government-society (*g-s* vertex) relationship is the most complex relationship involved with recruiting. During conscription, the government directs society to provide recruits, and under a volunteer force, it fulfills its responsibilities by enticing military service to society. In turn, society validates and credentials these governmental actions by responding with youths to join the service, as demonstrated by the *m-s* relationship. A balanced paradoxical trinity does not ensure marital victory outright, but rather that the state has optimized its potential for what Jason Lyall defines as "battlefield performance—the degree to which a state's armed forces can generate and apply coercive violence against enemy forces in direct battle."[8]

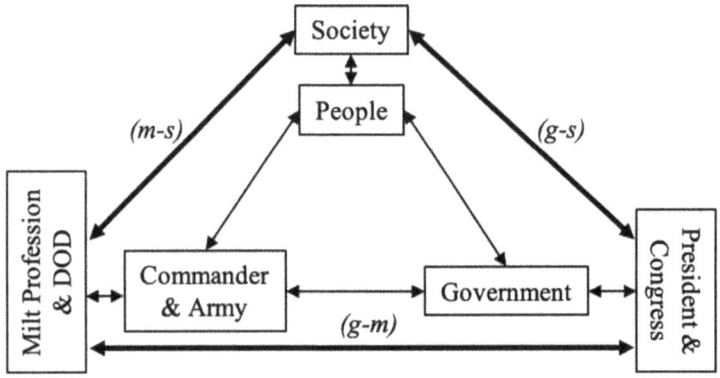

Figure 2. America's Paradoxical Trinity

---

8. Jason Lyall, *Divided Armies: Inequality and Battlefield Performance in Modern War*, Illustrated edition (Princeton, NJ: Princeton University Press, 2020), 9.

Republicanism as a Civic Virtue

Theories of security for democratic states traditionally fall into one of two camps. The Liberal school argues that the state's foremost duty is to protect individual citizens' rights and liberties. Liberalism prioritizes private life and sees the function of the military as subordinate to the pursuit of that life and protective of it. The challenge of the liberal society is that there may not be a sufficient number of people willing and committed to exercising their right of collective self-defense when the state is threatened. Alternatively, the civic-republican school argues that a citizen's engagement in public life is the first priority. In exchange for a citizen's commitment to the public good, society makes such life (and possibly death) satisfying to the individuals—the civic work is honorable and prestigious. The inherent tension in this arrangement is to ensure that the state does not suppress liberty to such an extent that the enthusiasm to protect the state is lost.[9] This debate as to which ethic has primacy informs civil-military relations and has been carried forward in modern times in two paradigms. Samuel Huntington, concerned with government encroachment and the military-industrial complex, argued for "Objective" civilian control resulting from an insulated military profession to enable a liberal society.[10] In contrast, recognizing the emerging threats of the nuclear age, Morris Janowitz argued for republicanism, where personal liberty was protected by "Subjective" civilian control, where a professional military remained aligned with—not separate from—larger society.[11]

Niccolò Machiavelli's writings in the early 1500s made him the first modern theorist of republicanism as a civic virtue within a larger society, arguing that good laws and good armies are the principal foundation of all states.[12] He explains that the citizen-soldier plays an

---

9. James Burk, "Theories of Democratic Civil-Military Relations," *Armed Forces & Society* (0095327X) 29, no. 1 (October 15, 2002): 7–29, https://doi.org/10.1177/0095327X0202900102, 11.
10. Huntington, *The Soldier and the State*, 83-95.
11. Janowitz, *The Professional Soldier*, 420-440.
12. Claire R. Snyder, *Citizen-Soldiers and Manly Warriors: Military Service and Gender in the Civic Republican Tradition* (Lanham, MD: Rowman & Littlefield Publishers, 1999), 19.

absolutely essential role in the linkage between ostensibly contradictory ideals. The citizen-soldier links the ideals where citizens govern themselves for the common good with the role of a militia that defends the citizens from external threats. Machiavelli explains, "Without one's own arms no principality is secure; indeed, it is wholly obliged to fortune since it does not have the virtue to defend itself in adversity. And one's own arms are those which are composed of either subjects or citizens or your creatures: all others are either mercenary or auxiliary."[13] While Machiavelli argued for republicanism in monarchies, the Enlightenment cast doubt on this conclusion.

The discourse of the 1600s questioned the existing political order and stratification of personal rights based on family bloodlines. Prominent in this ideological shift is the English political philosopher Thomas Hobbes, who argued "The Right of Nature," where *every* person, by virtue of their ability to reason, is entitled to personal liberty to act as they desire and in the preservation of their own life.[14] While such scholarship proved useful for rejecting the oppression of feudalism, the logic proved problematic for replacing monarchs with any political organization larger than a family. Rousseau resolved this dilemma by arguing in the 1700s that from this natural right evolved an almost sacred social right, where people benefited from a social order based on agreed covenants. In this way, people surrender their freedom to acquire the benefits of the social order. By doing this, people commit themselves to articles of association that include requiring citizens to give themselves absolutely so that the burdens are shared by all. In this way, each person is subordinate to the general will.[15] This logic of republicanism featured prominently in the political upheaval of 18th-century Europe.

According to Clausewitz, this republican virtue existed as both a personal condition and as a social resource available to the state in pursuit of its martial affairs. In this way, it is a variable within the para-

---

13. Niccolo Machiavelli, The Prince, 2nd ed. (Chicago, IL: University of Chicago Press, 1998), 57.
14. Thomas Hobbes, Hobbes: Leviathan (Cambridge University Press, 1993), 91-94.
15. Jean-Jacques Rousseau, *The Social Contract*, Modern Reprint (New York, NY: Penguin Classics, 1968), 50-59.

doxical trinity. This republican duality emerged during Emperor Napoleon Bonaparte's reign and changed the political character of the state and war. The Enlightenment increased the salience of inalienable human rights at the expense of monarchial control over its subjects and, in doing so, established that people comprised the state rather than being simply subject to it. Clausewitz documented this history by stating: "War, untrammeled by any conventional restraints, had broken loose in all its elemental fury. This was due to the people's new share in these great affairs of the state."[16] While this prose infers a strong sense of patriotism, Clausewitz was not so bold to infer that Napoleon's army was comprised entirely of citizen volunteers. Instead, he argued a theory of war where the modern state protected and perpetuated itself by having a strong military from the mobilization of the breadth of its resources, which included citizens. This contrasted with times past when a state's martial strength was a function of a class-based system based on its nobles' capacity to hire locals as soldiers. In Europe's post-revolutionary era of the 18th century, states' military strength became a function of the state's ability to mobilize its population directly. In this way, the philosophical argument that justified the state's recognition of the rights of its citizens also justified the compulsory fulfillment of the citizens' obligation to the state. Now, under this conceptualization, republicanism could be exercised in two ways. First, individuals who, because of their sense of republicanism, join the military and, in doing so, connect society with the military (m-s vertex). Alternatively, republicanism could be exercised corporately by the state when it mandates military service to members of society (g-s vertex), who in turn join the military (m-s vertex).

While most philosophers and social scientists debate a state's form of military service by anchoring their arguments against either a republican responsibility or personal liberty foundation, Eliot Cohen expands the inherent ethical tensions of governance into a third direction. By citing Clausewitz's dictum that war is a continuation of policy with other means, he explains that the state's ability to wage war (via

---

16. Clausewitz, *On War*, 593.

its military) makes its military institution also a political institution.[17] As such, politics and conceptions of ethics determine what type of military manpower method best suits any given state. Furthermore, through the influence of embedded politics, a state can move beyond a dogmatic application of a single concept of justice (i.e., individual liberty v. republican responsibility) to adapt its manpower model as a consequence of changes in the nature of war and the presence of an enemy. In this way, politics can explain why the U.S. military has continually changed forms of service (i.e., militia, conscripted, volunteer) to reconcile military necessity with social preference while retaining its belief in republicanism as a civic virtue.

As David Segal explained, "The American and French revolutions contribute to the expansion of the definition of citizenry and define participation in armed conflict as part of the normative definition of citizenship."[18] The founding fathers concurred with Washington, who felt that true citizenship and the preservation of liberty demanded a citizen's army, but that the state's authority to have an army must be restrained.[19] The newly independent nation of America codified this reasoning in its Constitution of 1787.[20] Informed by experience in the Revolutionary War, where nine of the thirteen colonies had implemented conscription, the foundational legal document of America gave states the right to raise militias and gave Congress both the right to federalize these state militias and to raise a separate national Army. In this way, Congress was a check on the President's authority to exercise the state's means of coercion at the expense of personal liberty. By design, America would be neither Athens nor Sparta, and would vary over time in its divergence from each type.

Since then, the Constitutional authority of conscription has been affirmed by Federal courts four times—known collectively as *Selective Draft Law Cases*—in response to a challenge coming each time the draft

---

17. Cohen, *Citizens and Soldiers*, 5-22.
18. Segal, *Recruiting for Uncle Sam*, 3.
19. Bacevich, "Who Will Serve?," 85.
20. "U.S. Constitution | Constitution Annotated | Congress.Gov | Library of Congress," accessed November 9, 2022, https://constitution.congress.gov/constitution/, Article 1, Section 8, Clause 12-13.

was reinstated. The first came in 1863, *Kneedler v. Lane,* where the Pennsylvania Supreme Court, in a 3-2 decision, found no legal basis for a lower court's injunction against the draft.[21] The second legal challenge came in 1918, eight months after the enactment of the Selective Draft Law of 1917, in *Arver v. United States,* and was heard by the U.S. Supreme Court. The unanimous decision cited principle (rather than legal precedent) as their justification by stating that the right of conscription is an attribute of national sovereignty and is in keeping with English and colonial history.[22] The enactment of the Selective Service Act of 1940 promptly resulted in appeals in four district courts. In each case, the right of conscription was upheld with expanded authority for use in peacetime due to the advances in technology that enabled massive surprise attacks. After the subsequent Japanese attack on Pearl Harbor on December 7, 1941, further legal challenges, and related opposition to conscription all but ceased.[23] From this point on, conscription was generally accepted as proper until the mid-1960s. The new legal challenges were resolved by the Supreme Court in the *U.S. v. O'Brien,* where the Court made it clear it considered the matter settled.[24] During the Vietnam War, some scholars rejected the *Selective Draft Law Cases* as a compelling justification because of their infrequent legal review. They argued that because conscription in America is a relatively rare phenomenon, it has not been subject to robust legal challenges and review. From 1787 until 1940—the first 150 years of the nation's history—conscription was law for just four years total, spread between the Civil War and World War I.[25]

The volume of case law aside, the consistency of the rulings over the 100-year span of legal challenges to conscription in America is insightful for two reasons. First, it shows that the state's exercise of republicanism as a civic virtue has existed as a tension between society

---

21. Leon Friedman, "Conscription and the Constitution: The Original Understanding," *Michigan Law Review* 67 (1969): 1493–1552, https://scholarlycommons.law.hofstra.edu/faculty_scholarship/19, 1548-1549.
22. Friedman, "Conscription and the Constitution," 1496-1497.
23. "Commission on an All-Volunteer Armed Force," 163.
24. "Commission on an All-Volunteer Armed Force," 166.
25. Friedman, "Conscription and the Constitution," 1552.

and the government (g-s vertex), neither of which has gained categorical deference. Second, the consistency of the court decisions demonstrates the belief that this sense of duty, recognized by the government and society, is both legitimate and necessary for the state. Taken together, one can argue that the government's exercise of republicanism in the form of the draft, over the objections of some, is legitimate if the reason is sanctioned by society. In modern times, this conclusion was shared by Chairman Gates of *The President's Commission on an All-Volunteer Force*—which argued for ending the draft in 1973 on the grounds of individual liberty—when he said, "While there is a reasonable possibility that a peacetime armed force could be entirely voluntary, I am certain that an armed force involved in a major conflict could not be voluntary."[26]

AMERICA'S NATIONAL STRATEGY AND ITS MILITARY STRATEGY

America's history of collective violence as a function of the state dates to its earliest events as separate colonies in the New World. From then to now, America employed several different military forces based on the moral authority of republicanism as a civic virtue. The Army is the most salient military part of this process. As noted above and by Russell Weigley, the military, as an institution, is inherently shaped by politics and the battlefield. The former is articulated as a national strategy, and the latter is addressed as a military strategy. Historically, U.S. national strategy reflected society's isolationist preferences and, as such, required a small standing military that expanded when required to "annihilate" (vice attrit or deter) the enemy, and then contract.[27] As a result, America's military strategy reconciled the enemy threat, social perceptions of justice, and the type of wars it fought by adapting its force design on several occasions; such as a militia, cadre-volunteer,

---

26. Bernard D. Rostker, "The Evolution of the All-Volunteer Force" (RAND Corporation, August 28, 2006), https://www.rand.org/pubs/research_briefs/RB9195.html, 1.
27. Russell F. Weigley, *The American Way of War: A History of United States Military Strategy and Policy*, Paperback Edition (Bloomington: Indiana University Press, 1977), 313-334.

and cadre-conscript. These force design changes were not linear, often oscillating from one type to another and occasionally reverting to the preceding system after the crisis had passed. This cycle would be broken when a significant geopolitical change forced a seismic national strategy adaptation in the 1950s. Studying military recruiting today requires an understanding of the military's force design history under two different national strategies and how this history informed the construction of the AVF. As illustrated by the Army, America's military force design history during the 200 years prior to the AVF is divided into two periods (early and modern) and summarized below.

America's Early Military

Although victorious over the British to gain independence, the fledgling nation's military strategy did not paint itself in glory. The Revolutionary Army relied on colonial militias that were reluctant to fight far beyond the borders of their parent colony for reasons of political principles and problems with logistics. The militias struggled with achieving mass because of a low number of volunteers and poor retention. This caused some colonies to resort to conscription. The cumulative result was that General George Washington struggled to wage a decisive campaign during the war—as Napoleon would do later and propel France to a continental power—and instead relied on a protracted war of attrition to defeat the British. Despite the shortcomings of the militia system, America's strong aversion to standing state armies perpetuated this system in the Articles of Confederation and, to a lesser degree, in the subsequent Constitution—which did relent slightly to include an additional authority to create a national army.

The sufficiency of this political-military design went untested for decades. With America engaged in small-scale Indian wars and European powers consumed by continental wars of defense and rebellion, the militia system proved adequate for the new nation's defense. When the U.S. suffered its own civil war, battlefield necessity demanded change, and Congress authorized America's first draft.[28] In

---

28. United States Congress, "An Act for Enrolling and Calling out the National Forces,

application, Union conscription has a debatable record; while providing needed manpower, the process invoked a civil divide as a result of political interference, a sense of social class as a reason for exemption, and the use of substitutes.[29] After the war, conscription ended, and America returned to a volunteer force design with a slightly larger standing professional army.

In the post-Civil War period, geographic isolation favored America, limiting the necessity for it to engage in armed conflict. As a result, the military changed little and returned to a small volunteer force while the world's economies and the methods of war were transformed by the Industrial Revolution. The drastic effects of the Industrial Revolution on warfare became most apparent in World War I, both on and off the battlefield. Born out of necessity when confronted by the emerging lethality of European powers in World War I, the U.S. military changed profoundly as a profession, in its use of industry, and its force design—by returning to conscription. When the U.S. again instituted a draft to rapidly build a military of sufficient size to aid Europe, it recognized for the first time the need to stratify who would serve based on larger national interests. As President Wilson declared at the onset, "The men who remain to till the soil and man the factories are no less a part of the army that is in France than the men beneath the battle flags."[30]

The resulting accumulation of national wealth from industrialization, especially after the 1930s, meant that the limitations of an agrarian economy and the safety of geographic distance were no longer the deciding factor in military affairs.[31] Whereas during the Civil War, the draft was intended to spur the American states to raise and equip their militias or to incentivize the wealthy to pay for individual substitutes, conscription now brought people directly into the

---

and for Other Purposes" (Congressional Record, March 3, 1863), Congressional Record. 37th Cong. 3d. Sess. Ch. 74, 75. 1863, https://glc.yale.edu/act-enrolling-and-calling-out-national-forces.

29. Timothy Perri, "The Evolution of Military Conscription in the United States," *The Independent Review* 17, no. 3 (Winter 2013): 429–39, 430-432.

30. Woodrow Wilson, "Message Regarding Military Draft" (Presidential Speeches, University of Virginia, May 19, 1917), https://millercenter.org/the-presidency/presidential-speeches/may-19-1917-message-regarding-military-draft.

31. Perri, "Evolution of Military Conscription," 437.

military for federal service by virtue of being able to fund a national army. As Timothy Perri explains, because of "the growth in the national government's relative size and power since World War I and especially since the 1930s, the problem of federal financing of the military was no longer as serious."[32] While politics continued to weigh heavily in the debate on conscription, changes in the nature of war now forced the state to adapt the republican virtue to modern circumstances. This necessity was not confined to just the U.S., as evidenced by the use of conscription by other nations at the time.

After the end of the war—because of a societal predisposition for a volunteer military, the economic necessity brought on by the Depression, and revulsion to the shocking scale of casualties from a European war—America returned to its historical pattern of a small volunteer military. Again, geography enabled isolationism, despite the new requirements of modern warfare. However, not lost on the military institution was the woeful inadequacy of the Army in 1915 and how much time and money it took to make the military proficient enough to fight in France as the Allied Expeditionary Force (AEF). While the military force suffered from under-resourcing in post-World War I America, the military profession and institution gained stature and influence. The high number of war veterans (made more salient by the protests of the Bonus Army), the public persona of battlefield heroes such as General Pershing, and the use of the military as the implementing agency for the Works Progress Administration (WPA) and the Civilian Conservation Corps (CCC) provided a means for the military to remain connected with society.[33] Although the U.S. had a small force that was not involved in a war, all three vertices of America's Trinity were active and in balance, setting the conditions to respond to the looming threat of a second global war.

---

32. Perri, "Evolution of Military Conscription," 437.
33. Debi Unger, Irwin Unger, and Stanley Hirshson, *George Marshall: A Biography*, 1st edition (New York, NY: Harper, 2014), 45-86.

America's Modern Military

America's military remained small and underfunded until the late 1930s, when it was confronted again with the complexities of the emerging conflict in Europe. Faced with the increasing aggression from the totalitarian governments of the Axis Powers, President Roosevelt (FDR) drove the passage of the Selective Service Act (known officially as the Burke-Wadsworth Act) through the House on August 12th, 1940, and then the Senate on September 16th—from a near party-line vote with steep opposition from Republicans who favored a continued isolationist foreign policy.[34] The central issue to reinstating conscription was whether having a small volunteer military could prevent a repeat of World War I, where a large number of casualties resulted from a foreign intervention that many Americans considered unnecessary. Much like America's long history of republicanism that was sometimes contested, America has a well-established modern history of *liberal internationalism* (interventionist foreign policy)—marked by active military engagement with various force designs (e.g., militia, volunteer, draft)—that was sometimes contested.[35] The debate about conscription in 1940 centered on what it foretold about the direction of American foreign policy, not on the suitability of republicanism as a civic virtue.

Unlike in times past, the required transformation of the military and society began before the Americans entered World War II. The military profession, having learned from the Spanish-American War and World War I, knew that the modern battlefield required a national effort that was not easily or rapidly mobilized.[36] Thus, Franklin Roosevelt enacted the Selective Service System (SSS), which was accompanied by a flurry of executive orders to refine the system and appease competing political demands in anticipation of wartime requirements. Chancellor Clarence B. Dykstra initially led the SSS from

---

34. Unger, Unger, and Hirshson, *George Marshal*, 106-111.
35. Mackubin Thomas Owens, "The Bush Doctrine: The Foreign Policy of Republican Empire," *Orbis* 53, no. 1 (January 2009): 23-40, https://doi.org/10.1016/j.orbis.2008.10.010, 35-39. an
36. Perri, "Evolution of Military Conscription," 436

the University of Wisconsin. He was later replaced by LTG Lewis B. Hershey, who came to personify the draft as he served for over 30 years as its head from August 1941 almost until it ended in 1973.[37] When fully operational, the Selective Service System would have 6,443 boards comprised of local citizens that were spread across every one of America's 3,070 counties.[38] As if to underscore the local nature of a national process, the induction notices opened with, "Greetings, Having submitted yourself to a local board composed of your neighbors...."[39] By the war's end, the SSS had registered 50,680,137 men and classified 36,677,024 as eligible for military service.[40] The SSS functioned outside of the military as a separate office of the U.S. government. In this manner, it coordinated with society (g-s vertex) to direct society's contribution to the military (m-s vertex). While imperfect, the American Trinity was well exercised during World War II.

From the beginning, the Selective Service System faced several justified criticisms. It suffered from the same challenges as its predecessor in World War I, including questions about whether it provided equitable sharing of the burden/duty to defend the country. There were significant variances between local boards in the granting of deferments and exemptions from service, providing the impetus for reformists to plead for a more centralized system. Also, lower-class youths were more likely to be rejected for health reasons (e.g., often resulting from chronic malnutrition), but once qualified for service, they were much more likely to be inducted.[41] By 1945, 40.3% of 23-year-old men were rejected as physically unfit; by age 34, over 50% were deemed unfit, and by age 38, disqualifications rose to 59.1%.[42] The class inequity was further magnified post-induction as the youths from lower classes were generally less qualified physically and by education, making them ineligible for more technical military special-

---

37. William A. Taylor, *The Advent of the All-Volunteer Force*, 1st edition (New York, NY: Routledge, 2023), 6.
38. Taylor, *Military Service and American Democracy*, 7.
39. Selective Service System, "Order to Report for Induction," February 13, 1943.
40. Taylor, *Military Service and American Democracy*, 8.
41. Ambrose and Barber, Jr., *The Military and American Society*, 212.
42. Taylor, *Military Service and American Democracy*, 26.

ties. Instead, they became infantrymen and suffered the brunt of fighting with high casualties and low morale.[43] In response to these criticisms, Hershey explained that local boards were preferred to any form of national centralization, as they represented a true form of democracy.[44]

Structural barriers compounded the inequality of local draft boards. In keeping with the racial segregation policies of larger America, blacks served with distinction in racially segregated units. With few exceptions (i.e., Tuskegee Airmen, 761st Tank Battalion, 92nd Infantry Division, 452nd Antiaircraft Artillery Battalion), these units were relegated to menial assignments outside of combat.[45] Black military participation was capped so as not to exceed their percentage of the general population, around 14%.[46] Women were exempt from the draft and excluded as volunteers from the four services, but were later, out of necessity, allowed to participate as auxiliaries (e.g., Women's Army Corps—WACs, Women Accepted for Voluntary Emergency Service—WAVES) where they made a demonstrable contribution.[47]

Because of these problems and the fatigue from World War II, the continuation of the SSS beyond the end of hostilities in 1945 would prove problematic. The U.S. emerged from World War II as a superpower with a burgeoning economy and its infrastructure intact. President Truman recognized the geopolitics of this position and realized that a return to an isolationist position, with its military force design of a small volunteer army, was untenable in the new world order. Instead, he declined to ask Congress for a renewal of the Selective Service Act and instead—propelled by Marshal's strong advocacy—petitioned for

---

43. Unger, Unger, and Hirshson, *George Marshall*, 200-205.
44. William A. Taylor, ed., *The All-Volunteer Force: Fifty Years of Service* (Lawrence, Kansas: University Press of Kansas, 2023), 24. In the face of increased opposition to the draft, more stringent national guidelines were published in 1969 with a televised central lottery for that year's call-ups; see Daniel E. Bergan, "The Draft Lottery and Attitudes Towards the Vietnam War," *Public Opinion Quarterly* 73, no. 2 (July 15, 2009): 38.
45. Jennifer Mittelstadt, "Military Demographics: Who Serves When Not All Serve?," in *At War: The Military and American Culture in the Twentieth Century and Beyond*, ed. David Kieran and Edwin A. Martini, War Culture (New Brunswick, NJ: Rutgers University Press, 2018), 87–107, https://www.degruyter.com/isbn/9780813584331, 91.
46. Taylor, *Military Service and American Democracy*, 28-29.
47. Mittelstadt, "Military Demographics," 97.

the authority to institute Universal Military Training (UMT); where qualified young men would enter the military for a brief period of training and return to civilian life, in a state more ready for those emergencies that required national mobilization.[48] On March 3, 1947, the Selective Service Act was allowed to expire, and Congress declined to pass UMT into law. The U.S. reverted to a dwindling volunteer force. By the end of 1947, the Army was 15% below authorized end-strength, falling short of requirements by 38,000 enlistments. With the concurrence of Congress, President Truman reinstated the draft on June 24, 1948, intending it to be a stopgap measure until the passage of UMT.[49]

The outbreak of the Korean War two years later and the recognition of approaching Soviet parity in nuclear weapons muted the calls to end conscription and squelched efforts to install a UMT system. This effectively closed the door on America's long tradition of expanding the military in times of crisis by mobilizing the citizen-soldier. The new national strategy of "deterrence" now called for a standing military in a constant state of readiness that would have to rely on conscription.[50] The Army, recognizing that the pattern of war was rapidly shifting to include conflicts below the nuclear war threshold, knew it would have to leverage America's scientific advantage to secure technologically advanced weapons in order to win the first battles against a numerically superior force.[51] The Selective Service System, now a partial mobilization tool, remained in place largely unchallenged for almost a generation. It functioned imperfectly but largely as intended, with relatively small and dynamic call-ups primarily because the draft provided a strong incentive for young men to enlist in the active or reserve components in order to exercise a degree of choice in their future military service.[52]

---

48. Unger, Unger, and Hirshson, *George Marshall*, 393.
49. Taylor, *The Advent of the All-Volunteer Force*, 11.
50. Weigley, *The American Way of War*, 366-337, 404-422.
51. Weigley, *The American Way of War*, 424.
52. Taylor, *The Advent of the All-Volunteer Force*, 8.

THE EMERGENCE OF THE AVF

Social tolerance of the draft became more nuanced when strong opposition to it emerged in the early 1960s. Philosophically, most Americans supported the draft, as evident by the fact that in 1969, a Gallup Poll found that 62% favored continuing the draft while only 31% preferred a volunteer military.[53] However, Johnson's escalation of the Vietnam War through increased troop commitment and carpet bombing—both of which drew select public ire—mobilized a constituency for presidential candidate Richard Nixon in an election cycle. The coming of age for America's baby boomers resulted in a massive demographic shift when the supply of young men to serve in the military far exceeded demand. By 1965, there were 50% more 18-year-old men than in 1955.[54] Military planners were well aware of this "pig in the python" effect, and the SSS responded with an increased number of draft deferments with an unintended result that seemed increasingly arbitrary to those not exempted.[55] In this way, military service had come to be viewed as a tax on the unlucky; any pretense of universal military service was gone. Additionally, beginning in 1963, the opposition to the draft was increasingly vocalized publicly by arguing that it was an infringement on civil liberties. Over time, the "clean-cut anti-draft Republicans" would join notable libertarian economists Milton Friedman and Martin Anderson to convince the Nixon administration to abandon the draft and move to a volunteer military.[56] These actions were moving America towards a new, unprecedented era by espousing a national strategy of deterrence that would be implemented by a military strategy without conscription.

As an extension of a campaign promise made 2½ weeks before the election, the opportunistic President Nixon appointed *The President's*

---

53. Worsencroft, "The Wrong Man in Uniform," 237.
54. Taylor, *The Advent of the All-Volunteer Force,* 20. The number of 18-year-olds available for military service would peak in 1959, but this was unknown at the time.
55. Bailey, *America's Army,* 13.
56. John M. Kinder and Jason A. Higgins, *Service Denied: Marginalized Veterans in Modern American History,* (Amherst, MA: University of Massachusetts Press, 2022), https://muse.jhu.edu/book/102909/, 160.

Commission on an All-Volunteer Force to study the feasibility of an AVF; as intended, it concluded that an end to conscription in America was both possible and preferred. The Commission, known commonly by the name of its chairman—former Secretary of Defense Thomas Gates—convened on May 15, 1969, and reported out nine months later (February 23, 1970) with unanimous concurrence from its fifteen members. Prominent on the committee were economists Milton Freedman (future Nobel Laureate) and Alan Greenspan (future Federal Reserve chairman), both of whom had long been public proponents for ending the draft.[57] Their prior work and economic arguments proved pivotal to the Commission's findings and recommendations.

The Commission's logic derived from economic arguments based on the declared premise that conscription was a violation of personal liberty as a discriminatory tax that was paid by only those few who were drafted rather than the population writ large. This belief was formalized in the report as two specified assumptions.[58] First, individual liberty was the paramount American value. Second, this value was best protected by free market principles. The Commission explained that "prevailing government accounting practices do not recognize the taxes paid in kind. Therefore, the tax on first-term servicemen never gets recorded in the budget either as revenue or as an expenditure."[59] The report argued that the result was that the costs incurred by the draftee and the nation were without documentation and, by extension, hidden from view. To quantify the value of this tax, the report detailed five hidden "costs" (see Table 1). By doing this, the Commission substantiated its argument and established the fiscal metrics to justify ending America's current period of conscription based on an economic assessment, and it stated that a free-market system was, in fact, cheaper and the best means to preserve individual liberty.[60]

---

57. Rostker, *I Want You!*, 66.
58. "Commission on an All-Volunteer Armed Force," 14-17, 23-34.
59. "Commission on an All-Volunteer Armed Force," 45.
60. Taylor, *The Advent of the All-Volunteer Force*, 63.

Table 1. Undocumented Cost of Conscription

Cost	Rationale
1. Leads to low servicemember retention	First-term re-enlistment rates for draftees pre-Vietnam were about one-fourth as high as for enlistees.
2. Promotes inefficient manpower utilization	DOD is not incentivized to pursue investing in labor-saving methods as conscription provides "cheap" manpower as actual personnel costs are undocumented.
3. Loss of value to civilian economy	Neither a lottery nor a selective system considers the lost contribution to the civilian economy that the draftee could have made.
4. Erodes ideals of patriotism and service	American youths are raised in an atmosphere where freedom and justice are held dear, the draft undermines identification with society's values.
5. Distorts personal and career plans	To avoid the draft, young men: -stay in school (college) longer -seek or avoid marriage -embrace a religious conviction -seek certain exempted occupations -relocate to another country

Source: Information from "Report of the President's Commission on an All-Volunteer Armed Force." (Washington, DC, February 1970), Nixon Foundation, 28-33.

To address the "infringement on personal liberty" argument, restore the image of the U.S. Armed Forces, reduce political tension, and provide a cost-effective alternative to the Selective Service System, the committee advocated for a volunteer force with three enabling recommendations: a) raise pay and compensation—especially for first term servicemembers, b) improve quality of life (e.g., better barracks and reduced KP), c) establish a stand-by draft system that required Congressional approval for activation.[61]

The Commission's argument that a volunteer force would be feasible and cheaper required it to meet four conditions. First, the composition of the force would remain largely unchanged in terms of demographics.[62] Second, the force would be smaller but just as effective because of increased competency from self-selection and higher retention.[63] Third, the active force would remain between two million

---

61. "Commission on an All-Volunteer Armed Force," 10. See also Griffin, Jr, and Mountcastle, The U.S. Army's Transition, 115-117.
62. "Commission on an All-Volunteer Armed Force," 12, 15.
63. "Commission on an All-Volunteer Armed Force," 41.

and three million persons.[64] Lastly, the percentage of volunteers from society for the service would remain constant, and there would be the same level of propensity to serve across society.[65] The report did not address the consequences should these essential conditions deteriorate after the enactment of a volunteer force.[66] While valid at the time of the report, each of these conditions would prove problematic over the subsequent fifty years.

Regarding the third condition, the Commission based its modeling on an active-duty force of 2 million to 3 million servicemembers. This force size was determined as appropriate for the following reasons: economy of scale, cost offset from increased personal income tax revenues of servicemembers, and sufficient to meet operational requirements until mobilization of the reserves and the activation of the recommended stand-by draft.[67] In these force structure considerations, the size of the Army was of central concern as it was the only service that consistently required draftees to meet its strength objectives. The committee's analysis projected that the Army would stabilize at 35% of the personnel in DOD (based on a historical average of the period between the Korean and Vietnam wars) and was expected to have the greatest recruiting challenge in a volunteer force.[68] The Gates Commission did not consider a smaller force feasible for the responsibilities of a post-World War II America.[69] Since then, the committee's active-duty strength condition has been invalidated as force structure has significantly declined (see Figure 3). The AVF's active-duty end-strength stayed over 2 million servicemembers until 1991. Then, in the wake of the collapse of the Soviet Union, the end-

---

64. "Commission on an All-Volunteer Armed Force," 5, 35, 125.
65. "Commission on an All-Volunteer Armed Force," 49-50.
66. For example, per the Gates Commission, having a +2m servicemember force structure with a socially representative composition were two of the required conditions for a volunteer force. These same two conditions were assumed when refuting some of the objections to a volunteer force. Logically speaking, if these two conditions ceased to exist, then they no longer serve as a valid basis for refuting objections—thus restoring the objections' validity.
67. "Commission on an All-Volunteer Armed Force," 36, 63, 97-98, 120, 154-155.
68. "Commission on an All-Volunteer Armed Force," 35-37, 41.
69. Lawrence B. Wilkerson, "Efficiency," in *The All-Volunteer Force: Fifty Years of Service*, ed. William A. Taylor (Lawrence, Kansas: University Press of Kansas, 2023), 183.

strength was reduced to less than 2 million and then continued to decline to 1.3 million in 2022.

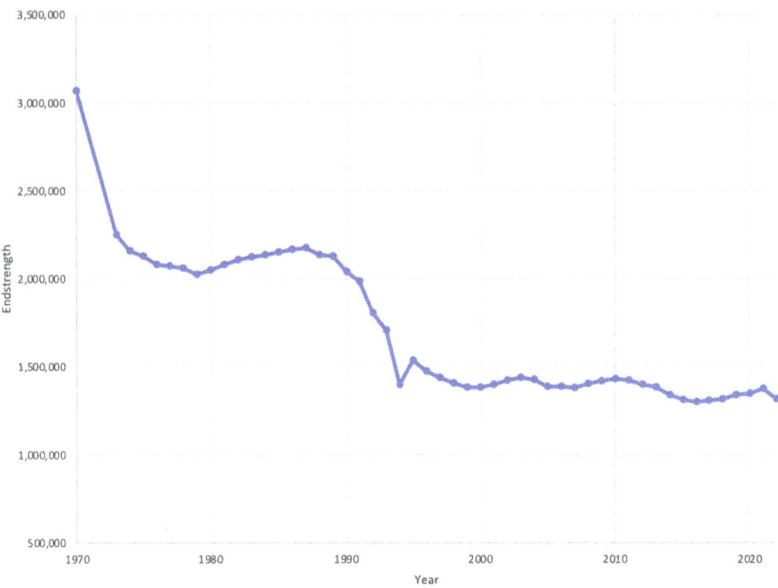

Figure 3. DOD Active-Duty End Strength 1970-2022
Source: Data from Department of Defense, "Defense Manpower Data Center."

The last condition, which was that the percentage of volunteers for military service coming from American society would continue for the AVF, proved most fragile and consequential. In countries that exercise conscription, the draft serves as the primary means for securing personnel for the armed forces. In America during World War II, such was the case, as conscription not only ensured a sufficiently sized military but also allowed for an efficient management of a large number of people during national mobilization. While arguably not a flawless system, the SSS in World War II served as a deliberate process to obtain the desired breadth and depth of social representation in the military. As General Marshal explained in a 1944 letter to General Eisenhower—who was critical of the quantity and quality of incoming Soldiers, "the magnitude of our worldwide task and the limitation of manpower require the specific assignments of every man we are authorized, and all are still assigned on the 'Troop Basis'."[70] However, in the post-war world, the requirement for a large standing Army remained but without the necessity of a national mobilization. While U.S. serviceperson s were heavily engaged in occupation duty and combat operations, such as in Korea and Vietnam, U.S. foreign policy did not require perpetuating the near-nationalized economy and enormous military. As a result, the SSS changed to assume an essential but secondary role in ensuring the services achieved their end-strength requirements.

During the Vietnam War, the threat of being drafted drove many eligible men to volunteer for military service.[71] In exchange for agreeing to a three-year voluntary enlistment (versus a two-year term of conscription), the inductee could exercise a choice of component (active or reserve), service branch (Army, Air Force, Navy, USMC), and occupation (pending availability and qualification). These "induced" voluntary enlistments were also thought to lessen the bias and political behavior of the local draft boards, which demonstrated significant variability in granting deferments.[72] The Gates Commission estimated that 77% of DOD and 65% of the Army" were "true volunteers" who entered service because of "a sense of duty, a desire for adventure or travel, society's esteem for military service, a desire for training."[73] The members felt that others wanted to join but could not afford to do so at the current low rate of pay. The economic argument concluded that pay and compensation increases for a voluntary force need only be sufficient to induce another 84,000 men to enlist voluntarily, of which 51,000 would do so for the Army, to secure the number of personnel needed above those that were already enlisted annually as "true volun-

---

70. "Troop Basis" was the title of the approved protocols that determined what civilian occupations warranted a deferment from service and how inductees' previous civilian occupations would determine their military assignment.
71. Taylor, *The Advent of the All-Volunteer Force*, 101.
72. Taylor, *Military Service and American Democracy*, 98-99.
73. "Commission on an All-Volunteer Armed Force," 49. Of note, when the Commission made cost estimates for the AVF the % of Army "true volunteers" was higher at 65% (page 50), when making cost estimates for continued selective service the "true volunteer" number was reduced to 58% (page 40). Intentionality aside, the result was a reduction in the estimated cost of implementing the AVF.

teers" (approximately 452,000).[74] This led the Commission to recommend pay and compensation increases to remove historical inequalities between first and second-term soldiers (a 50% difference) and to ensure sufficient volunteers to maintain a force of 2.5 million service members.

Today, as evidenced by increasing recruiting challenges for a smaller force, the percentage of "true volunteers" in society is far below the number the Gates Commission identified in 1970—when servicemembers were paid far less (when controlling for inflation). The presence of patriotic enthusiasm has proven to be a dynamic condition, lower today than in 1973 and declining at an increasing rate. In 1980 (with an end-strength greater than 2 million), quantitative analysis identified patriotism as the predominant reason for joining the armed forces.[75] Since 1984 the DOD has tracked volunteerism through its *Youth Propensity Poll*. The results indicate that the propensity to serve fluctuates significantly and that by 2021 the propensity to serve in the military was just half that of 25 years earlier (see Figure 4). Another indicator of a decline in "true volunteers" is evident as the U.S. Army failed to meet its recruiting requirement in 2022, falling 15,000 short of its goal of 60,000.[76] These indicators of a decline in the density of "true volunteers" motivated by patriotism and a sense of duty, demonstrate that it is subject to change with significant consequences.

---

74. "Commission on an All-Volunteer Armed Force," 50.
75. James Burk, "Patriotism and the All-Volunteer Force," *Journal of Political & Military Sociology* 12, no. 2 (1984): 229–41, https://www.jstor.org/stable/45293434, 236.
76. Lolita C. Baldor, "US Army Misses Recruiting Goal; Other Services Squeak By," *U.S. News and World Report*, October 1, 2022, https://www.usnews.com/news/politics/articles/2022-10-01/us-army-misses-recruiting-goal-other-services-squeak-by. See also Lolita C. Baldor, "Army Misses Recruiting Goal by 15,000 Soldiers," *Army Times*, October 2, 2022, https://www.armytimes.com/news/your-army/2022/10/02/army-misses-recruiting-goal-by-15000-soldiers/.

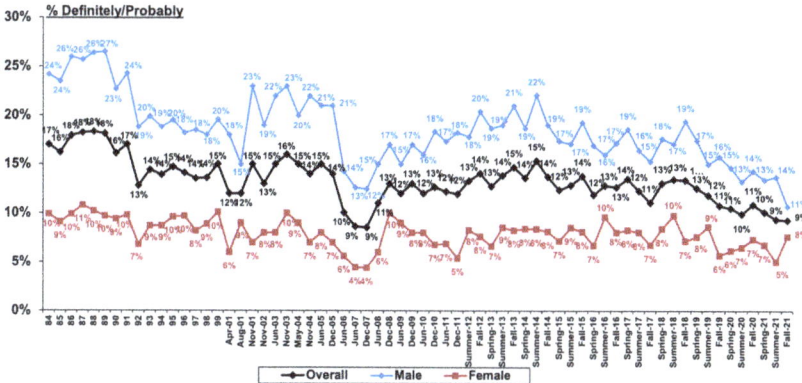

Figure 4. Historical Propensity of Youth to Serve in the Military
Source: Office of People Analytics, "Fall 2021 Propensity Update," August 9, 2022.

The committee's recommendation to end conscription (enabled by increased compensation, better quality of life, and a stand-by draft), while popular with many, was not without criticisms. The committee categorized the arguments against ending the draft as nine objections (see Table 2)—the second objection was an explicit recognition of the need to preserve republicanism as a civic virtue—and addressed them in the second chapter of their report, with references to other supporting chapters. The report stated that the elimination of SSS would be "a major social change, but it will not produce a major change in the personnel of our armed forces. The majority of men serving today are volunteers."[77] This assertion that the composition of the military as a volunteer force would remain unchanged in character and quality compared to the then-existing conscripted force is an essential part of the counterarguments to the nine objections. Continuity of the military's representative composition, as explained in the counterarguments, was derived from four *inferred* or unstated assumptions (tautologically, two of which were also required conditions of the proposed volunteer force—see above).

---

77. "Commission on an All-Volunteer Armed Force," 12.

Table 2. Initial Objections to an All-Volunteer Force

Objection	Counter Argument
1. The U.S. cannot afford an AVF.	Conscription has large hidden costs.
2. An AVF cannot expand in time to respond to a crisis.	Expansion risk offset by the reserves and a stand-by draft.
3. An AVF undermines patriotism by weakening the tradition of citizen obligation.	When not all can serve, a voluntary decision to serve is the best answer.
4. The presence of draftees guards against a military ethos that could threaten civilian control.	In the U.S. and England, there is a strong tradition of civilian control over volunteer armies.
5. Higher AVF pay will cause an over-representation of blacks, resulting in white apprehension of the military and black resentment of the burden of defense.	Analysis indicates that the racial composition will not change in a volunteer force.
6. An AVF will attract the poor, becoming a mercenary force.	Analysis indicates that the economic background composition will not change in a volunteer force.
7. An AVF will stimulate foreign military adventure by the executive branch.	The decision to commit the military will be the same regardless of force design.
8. AVF will be less effective by virtue of being filled with less skilled volunteers.	The dignity of a volunteer force will attract sufficiently skilled volunteers.
9. Defense bills will not grow to support an AVF, forcing military cutbacks.	Funding levels for Defense that reflect taxpayer preferences are in accordance with a noble democratic tradition.

Source: Information from "Report of the President's Commission on an All-Volunteer Armed Force." (Washington, DC, February 1970), Nixon Foundation, 11-22.

The first inferred assumption was that the force structure would remain greater than 2 million servicemembers. The Commission's computations were based on a recommended active-duty force structure between 2 million and 2.5 million people, 35% (700,000) of which would comprise the Army based on historical norms. In this way, the density of veterans in society would continue to connect the military with the people and the government.[78] A force of this size would ensure a military that mirrored society (i.e., race, education, aptitude, and socioeconomic status). Given the existence of a 2-million-person

---

78. "Commission on an All-Volunteer Armed Force," 151-152.

force, the following three assumptions were implied without question. The second inferred assumption was that recruiting would not affect representativeness, particularly regarding the geographic origin of accessions. While the committee acknowledged that recruiting efforts would need to increase with a volunteer force, it did not consider special measures to ensure the same geographic representation achieved by the SSS's 6,443 local draft boards spread across all of America's 3,070 counties.[79] Instead, it recommends that additional recruiters be placed in those cities with the highest induction rates.[80]

The third inferred assumption was that the military is not an agent responsible for maintaining a racially representative force. The Committee, while sensitive to issues of Blacks in a volunteer force, was dismissive of the hard and necessary work required to prevent discrimination in accessions. It offered that in the event of such problems, "citizens who are concerned with racial imbalance in this or that sector must work to open opportunities for blacks in all occupations."[81] Lastly, the committee assumed, but did not state, that pursuing volunteers would act as a form of natural selection and, as such, would ensure a representative force. Because of these assumptions, the report gave almost no consideration to deliberate actions to ensure the military would continue to be representative of the population it served, aside from addressing concerns regarding the percentage of Blacks that would serve. Ironically, the one exception to this demographic indifference is when the report dismisses the importance of veterans in a community, stating that "occupation, income, region, education, political party, age, race, and other sociological attributes" were better predictors of attitudes towards the military.[82] Since these four assumptions of a volunteer force were inferred as logical facts, the Committee's report did not address the consequences should these conditions change. Instead, the report focused on why an All-Volunteer Force was appropriate and desirable.

---

79. Selective Service System information from Taylor, Military Service and American Democracy, 7.
80. "Commission on an All-Volunteer Armed Force," 85.
81. "Commission on an All-Volunteer Armed Force," 150.
82. "Commission on an All-Volunteer Armed Force," 152.

In the end, the Gates Commission and other similar research endeavors by the Department of Defense, think tanks, and academics provided a body of scholarship and literature for President Nixon to end America's longest period of conscription.[83] In a seminal work, Bernard Rostker summarizes the five reasons why the United States moved to a volunteer force.[84] First, the norm of America's history is voluntary military service. Second, a youth bulge in the eligible population exceeded the military's requirements, removing any pretense of universality. Third, the Vietnam War was unpopular. Fourth, a long-running argument from the social elite and Republicans characterized compulsory service as immoral.[85] Finally, declining discipline in the Army led its leaders to desire change. These conditions, while significant, were more an indictment against the war in Vietnam rather than a majority opinion in America against conscription.

The Gates Commission's report provided a rationale and method to resolve opposing pressures related to creating an All-Volunteer Force; it did not represent a consensus on national defense policy. Army senior leaders (as the service most affected by this change) did not advocate the transition to a volunteer force. Like their predecessors confronted with Truman's decision to desegregate the Army, they harbored reservations based on pragmatic assessments. However, like their predecessors, in a statement of personal honor and professionalism, they kept these reservations private and worked tirelessly to implement the change directed by civilian leadership (g-m vertex).[86]

---

83. Prominent among the supporting contributions are the Astarita Report (Department of the Amy), Westmoreland's review of the profession, research from the Center for Naval Analysis at the University of Rochester, RAND Corporation, economists Walter Oi and Stuart Altman, and the offices of the Assistant Secretaries for Systems Analysis (ASA-SA) and for Manpower and Reserve Affairs (ASA M&RA). See Finney and Mayfield, Redefining the Modern Military, 6. See also Rostker, I Want You!, 67.
84. Rostker, *I Want You!*, 2. See also Rostker, "The Evolution of the All-Volunteer Force," 1.
85. Worsencroft, "The Wrong Man in Uniform," 160.
86. Taylor, *Military Service and American Democracy*, 127. See also Griffin and Mountcastle, *U.S. Army's Transition*, 211.

THE ALL-VOLUNTEER FORCE IN APPLICATION

Over the 50 years since the AVF's inception, demographics, social culture, warfare, and politics have changed. In response to these stressors, the AVF has evolved and adapted, successful in some respects while achieving marginal results by other metrics. Typically, change is examined by establishing uniform blocks of time in which historical events are summarized. However, a review done in this manner often obscures causality as it dissociates change from significant historical political events and deliberate executive decisions that altered the AVF. More useful is Carter's rubric, which illustrates how the AVF has changed in response to the environment. He defines four distinct periods for the AVF, labeled in popular vernacular as versions *1.0* through *4.0* (see Table 3).[87] At each stage, the AVF adapts to a new version in response to changes in the role of the government, the military, and society (the components of America's Paradoxical Trinity).

Table 3. Adaptation of the All-Volunteer Force

Version	Period	Environment	Design
AVF 1.0	1973-1991	-Post Vietnam, hollow Army -Cold War	-Large force -Reagan build-up -Technology in big weapons (Abrams tank, Bradley infantry carrier, Apache helicopter, Paladin artillery, Patriot air defense)
AVF 2.0	1991-2001	-USSR collapses -Peacekeeping Operations	-Small force, -"Peace Dividend" pursued -Technology is networked (C2, precision munitions)
AVF 3.0	2001-2015	-Global War on Terror -Large-scale commitment	-Too small force -Fractured the reserve forces -Heavy use of contractors -Technology diffused & cheap (IEDs, cell phones, drones)
AVF 4.0	2015-present	-Return Great Power competition -Recruiting problem	-Dwindling force -TBD....

Source: Information from Phillip Carter et al., "AVF 4.0: The Future of the All-Volunteer Force" (Washington, DC: Center for a New American Security, March 28, 2017).

---

87. Carter et al., "AVF 4.0," 2-3.

AVF 1.0

As a starting point, *AVF 1.0* began in 1973 and immediately encountered problems with readiness that, fortunately, were not made worse by challenges from a rival geopolitical power. Five years later, the AVF's continued problems obtaining sufficient and representative accessions, with higher-than-expected costs, were causing people to question its validity and moral authority. The planning assumptions of the Gates Commission seemed suspect, and there were calls for consideration of other types of force design—including but not limited to a return to conscription.[88] So severe were these problems that in 1980, General Myer, the Army Chief of Staff, publicly stated that America had a "hollow Army."[89] Taking notice of such candor, Congress reinstated the SSS by authorizing 124 employees and requiring 18-year-old men to register, but stopped short of creating active boards, a classification system, or initiating inductions.[90] In 2022, the national registration rate for men aged 18 to 25 was 84 percent.[91]

From the "hollow Army" low point, the AVF evolved through the 80s under the Reagan build-up to perform exceptionally well in the first Gulf War. It was a large force designed to fight short wars with overwhelming force. The coherence or balance of the American Trinity remained primarily enabled by the number of veterans in society and the legacy effects of the previous force structure (18 Divisions, 700,000 Soldiers) and policies. Assessments and projections of the AVF during this time were favorable. Although the age cohorts had shrunk, projections on meeting accession requirements (for a force greater than 2 million) were deemed adequate without a decline in quality. Compen-

---

88. William R King, "The All-Volunteer Armed Forces," *Military Review* LIX-- September 9 (1977): 85–94, https://www.armyupress.army.mil/Portals/7/PDF-UA-docs/King-UA.pdf, 86, 95. See also Morris Janowitz and Charles C. Moskos, "Five Years of the All-Volunteer Force: 1973-1978," *Armed Forces & Society* 5, no. 2 (January 1, 1979): 171–218, https://doi.org/10.1177/0095327X7900500201, 200-215.
89. Bailey, *America's Army*, 172-173.
90. Since reactivation in 1980, the SSS has gone unused, with comparatively few assigned personnel in a few locations. "Historical Timeline," Selective Service System, accessed October 17, 2023, https://www.sss.gov/history-and-records/timeline/.
91. Selective Service System, "Selective Service System Annual Report to the Congress of the United States," Government (Arlington, VA: Selective Service System, 2022), 7.

sation was advised to increase by 10% over the next decade to achieve this. Noted as a shortcoming at the time was a failure of the AVF to achieve ethnic representativeness, although the disparity was not significantly different than what was present during the draft.[92] During the post-war period, the social standing of the military was restored, and its battlefield competence was validated.

AVF 2.0

By 1991, having stabilized recruiting and vanquished its Vietnam image with a clear victory in Iraq, *AVF 2.0* began and marked a pivotal shift in its structure (size and relationship with the reserves) and its design (theory and method of warfare).[93] The fall of the Soviet Union led to political cries for a peace dividend from reduced military expenditures. By fiat, the military was downsized again—now half of its 1973 strength[94]—and was surprised by its growing involvement in peacekeeping operations. As part of this cost-saving effort, scores of military installations were concurrently closed under the Base Realignment and Closure (BRAC) process, as codified in statute. From 1977 to 1988, not a single major installation was closed, but since 1989, 330 installations were targeted for closure and another 173 for realignment.[95] Economic efficiency and the achievement of economies of scale served as the foundational evaluation criteria for which military bases remained. While the BRAC targets were not fully realized, 72% (364,000 of 504,000 targeted acres) of the property has left DOD control, with the remaining pending environmental remediation.[96] In this way, the military's physical footprint in America became more concentrated,

---

92. Aline O. Quester and Robert F. Lockman, "The All-Volunteer Force: Outlook for the Eighties and Nineties" (Alexandria, VA: Center for Naval Analysis, March 1984), https://apps.dtic.mil/sti/pdfs/ADA153703.pdf, 12-13.
93. Moskos and Burk, "The Postmodern Military," 163–174. See also Segal, *Recruiting for Uncle Sam*, 5, 14.
94. David Coleman, "U.S. Military Personnel 1954-2014: The Numbers," Research, July 24, 2014, https://historyinpieces.com/research/us-military-personnel-1954-2014.
95. Paul Taibl, "U.S. Base Closures Bring Post-Cold War Jitters," Forum for Applied Research & Public Policy 10 (January 15, 1995): 24–28.
96. Barry W. Holman, "Military Base Closures: Observations on Prior and Current BRAC Rounds" (Washington DC: Government Accountability Office, May 3, 2005), 1.

and its veteran network with society shrank. In the absence of a veteran population, the role of the veteran (as a parent, family member, youth mentor, or community member) in influencing a person to join the military was realized.[97]

During this time, the employment of technologically advanced weapons moved to the forefront within the profession, allowing the military to improve its management and substitute advanced technology weapons for fewer uniformed service members on the battlefield.[98] So profound was the advancement of technology on the battlefield that military theorists began to debate the possible presence and significance of a "Revolution in Military Affairs."[99] The second-order effect of this force reduction and technological shift was to render obsolete the role of the reserves as envisioned by the Commission in 1973. The active reserve force was not used to buy time for mobilization of the ready reserve; instead, it was used to buttress shortages in the active component.[100] These environmental and accompanying structural changes created vulnerabilities in the AVF that did not go unnoticed. A report to Congress noted that ongoing force reductions were not commensurate with operational requirements. Specifically, during the 1989-1997 period, the Army and Air Force's force structure was reduced by 45 percent each, the Navy by 38 percent, and the Marines by 12 percent. According to the Army's Chief of Staff, General Dennis Reimer, the Army reduced manpower by 36 percent while increasing the number of deployed operations by 300 percent.[101] In the face of declining enlistments during a strong economy and reduced retention resulting from a high operational tempo, Congress incentivized accessions with increased funding for recruiting, pay, and bonuses. These achieved the desired effect of restoring the quality and specified (smaller) quantity of recruits by 2001, while scholars noted

---

97. Government Accountability Office, "Military Personnel," 82.
98. Segal, *Recruiting for Uncle Sam*, 5. See also Firmin, "Socioeconomics," 144-154.
99. Downing, *The Military Revolution*, 11.
100. Bailey, *America's Army*, 31.
101. Michael Ryan, "Military Readiness, Operations Tempo (OPTEMPO) and Personnel Tempo (PERSTEMPO): Are U.S. Forces Doing Too Much?," Congressional Research Service (Washington, DC: The Library of Congress, January 14, 1998), http://www.congressionalresearch.com/98-41/document.php, 2, 3.

that these challenges were likely to continue.[102] By 2005, the Government Accountability Office (GAO) scored military compensation at the 70th percentile of comparably educated civilians.[103] Despite this apparent correction in recruiting, other scholars noted the emergence of structural flaws in the AVF. Condoleezza Rice, noted political scientist and later advisor to the National Security Advisor, declared: "The AVF, a daring experiment, was a poorly conceived solution to the multiple dilemmas of American military manpower policy. Its failure has been marked not by protests and riots but by a perceptible decay in the efficiency of the American armed forces and a decrease in their size."[104] While the military episodically received sufficient recruits from society (m-s vertex) to meet its accession requirements, the military's force structure was incongruent with the government's needs (g-m vertex) as defined in the National Security Strategy of Engagement.

AVF 3.0

The transition to *AVF 3.0* began in response to the AVF's performance following the attacks on September 11, 2001. The subsequent wars underscored the significance of the above-noted accession problems and forced its adaptation. The AVF, while never completely failing, struggled with the wars in Iraq and Afghanistan; where an even smaller military had to fight unanticipated counterinsurgencies, integrate overtaxed reservists in an unplanned manner, and rely heavily on contractors.[105] Although highly competent with technologically advanced command, control, and weapons, the military struggled with

---

102. Lawrence Kapp, "Recruiting and Retention in the Active Component Military: Are There Problems?," Government (Washington, DC: Congressional Research Service, February 25, 2002), https://crsreports.congress.gov/product/pdf/RL/RL31297, 34-36.
103. Government Accountability Office, "Military Personnel," 94.
104. Cohen, *Citizens and Soldiers*, 185.
105. Jeffrey E. Philips, "Reserve Components," in *The All-Volunteer Force: Fifty Years of Service*, ed. William A. Taylor (Lawrence, Kansas: University Press of Kansas, 2023), 215. See also Isenburg, "A Government in Search," 91. See also "Department of Defense Personnel Reform," 33-38.

retention and recruiting in sufficient numbers to expand as required. As a result, personal compensation soared.[106]

The DOD's neglect of the Total Force policy since the 1990s (when the role of reserves changed from an interim force until mobilization of the ready reserves)—due in part to its politically sensitive nature—became painfully apparent during the wars in Iraq and Afghanistan. As Christopher Parker explained, "Although conceptually admirable, the Abrams Doctrine overestimated the Reserve Component's ability to affect the popular will, and it was unable to prevent the fiasco in Iraq. All of this has resulted in a very sick Trinity and a Nation ill-prepared to prosecute the protracted, expeditionary campaigns it is likely to face in the future."[107] Destabilizing reserve force structure changes repeatedly served to compensate for accession and end-strength shortcomings. According to the Government Accountability Office, "the services rebalanced about 10,000 military spaces both within and between the AC and RC in fiscal year 2003 and planned to rebalance another 20,000 spaces each in fiscal years 2004 and 2005. Between fiscal years 2005 and 2009, the Army intended to rebalance over 100,000 spaces of force structure."[108] Others criticized the AVF and called for change on the grounds that when tested in a larger conflict it lacked sufficient troops, and that the hardships borne by its members and families were not equally shared across society, and the affluent and elite were less likely to have served.[109] Disregarding these existential problems, political appointees in 2023 continue to state publicly that the current size of the armed forces was sufficient to meet requirements and then add as a caveat that "the force is getting stretched thin."[110] Outside the military profession, economists

---

106. Kieran, "The Patriot Penalty," 182. See also Bailey, *America's Army*, 252.
107. Christopher Parker, "Lack of Will: How the All-Volunteer Force Conditioned the American Public," *Military Review*, October 2023, 44–56, https://www.armyupress.army.mil/Journals/Military-Review/English-Edition-Archives/September-October-2023/, 55.
108. Government Accountability Office, "Military Personnel," 19.
109. Heidi Golding and Adebayo Adedeji, "The All-Volunteer Military: Issues and Performance" (Washington, DC: Congressional Budget Office, July 2007), https://www.cbo.gov/sites/default/files/110th-congress-2007-2008/reports/07-19-militaryvol_0.pdf, vii.
110. Steve Beynon, "Soldiers Are Getting Burned Out. Army Leadership Knows It's a Problem.," Military.Com, October 16, 2023, sec. Daily News, https://www.military.com/

continued to affirm the feasibility of the AVF by explaining that the founding analysis remained valid—it was cheaper than the draft, and with additional compensation, enough personnel would come forward to meet demand.[111] Similarly, other scholars advocate for more efficient recruiting and induction systems to better realize the economists' conclusions.[112] Missing from these analyses were explanations of why recruiting has become more challenging despite unprecedented compensation, a smaller demand signal, and better retention.

AVF 4.0

As the wars in Iraq and Afghanistan wound down, it became apparent that for the U.S. to be capable of responding to future wars, significant personnel problems would need to be addressed.[113] This necessitated the call for an AVF 4.0, which began with Secretary of Defense Ashton Carter's initiative in 2015, calling for strategic concepts on which to build the "Force of the Future."[114] Later, he explained that part of the reason for changing the AVF was that it lacked geographic diversity, resulting in "too many of America's young men and women having no personal connection to our military. As a result, they give no real consideration to the possibility of joining us."[115] Since 1990, the DOD has been aware that from a regional perspective, the South has overproduced accessions, while the West, Midwest, and Northeast

---

daily-news/2023/10/16/senior-army-leaders-agree-soldiers-need-more-time-home-theres-no-plan-make-it-happen.html.
111. John T Warner and Beth J Asch, "The Record and Prospects of the All-Volunteer Military in the United States," *Journal of Economic Perspectives* 15, no. 2 (May 1, 2001): 169–92, https://doi.org/10.1257/jep.15.2.169, 187-190.
112. Richard Brady, "Recruiting the All-Volunteer Force: New Approaches for a New Era," Nonprofit, The Heritage Foundation, October 18, 2022, accessed 5 January 2023, https://www.heritage.org/military-strength/topical-essays/recruiting-the-all-volunteer-force-new-approaches.
113. Segal, *Recruiting for Uncle Sam*, 167-170.
114. Carter et al., "AVF 4.0."
115. Matthew S. Goldberg et al., "Geographic Diversity in Military Recruiting" (Alexandria, VA: Institute for Defense Analyses, November 2018), https://apps.dtic.mil/sti/pdfs/AD1122506.pdf, iii.

have underproduced.[116] The cause of this or the consequences have not been examined.

While a return to conscription is seen as an infeasible and implausible solution, adaptation to the AVF is still required.[117] The debate as to why and how is ongoing. What *AVF 4.0* will look like remains to be determined, but it should address several criticisms that emerged from the long wars. In summary, today's AVF has been criticized for: a) the underrepresentation of minorities in many specialties and their limited advancement to senior leadership positions, b) a misaligned Total Force, with the active-reserves overtasked and the individual-reserves ineffective, c) an Active Component that is too small and expensive—forcing heavy reliance on incentives and the use of contractors for combat operations, d) insufficient volunteers, an absence of citizens feeling an obligation to serve, e) inconsistent recruit quality, too small of a talent pool available in civilian society, f) enabling military adventurism by political leaders.[118] The aggregated effect of these six types of problems has led scholars to conclude that there is, in fact, a critical civil-military divide in America. As Beth Bailey eloquently explains, the presence of this divide renews discussion of the AVF's founding dilemma.

> The debate about race, class, and equity, however, though legitimate and well-grounded in history, obscures a more significant question. Is it just or fair for a small number of Americans to bear the heavy burden of military defense, while the rest of the nation is asked no sacrifice? As a vast majority of Americans remain untouched by war, not even

---

116. Matthew S. Goldberg et al., "Geographic Diversity in Military Recruiting" (Alexandria, VA: Institute for Defense Analyses, November 2018), https://apps.dtic.mil/sti/pdfs/AD1122506.pdf, 14. Authors noted that data before 1990 was incomplete and without credible sources, and thus was rejected from their analysis.
117. Jomana Amara, "Revisiting the Justification for an All-Volunteer Force," *Defense & Security Analysis* 35, no. 3 (July 3, 2019): 326–42, https://doi.org/10.1080/14751798.2019.1640425, 339.
118. Ulrich, "The Civil-Military Gap," 288, 294. See also Taylor, *The Advent of the All-Volunteer Force*, 88. See also Bailey, *America's Army*, 259. See also Carter et al., "AVF 4.0." See also Rostker, *I Want You!*, 691. See also Taylor, Military Service and American Democracy, 180.

subject to the shared risk of the draft, or the obligation of service, the lives of others—those who volunteer—are disrupted or destroyed.[119]

While Bailey identifies the inflammation of the historical tension behind current civil-military relations, it overlooks two central questions at the core of this problem. First, why do present-day elites (and their children) not respond to calls for military service? Second, what should America do about this problem?

CONCLUSION

In summary, three findings emerge by applying Clausewitz's Paradoxical Trinity to examine American civil-military relations as they relate to the current AVF recruiting crisis. First, while a sense of individual liberty has always been a defining characteristic of Americans, the preeminence of republicanism in matters relating to military service has been at the forefront of the U.S. way of war. Until World War II, the government only compelled this virtue with conscription during times of war. Post-World War II geopolitics and advances in military technology necessitated a large standing peacetime force, so conscription continued. In the 1970s, demographics, politics, and dissatisfaction with the Vietnam War caused the ascendency of liberalism in the policy of force design, but it did not diminish a national sense of republicanism as a civic virtue. The AVF was implemented in 1973 based on the justification that young Americans' republicanism could be better harnessed for military service if the military offered a sufficient wage to volunteers. Concurrently, the AVF analysis assumed that the propensity of "true volunteers" for military service under conscription would remain relatively constant in a volunteer force as an individual expression of republicanism, regardless of compensation level. The scope or breadth of this virtue 50 years later is in question. Second, the economic rationale for the feasibility of the AVF required a military greater than 2 million people to ensure a societal connection with the military as a representative force. Today, the DOD has fewer than 2

---

119. Bailey, *America's Army*, 259.

million servicemembers, there is a marked decline in the expression of republicanism as a civic virtue, and it is less representative of the United States now than in 1973 in several dimensions. Third, paradoxically, while the AVF today is smaller and better compensated than at any time in the past, it struggles with recruiting more than at any time in the past. These conditions indicate a misalignment or breakdown of America's Paradoxical Trinity regarding accessions.

There is a need for research in three areas. First, why is the decline of the civic virtue of republicanism disproportional to the reduced accession requirements for today's smaller military, and by extension, what caused its decay? Second, in what aspects does the AVF fail to meet the requirement for social representation? Third, how do the military's smaller and less representative accessions contribute to and suffer from a civil-military divide? Answers to these questions will be pursued in the following chapters.

CHAPTER 3
THE CROOKED SMILE: WHERE THE NEW WARRIOR CASTE IS FROM

> *With this enthusiasm of the majority, the few that did not like it feared to appear unpatriotic by holding up their hands against it and so kept quiet.*
>
> –Thucydides, *A History of the War*

THE RECENT MULTI-YEAR RECRUITING PROBLEM FOR THE ALL-VOLUNTEER Force (AVF) has caused much introspection among scholars and military leaders regarding whether there is a more significant, foundational problem with its design. The recent recruiting problems provided another criticism of a military personnel system that proved wanting during recent conflicts. The institution's practiced explanation for recruiting shortfalls has been that the Department of Defense competes for talent, and those most qualified for military service have several other options. The military's pat response to the obstacles that hinder the successful recruiting of said talent has been to increase compensation to entice more enlistments.[1] However, this explanation and proposed corrective measures are increasingly invalid. So significant is the recruiting problem today that General David Berger, as the Commandant of the Marine Corps, stated that "military leaders have few levers to pull to increase the number of Americans eligible for service, and the biggest and most immediate lever—lowering standards—is not one military leaders or most Americans want to pull. To effect enduring change requires understanding and addressing the declining propensity to serve."[2]

The recruiting results in 2022 were the Army's worst in terms of aggregate number inducted and in proportion to end-strength over the 50-year history of the AVF. Given that today, the military is smaller—requiring fewer accessions (see Figure 5), and servicemembers receive more in personal compensation than ever before, the cornerstone research question is why the AVF's recruiting is increasingly less effective categorically and regarding geography. While insufficient compensation may explain part of the recruiting problem, this seems inadequate given the magnitude of the problem, and the current accession requirement is less than in past times. Historically, not all volunteers for military service did so for economic gain. Given the smaller number of young people now needed for the military, and competitive compensation is provided now for those that enlist, the research question changes from; "How can DOD entice more enlistments?" to "Why are the recruiting efforts of the DOD increasingly less effective?" This chapter contributes to the answer by arguing that military recruiting suffers from a destructive cycle driven by market efficiency, resulting in a geographically nonrepresentative force. As this imbalanced condition increased over time, it caused a corresponding uneven geographic reduction in republicanism (where citizens participate in military service as a civic duty), further fueling nonrepresentative accessions. The net effect is twofold. First, AVF recruiting becomes increasingly difficult as it draws from an ever-smaller footprint. Second, AVF acces-

---

1. Kapp, "Recruiting and Retention," 35.
2. David H. Berger, "Recruiting Requires Bold Changes," *Proceedings* 148, no. 11 (November 2022): 1437–45, https://www.usni.org/magazines/proceedings/2022/november/recruiting-requires-bold-changes.

sions based on cost-efficiency (i.e., easiest/cheapest to recruit) come at the expense of the long-term social system effectiveness derived from a representative military that increases citizen efficacy in civil-military relations. The result is a New Warrior Caste, whose members are characterized by family lineage and geography. The argument is supported by an analysis of the Army's accessions by state from 1973 to 2022 to measure any potential change in geographic representation over time. The chapter concludes with a summary and recommendations.

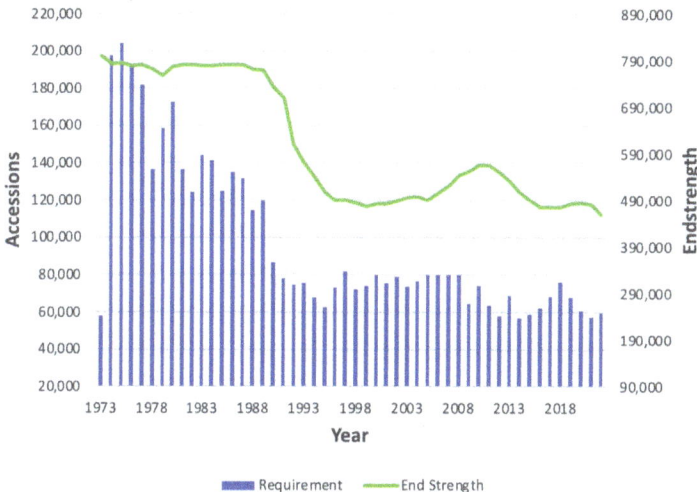

Figure 5. Army Accessions and End Strength 1973-2022
Source: End strength data from Department of Defense, "Defense Manpower Data Center." Accession requirement and achieved data for 1973 from Griffin, Jr, and Mountcastle; for 1974-2021 data from United States Army Recruiting Command; for 2022 data from DOD Public Affairs.

Structuralists, who see the AVF as a bureaucratic process rather than a dynamic system, reject this hypothesis outright. They counter with an economic argument that accession shortfalls reflect an imbalance in the value proposition—military compensation is below the market price for labor. While increased servicemember pay and benefits (and reduced requirements) have episodically countered several difficult recruiting periods, this explanation—used often by the DOD as justification for increased funding—is shortsighted for two reasons. First, it is dismissive and potentially destructive of the foundational need for republicanism in the AVF (see Chapter 2). Second, this counterargument assumes that there are no fiscal limits to military personnel compensation. Today, with servicemember pay and compensation at record highs, the outlays have reached the point where personnel costs exceed monies spent on operations and training. The Department of Defense's (DOD) budget is the largest single discretionary expenditure of the Federal Government, placing it at continued risk of reduction in the face of other competing federal fiscal requirements that include social programs, deficit spending, and financing of the national debt.

Within the DOD's budget, personnel costs are the fastest growing activity of each service's budget—leaving little room for further large pay and allowance increases to make military service more economically attractive without subtracting from core functions. In 2023, the Army requested a budget of $177.5 billion, which allocated $69.1 billion (38.5%) for personnel costs. To put this in perspective, this represents an amount almost equal to the Army's total operations and maintenance costs of $69.7 billion (39.2%) and is greater than the Army's personnel budgets in fiscal year (FY) 2021 and 2022—when the Army had more personnel.[3] In 2024, with an end-strength lower than 2023, the DOD requested a budget increase of $6.7 billion for military personnel.[4] The resulting increased enlistment bonuses could not entice sufficient volunteers to meet the personnel demands of the wars in Iraq and Afghanistan.[5] After 50 years of experience with the AVF, compensation is now much more competitive with civilian work, with the effect of increased compensation on recruiting declining almost exponentially. Based on data from 2000-2010, the analysis estimates that compensation requires a 10% servicemember wage increase— above the increase in civilian wages—to gain an increase of 11.5% in

---

3. Camarillo, "Army FY 23 Budget Overview."
4. Meghann Myers, "Military Services Grappling with Filling Their Ranks in Budget Request," *Military Times*, March 13, 2023, sec. Your Military, accessed 15 March 2023, https://www.militarytimes.com/news/your-military/2023/03/13/military-services-grappling-with-filling-their-ranks-in-budget-request/.
5. The size of the conflicts in Iraq and Afghanistan are considerably smaller than those anticipated in Large Scale Combat Operations (LSCO) required in the current era of returned Great Power Competition.

high-quality recruits.[6] The emphasis on an economic approach to incentivizing personnel to join the AVF appears to have exhausted its utility during peace and war.

FOUNDATIONAL SCHOLARSHIP ON AVF COMPOSITION

For the U.S., the demonstration of republicanism—as a shared sense of duty to the state—was expected; what was subject to debate was the best way to harness this virtue. Historically, America has relied on volunteers to fulfill its military personnel requirements. The episodic implementation of conscription reflected the core belief within the U.S. in a shared military civic duty and the need for social consequences for those deviating from this norm. The significance of the belief in corporate republicanism and the associated effects on the American Paradoxical Trinity cannot be overstated. The widespread presence of republicanism as a motivation for military service facilitates adequate and representative military accessions (volunteer or conscription) to meet national security requirements and, in doing so, improves democratic civil-military relations in three ways. First, through military participation, the populace feels that citizenship is "earned" through military service and that republicanism should be exercised by participation, creating greater citizen efficacy.[7] The Gates Commission's report argued for a volunteer force explicitly cited the "dignity" of service as an essential rationale that would ensure sufficient volunteers with only moderate cost increases (see Table 2 in Chapter 2).

Second, when the military obligation is personal—through the participation of self, family, or close friends—citizens exercise greater

---

6. Beth Asch, *Navigating Current and Emerging Army Recruiting Challenges: What Can Research Tell Us?* (Santa Monica, CA: RAND Corporation, 2019), https://doi.org/10.7249/RR3107, 12. See also John T Warner, "The Effect of the Civilian Economy on Recruiting and Retention," in Report of the Eleventh Quadrennial Review of Military Compensation (Washington, DC: Department of Defense, June 23012), 71–91, https://militarypay.defense.gov/Portals/3/Documents/Reports/SR05_Chapter_2.pdf, 71.

7. Min Jae Choi, Seung Wook Yoo, and Zack Bowersox, "Conscription and Political Participation: How Conscription Policies Affect Voter Turnout," *Armed Forces & Society* (0095327X) 50, no. 1 (January 2024): 316, https://doi.org/10.1177/0095327X221112028.

political participation regarding military matters.[8] Several studies have documented that the presence of a veteran (as a parent, extended family, or a direct leader such as a coach/counselor) significantly favorably influences a young person's consideration of military service.[9] Thus, as an aging veteran population from the large wartime militaries (from World War II through Vietnam) dwindles, one could expect a decline in republicanism as the number of exemplars declines.

Lastly, at the aggregate level, the more the military is representative of society, the greater the "pacification effect" (decreased propensity for democracies to take military action) upon the government.[10] Since 1990, scholars and the DOD have noted a decline in republicanism as measured by a sense of patriotism and propensity to join the military (see Figure 4 in Chapter 2).[11] In theory, a reduction in republicanism as a civic virtue, resulting from a smaller military and subsequent veteran population, would occur proportionally across the U.S. if the military had representative accessions. A representative military and associated veteran population would enable citizen efficacy in military affairs across the breadth of society.

The scholarship and literature on the state of republicanism in the AVF and how this relates to its representativeness provide reference points for measuring the changes explaining the current accession problems and the resulting emergence of a new warrior caste.

---

8. Daniel E. Bergan, "The Draft Lottery and Attitudes Towards the Vietnam War," *Public Opinion Quarterly* 73, no. 2 (July 15, 2009): 383, https://doi.org/10.1093/poq/nfp024.

9. Jason K. Dempsey, *Our Army: Soldiers, Politics, and American Civil-Military Relations* (Princeton, NJ: Princeton University Press, 2010), 175. See also Jeb Blount, Fanatical Military Recruiting: The Ultimate Guide to Leveraging High-Impact Prospecting to Engage Qualified Applicants, Win the War for Talent, and Make Mission Fast, 1st edition (Hoboken, New Jersey: Wiley, 2019), 1-6. See also Kristy N. Kamarck, "Diversity, Inclusion, and Equal Opportunity in the Armed Services: Background and Issues for Congress" (Washington, DC: Congressional Research Service, October 24, 2017), https://crsreports.congress.gov/product/pdf/R/R44321/12, 53.

10. Joseph Paul Vasquez III, "Shouldering the Soldiering: Democracy, Conscription, and Military Casualties," *Journal of Conflict Resolution* 49, no. 6 (December 2005): 853.

11. See also Brady, "Recruiting the All-Volunteer Force," October 18, 2022.

CHAPTER 3

The All-Volunteer Force and [r]epublicanism

To fulfill a campaign promise to end the draft, President Nixon, on March 27, 1969, asked former Secretary of Defense Thomas Gates to lead a commission on transitioning America to an All-Volunteer Force. The now-famous "Gates Report" was released ten months later as a blueprint for the transition from the Selective Service System, which had been in place almost uninterrupted since 1939, to a volunteer force. Objections to the Gates Report centered on risks to civil-military relations from a loss of republicanism virtue in society (where each citizen accepts a personal duty to the state); and that an AVF would not represent American society in terms of economic status, education, geography, and especially race.[12] The preeminent military sociologist Morris Janowitz noted at the time that:

> The military [professionals] think of themselves as civil servants in a national service, and that is an essential ingredient of civilian control. To be paid adequately is essential for one's prestige, but the military resists the idea that civilian society should assume that they are in the military merely or primarily because of considerations of the marketplace. Such a definition leads them to feel that they are mercenaries and not professionals subject to internal and external control. A volunteer armed force will be much less likely to think of itself as mercenary if military service is seen as part of a broader system of community and national service based on voluntary participation."[13]

The transition from the Selective Service System to the All-Volunteer Force was rough. In 1973, as the draft ended, the Army missed its comparatively small recruiting requirement by 23.9%, leaving the active force 14,000 personnel short of its end-strength authorization.[14] In tacit recognition that republicanism would not provide sufficient volunteers, the Army initiated several changes to make military service

---

12. Taylor, *The Advent of the All-Volunteer Force*, 59-63.
13. Janowitz, *The Professional Soldier*, liii.
14. Griffin, Jr, and Mountcastle, *The U.S. Army's Transition*, 213-220.

more marketable and appealing. These actions included doubling the number of recruiters, advertising better compensation, and improving servicemembers' quality of life (e.g., reduced KP and better living accommodations).[15] Despite these actions, in the subsequent 50 years, the Army missed its recruiting target 25 times, with increasing frequency after 2000, despite a generally decreasing requirement (see Figure 6).

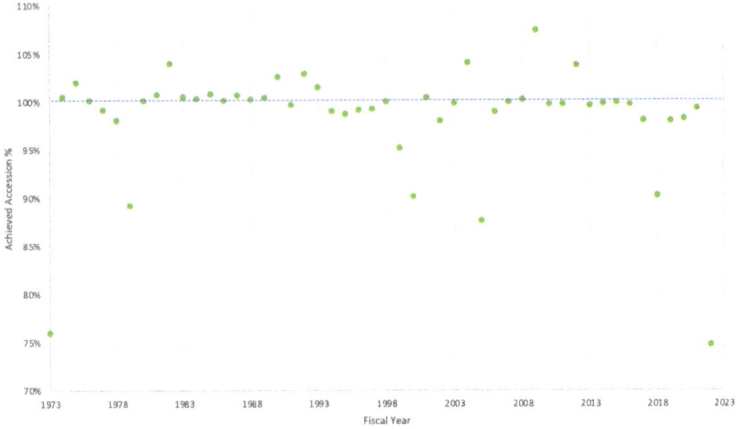

Figure 6. Army Attainment of Accession Goals 1973-2022
Source: Accession requirement and achieved data for 1973 from Griffin, Jr, and Mountcastle; for 1974-2021 data from United States Army Recruiting Command; for 2022 data from DOD Public Affairs.

While 1973 marked a low point for Army recruiting, it also was the high-water mark for Army end-strength at 800,973—the largest force in the 50-year AVF's history.[16] Over the AVF's history, two conditions have offset the consequences of a shrinking military and difficult recruiting. First, modern technology has made the U.S. and other militaries more lethal and, in doing so, enabled them to function with fewer people. Second, the collapse of the Soviet Union in 1989 created the political conditions to justify a smaller military as appropriate,

---

15. Griffin, Jr, and Mountcastle, *The U.S. Army's Transition*, 60-67, 119-124.
16. Karl E. Cocke, ed., Department of the Army Historical Summary: FY 1974 (Washington D.C.: Center of Military History, 1978), https://history.army.mil/books/DAHSUM/1974/ch02.htm, 3.

given the implosion of a foe.[17] Of note, as the military became smaller and required a decreasing percentage of the population to serve, the demands on the Army increased. From 1989-1997, the Army saw a 45% decrease in force size and a 300% increase in operational deployments.[18]

Until 9/11, the declining size of the Army and increased servicemember pay had allowed the AVF to recruit sufficient numbers. This condition, coupled with the U.S. military's battlefield success in 1991 (with a 1.9 million servicemember end-strength, see Figure 3 in Chapter 2) using advanced technology weapons, arguably masked a decline in society's sense of civic obligation to military service. James Burk notes that since World War II, "there has been a gradual erosion of the idea that citizens have an unlimited obligation to bear arms in the defense of their countries. Today [2002], the unlimited obligation still exists as an abstract ideal but is limited in practice."[19]

The silence grows in the absence of a public debate about who and how many should serve in the military. As these operations occurred without a formal declaration or authorization from Congress and the associated public discourse, such unencumbered commitments presaged what scholars would later label as "military adventurism by the executive branch." David Barno and Nora Benshal noted this contradiction and offered that the success of the AVF,

> masks its one profound disadvantage: It has become too easy for most Americans to believe that they are no longer responsible for fighting the nation's wars. It has unintentionally sent the message that "someone else" will take those risks and fight those fights. Since fewer than 1 percent of the population serves in the military, and most of those who now serve are related to someone who has served, the civil-military gap has expanded into a massive chasm.[20]

---

17. Burk, "Thinking Through the End," 27.
18. Ryan, "Military Readiness, Operations Tempo," 2.
19. James Burk, "Theories of Democratic Civil-Military Relations," *Armed Forces & Society* 29, no. 1 (October 2002): 19, https://doi.org/10.1177/0095327X0202900102.
20. David Barno and Nora Benshal, "The Deepest Obligation of Citizenship: Looking Beyond the Warrior Caste," War on the Rocks, May 15, 2018, accessed 13 March 2023,

Although the U.S. has largely concluded operations in Iraq and Afghanistan, the force-to-mission imbalance continues today, with the active reserve regularly filling end-strength shortfalls—resulting from inadequate accessions—in the active component.[21] While the absence of a declaration of war for the conflicts during the AVF's history is argued to be the proximate cause for the lack of public debate that would have bolstered civil-military relations, the root cause could be the absence of republicanism necessary to provide representative accessions in the military. Had a sense of republicanism provided adequate accessions, this would have arguably created the citizen efficacy needed to rebalance America's Paradoxical Trinity and reconcile its military actions. Responding to reduced republicanism with market-based recruiting for a smaller military force calls into question whether the AVF meets the required condition of being representative.

The AVF and Representativeness

When a society has a common civic virtue of shared military sacrifice (republicanism), then its military force (assuming it is of adequate size) should be representative of the society it serves. A representative force increases the likelihood that members of society can identify with it. When this happens, society is more likely to provide the essential resources of money and personnel.[22] Although the importance of a representative military is well established in philosophy and is explicitly argued in the Gates Report, the scholarship on the AVF regarding the consequences of any deviation from this specified condition is less robust.

The existing research on the military's representativeness primarily focuses on the officer corps and builds upon one of two pre-AVF concepts. Morris Janowitz argued for a representative officer corps to

---

https://warontherocks.com/2018/05/the-deepest-obligation-of-citizenship-looking-beyond-the-warrior-caste/.
21. Gil Barndollar and Matthew C. Mai, "America's Army Is Shrinking. Its Missions Aren't," The Hill, August 11, 2023, accessed 15 August 2023, https://thehill.com/opinion/national-security/4148419-americas-army-is-shrinking-its-missions-arent/.
22. Feaver, *Thanks for Your Service*, 45, 201.

"subjective" control of the military.[23] In contrast, Samuel Huntington called for a disassociated officer corps to enable "objective" control over the military.[24] These two paradigms and the role of officers in accessions are discussed in Chapter 5. Much less attention has been given to the rank and file and how it also connects to society (m-s vortex) and, in turn, affects the civil-military relations required for adequate accessions. The importance of the m-s vertex relationship of America's Paradoxical Trinity was explained by then CSA, GEN Fred Weyland in 1976,

> Vietnam was a reaffirmation of the peculiar relationship between the American army and the American people. The American Army really is a people's army in the sense that it belongs to the American people who take a jealous and proprietary interest in its involvement. . . . In the final analysis, the American Army is not so much an arm of the executive branch as it is an arm of the American people. The Army, therefore, cannot be committed lightly.[25]

Not surprisingly, the most heated debates about who serves military service occur when the shared burden of military service is suspect. During the Civil War, the ability of wealthy men to pay another to take their place caused riots and was seen as a corruption of republicanism as a national civic virtue. Fast forward to the 20th century's Selective Service System (SSS), and again, allegations of unfairness and protest arise, this time from the metering of deferments. Not surprisingly, the AVF was expected to be representative of America through volunteer participation. In this way, the burden of military service would be more equally shared and better supported, and the Army as an institution could serve as a method of amalgamating a diverse citizenry (see Chapter 2).

Time has shown that the condition of a representative AVF (alternately stated as a diverse military) has increasingly gone unrealized.

---

23. Janowitz, *The Professional Soldier*, 80, 442-444.
24. Huntington, *The Soldier and the State*, 33-34, 46, 464.
25. Williams, Cimbala, and Sarkesian, *US National Security*, 206.

For a variety of reasons, the American Paradoxical Trinity has caused the AVF to change over its 50-year history; organized for discussion as versions *1.0* to *4.0* (see Table 3 in Chapter 2).[26] Often noted as illustrative of the declining diversity in accessions is the divergence of Ivy League universities from involvement with military service. When the AVF was founded, Harvard had hundreds of ROTC cadets, today, there are fewer than a dozen. In World War II, Columbia produced 20,000 naval officers (more than the U.S. Naval Academy at Annapolis); now it has 10 students enrolled in ROTC.[27] In separate works, author Thomas Ricks and political scientist Ole Holsti identified "fault lines" between the military and civilian society, resulting in an estrangement that has implications for military effectiveness and civilian oversight.[28] The historian Andrew Bacevich concludes that today, a cultural divergence has evolved since the founding of the AVF, where elites—the most influential members of society—seldom serve but clamor for military participation on social issues.[29] During these changes, the disparity between states in fulfilling Army accessions has not gone without notice; episodic scholarship identified this condition but has not considered the cause or consequences.[30]

The "Peace Dividend" enabled by the fall of the Berlin Wall in 1989 marked a profound change in the AVF to version *2.0*, as it rapidly reduced in end-strength. The sharp drop in accession requirements provided a surplus of applicants and created a window of time to retool recruiting to address any imbalances. Twenty years later, in AVF *3.0*, the second-order effects of this drawdown and the unaddressed consequences of market-based recruiting have become apparent in military accessions. The government, sensing a problem with personnel willing to serve in the military, directed in the 2017 National

---

26. See Chapter 2, "A Place for Virtue: The Role of Civic Duty in the All-Volunteer Force." See also Carter, "AVF 4.0."
27. Kelly Field, "After Repeal of 'Don't Ask,' Elite Colleges Reconsider ROTC," *Chronicle of Higher Education* 57, no. 19 (January 14, 2011): A1–18.
28. Williams, Cimbala, and Sarkesian, *US National Security*, 307.
29. Bacevich, "Tradition Abandoned," 16–25.
30. For example, see CFR Editors, "Demographics of the U.S. Military," *Council on Foreign Relations, Backgrounder*, July 13, 2020, https://www.cfr.org/backgrounder/demographics-us-military. See also Chuck DeVore, "States That Defend Us."

Defense Authorization Act (NDAA) the formation of a commission to "conduct a review of the military selective service process and to identify and consider methods to increase participation in military, national, and public service in order to address national security and other public service needs of the Nation."[31] In a 255-page report released in 2020, the Commission called for 49 recommendations so "that 5 million Americans will begin participating in military, national, or public service each year. So that, by 2031, more than enough qualified individuals will seek to serve in the Armed Forces, minimizing the need for traditional military recruiting."[32] Unlike the Gates Commission Report, the recommendations went without action, and the current system—and its associated problems with representative recruiting and declining republicanism—persist.

Today, the propensity of youth (age 17-24) to serve in the military is at its lowest point since 2007, when combat operations in Iraq and Afghanistan reached a low point in public support (see Figure 4 in Chapter 2). The low number of enlistments seems at odds with concurrent research that concluded that Americans are divided almost equally on why they believe youth volunteer for the military. Research shows a clear bivariate condition exists in society, where 43% of adult respondents believed compensation was the principal motivator, and 47% considered duty and patriotism the principal motivation for joining the military. The findings also noted that the respondents' liberal versus conservative political beliefs covaried, respectively, with the perceived motivation for military service. Only 10% considered military service as the choice of last resort, and this answer was most prominent among the most politically liberal. The authors concluded that, contrary to previous predictions about the transition to the AVF, the citizen-soldier tradition as an ideal type remains popular in society but does not manifest as a desire to serve.[33] The article did not consider how the distribution of political beliefs varied by geography

---

31. Commissioners, et al., "Inspired to Serve, Executive Summary to the Final Report of the National Commission on the Military, National, and Public Service." (Washington DC, March 2020), www.inspire2serve.gov, 5.
32. Commissioners, et al., "Inspired to Serve," 7.
33. Ronald R. Krebs and Robert Ralston, "Patriotism or Paychecks: Who Believes What

or whether these findings were reflected in those who enlisted in the military.

Jason Dempsey also argues that there is reason for concern regarding military accessions. While noting that the South became increasingly conservative since the advent of the AVF and that senior military leaders are more conservative, he concludes that the enlisted force is not significantly different from the general population in terms of alignment to political parties but is more conservative—a condition he attributes to self-selection.[34] The author did not consider how the geographic representation origin of servicemembers may affect the results; the analysis assumed a proportional distribution across the military. Potentially, the oversight void created by the dissolution of the SSS created the conditions for military recruiting to pursue efficient market-based accessions at the expense of fulfilling its institutional responsibility to have representative accessions.

In summary, scholarship has identified that the Gates Commission's report justified its economic argument for the AVF by assuming a continuing presence of a high number of "true volunteers" who were driven to military service by a sense of civic duty. This virtue was to be perpetuated by a representative veteran population resulting from an active force that remained above two million (with an Army greater than 700,000). The committee and subsequent work have not considered the effect on "true volunteers" should the military force drop below this number. Similarly, the Gates Commission and notable scholars cite the need for a representative military as the cornerstone of effective civil-military relations. Recent scholarship has identified that the military increasingly recruits from the southeast, a condition accepted as logical given that it has the highest return on investment and is politically conservative, but scholars have not concluded how this pattern affects the founding assumptions of the AVF.

About Why Soldiers Serve," *Armed Forces & Society* 48, no. 1 (January 2022): 25–48, https://doi.org/10.1177/0095327X20917166.

34. Dempsey, *Our Army*, 181-186.

METHODS AND DATA

As an indicator of decreasing representativeness in the AVF, the following analysis examines military accessions over time based on their state of residence at the time of enlistment. This analysis uses official records from Congress, DOD, DA, and the US Army Recruiting Command (USAREC) and other national-level data as specified (e.g., The Census Bureau). The Army's accession data is used as an exemplar of the DOD in this analysis for the reasons explained in Chapter 1. For clarity, excluded from the data set (n) are accessions from territories, districts, overseas, or locations coded as unknown. The numbers associated with these exclusions were not statistically significant. Change is determined by comparing the Army's accession data from FY 1990 to those of FY 2022 using the chart function of Microsoft Excel (version 16.91). The latter represents the last year of *AVF 1.0*, before the drawdown associated with the collapse of the USSR and the period of *AVF 2.0*. The latter data point is the most recent data source and is the period of the nation's most significant recruiting problem.

ANALYSIS

If the American Paradoxical Trinity functioned as intended when the AVF was created, it would have ensured that the AVF's adaptation over the last 50 years complied with the Gates Report's specified condition for a representative force (see Chapter 2). If the AVF's recruiting enterprise has dysfunctionally adapted over the last 50 years, then accession demographics would be increasingly skewed by other characteristics besides family lineage. If other skewed characteristics have emerged to define accessions, then the presence of a new type of warrior caste is serving.

In 1990, the Army inducted 89,140 new Soldiers; Figure 7 breaks this number down by state of residence at the time of enlistment. Not surprisingly, states with large populations (e.g., California and Texas) provided the most enlistments. More telling in terms of sharing the civic burden of defense is found by considering the number of Army enlistments to each state's population per capita. Taking the 1990 U.S.

Census population numbers divided by the number of Army enlistments, the national rate of enlistment is 36 per 100,000 (100k). When the per capita rate of accessions is identified by the state, a disparity in the composition of the AVF becomes apparent (see Figure 8). When viewed this way, a geographical pattern emerges, with a higher concentration of Army enlistees coming from the southeast and south-central states and an additional cluster of over-representation in the central northern states. Of note, the two most populous states—New York and California—are among the states with the lowest per capita contribution to the Army. In 1990, the civic burden of national defense was not shared equally across the United States.

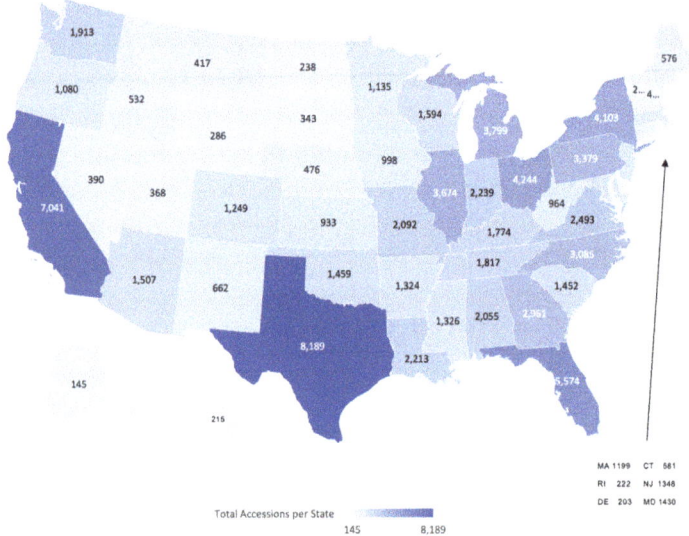

Figure 7. Army Enlistments by State, 1990
Source: Data from Freedom of Information Division, Department of Defense. For clarity, enlistments from U.S. territories, districts, overseas, and unknown locations were excluded, n=89,140.

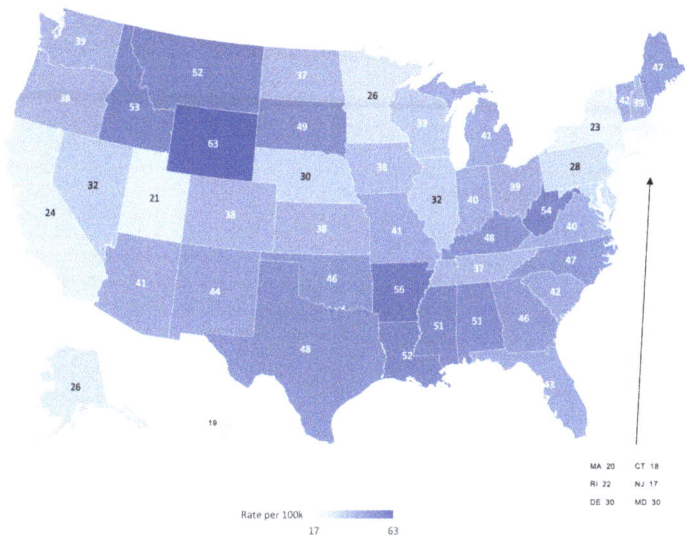

Figure 8. Army Enlistment, per 100k, by State, 1990
Source: Data from Freedom of Information Division, Department of Defense, and United States Census Bureau, "State Population Estimates: Annual Time Series, 01 July 1990 to 01 July 1999." For clarity, enlistments from U.S. territories, districts, overseas, and unknown locations were excluded, n=89,140.

Over the next 25 years, the lack of geographic representation in the Army, identified in 1990, worsened (see Figure 9). Since enlistment requirements have declined since 1990 while populations increased, the aggregate rate per 100,000 people has declined to 13 (n=43,860). The comparison of 1990 to 2022 accessions between states at the per capita rate remains telling. Today, more so than 32 years ago, the southeast United States provides a disproportional percentage of the Army and a steep decline in accessions from the northern central states. Within USAREC, the term of art for the current over-accessions region from the southern region is "the crooked smile."

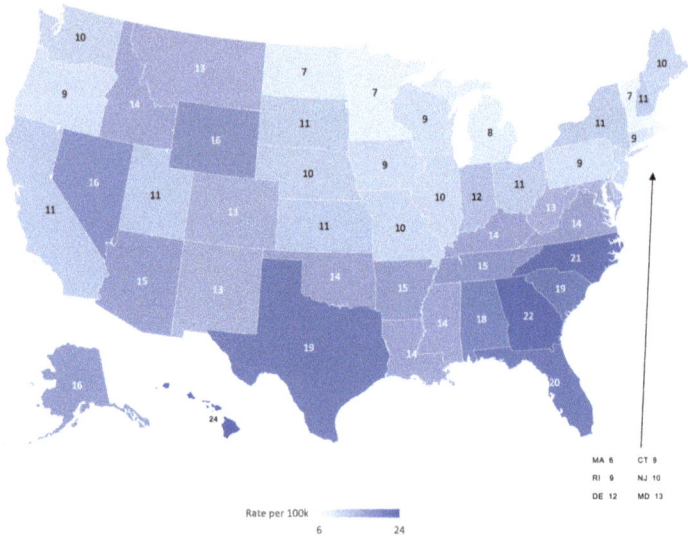

Figure 9. Army Enlistment, per100k, by State, 2022
Source: Data from Freedom of Information Division, Department of Defense, and United States Census Bureau, "State Population Totals and Components of Change: 2020-2022."[35] For clarity, enlistments from U.S. territories, districts, overseas, and unknown locations were excluded, n=43,860.

Potentially, the South, which has been considered more politically conservative than the rest of the country, would provide a greater proportion of enlistments by virtue of the self-selection of youths into an institution that is conservative. In 2019, Gallup found that "in 25 states, the conservative advantage is significantly greater than the national average, including 19 'highly conservative' states in which conservatives outnumber liberals by at least 20 percentage points." While there is an ideological difference between conservative v. liberal in the U.S., the shrinking delta indicates a condition in decline geographically, with the aggregate difference in ideological identification between liberals and conservatives narrowing to nine percentage points from twenty-one points in 2004.[35] For comparison, each state's ideology score (based on the ratio of those identifying as liberal or conservative) is converted to a five-point scale. States where the

---

35. Gallup, "Conservatives Greatly Outnumber Liberals in 19 U.S. States," February 22, 2019, accessed November 08, 2023, https://news.gallup.com/poll/247016/conservatives-greatly-outnumber-liberals-states.aspx.

conservative-liberal gap is 20 points or greater are considered "highly conservative" and scored as a 5. The "more conservative than average" states have gaps of between 15 and 19 points," scored as a 4. About "average" states' residents prefer the conservative description by seven to 14 points (score 3). Those with gaps of zero to six points are considered "less conservative than average" (score 2). States that are more "liberal than conservative" are scored as 1. By comparing this Likert ideological scale to accessions, no significant relationship emerges when the top and bottom five states for Army accessions in 2022 are compared with their political ideology (see Table 4). While states with low accessions may be liberal, a rise in geographic conservatism does not predict increased Army accessions.

Table 4. Comparison of Army Accessions in 2022 to Political Ideology

Rank (per 100k)	State	Conservative Score	Conservative Ranking
1	NC	4	23
2	GA	5	19
3	TX	4	21
4	FL	3	27
5	NV, WY*	3, 5	31, 5
46	MI	3	30
47	NH	1	45
48	ND	5	17
49	MN	3	35
50	MA	1	50

Source: Accessions rate computed from Data from the Freedom of Information Division, Department of Defense. Data for Conservative scores from Gallup, "Conservatives Greatly Outnumber Liberals in 19 U.S. States," 2019.
* Tied rankings of accessions per 100k.

The boxes and whiskers of the chart numerically represent the significant change between the two preceding maps (in Figure 8 and Figure 9). Because of a smaller Army and growing population, the rate of accessions per 100,000 declined from 36 in 1990 to 14 in 2022, illustrated by the orange box plot lower on the y-axis (see Figure 10). The disparity in accessions per 100k population from each state in 1990 compared to 2022 increased, as illustrated by 2022's orange boxplot's measure of the outer quartiles (whiskers) being proportionally longer than those of 1990's blue boxplot. The larger interquartile range of 1990 compared to that of 2022 indicates a decline in the number of states close to the median value of enlistments per 100k population. This is alternately explained as the deviation from the median rate of enlistments per 100k population increased from 1990 to 2022. In 1990, the aggregate states' enlistment per capita followed a near-normal distribution, with a slight positive skew. By 2022, the distribution curve of States' accession contribution (per capita) is narrower in the center quartiles (as shown by the proportionally smaller orange boxes) with longer tails—Army accessions by state in 2020 are increasingly moved from the median (greater variance from state to state). The whiskers in 2022 show an increased positive skew compared to the near balance in 1990, indicating that fewer states are over-accessing, but those that do are achieving to a larger degree than in 1990. The narrow-peaked distribution curve of 2022 is such that the accessions of one state emerge as an outlier (Hawaii) with a near second (Georgia at 22), whereas there were no outliers in 1990. Put simply, in comparison to 1990, the boxplots quantify that by 2022, fewer states are increasingly fulfilling the requirement for Army enlistments, while those states that are under-accessing citizens into the Army are doing so to a greater degree. From 1990 to 2022, the burden of personnel for the military has been increasingly unequally distributed geographically in the U.S.

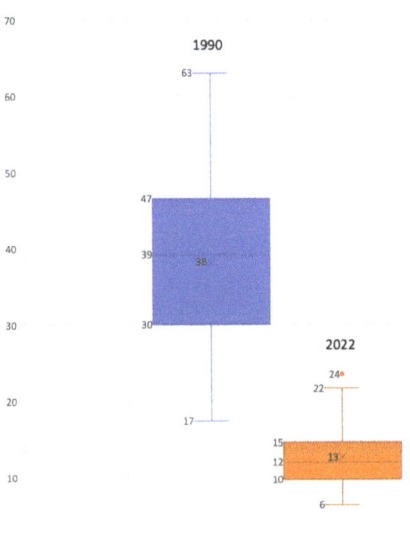

Figure 10. Boxplot State Variance, per 100k Army Enlistments, 1990 and 2022

FINDINGS

The U.S. Army's Recruiting efforts, when viewed over the last 35 years of the AVF, indicate that the lack of geographic and economic representation is neither episodic nor a statistical anomaly. Instead, the condition of the military as a representation of society has deteriorated over the last three decades because of the overrepresentation of both generational veterans ("the family business") and those from select states. This combination indicates the emergence of a new warrior caste, with an Army that is the least representative of the public it serves since President Truman desegregated the Armed Forces in 1948.[36] While the debate over the utility of a warrior caste officer corps has continued since Janowitz and Huntington introduced their respective theories, the presence of today's new warrior caste in the enlisted rank-and-file military is in direct contravention of two AVF's required conditions and two inferred assumptions.[37] Regarding the two required conditions: a) the active-duty military had fallen below the required condition of >2m personnel to 1.4m (see Chapter 2), while b) the accession trend line since 1990 indicates that a consistent percentage of youth who are "true volunteers" did not exist in 1990, and the density has declined through to 2022. The Gates Report refuted criticisms of a volunteer force by assuming that: a) natural selection would produce a representative force and, b) this would not be altered by market-based recruiting. Identifying today's non-representative new warrior caste—defined by increases in generational-family enlistments and the disparity in states' per-capita enlistments from 1990 to 2022—invalidates these two inferred assumptions when the AVF was founded. The long and consistent development of the New Warrior Caste explains the DOD's current and persistent recruiting problem and identifies two 2nd order consequences that America's Paradoxical Trinity will likely confront.

---

36. Detailed discussion and analysis follow in Chapter 4.
37. For a detailed discussion of the AVF's four inferred and two specified assumptions, as well as the four required conditions, see Chapter 2.

2nd Order Consequences of AVF Recruiting

First, the identification of a New Warrior Class means that the military recruiting system contravenes and reduces America's espoused value and need for republicanism as a civic duty shared by all—the root source of "true volunteers" assumed by the Gates Commission. The comparison of the states' per capita enlistments in 1990 and 2022 indicates that, despite the wide latitude granted to the Army for recruiting, the resulting accessions do not represent America. Children of veterans and those from the Southeast United States are over-represented in the AVF today.[38] This unbalanced induction has a near multiplicative negative effect on future recruiting by creating an over-representation of veterans in select locations (productive recruiting areas) at the expense of creating veterans in other areas. In 2022, the number of Americans likely to have a close connection to a veteran varies between 0.80% and 10%, a far cry from the near-ubiquitous presence of veteran family members following WW II.[39] The fewer communities with Army veterans, the smaller the geographic dispersion of veteran family members, coaches, and teachers present to influence the next generation to serve and connect the public to its military.

Over time, this creates a downward spiral where subsequent recruiting becomes more concentrated in a shrinking pool of applicants, and the social artifacts legitimizing a tradition of military service as a shared and common civic virtue are removed. Adrian Lewis argues that "the people in America are no longer a single group but highly fractionalized into tribes where each, as a component of society, pursues their own relationship with the military and the state."[40] The result is both a fractured society and the military becoming increasingly isolated from society.[41] Chapter 4 considers whether recruiting

---

38. Ironically, this is the area that has the most medically unhealthy youth, see Daniel B. Bornstein et al., "A State-by-State and Regional Analysis of the Direct Medical Costs of Treating Musculoskeletal Injuries among US Army Trainees," Progress in Cardiovascular Diseases 74 (September 1, 2022): 53–59, https://doi.org/10.1016/j.pcad.2022.10.008.
39. Feaver, *Thanks for Your Service*, 61.
40. Lewis, "Military Culture," 234.
41. Beehner and Maurer, "Introduction," 2.

for the AVF defines a New Warrior Caste in ways besides family history and geography.

Second, as the world's superpower, the U.S. will at some point have to reconcile the size of the force it needs and wants against the military force design and recruiting resources necessary to fulfill this requirement. From 1787 to 1939, the U.S. military, under government supervision, functioned as a small cadre-enabled volunteer military force until times of crisis, with few exceptions. By exception, on four occasions, the President called upon Congress for statutory authority to create a large army via conscription. Each time, the Congressional authorization process unfolded with much public debate and some protests; in this way, the vertices of America's Paradoxical Trinity were exercised, and it was rebalanced so that military service was seen as legitimate. When conscription ended in 1973, the SSS (as an independent government agency with representation from each county in the U.S.) ceased supervising military accessions. By 1990, the military had shrunk despite increased requirements and proved incapable of the required expansion during wartime. In recent years, Congress has repeatedly mitigated the Army's accession problems by reducing the size of the force, increasing compensation, and accepting pledges from military leaders to use better recruiting methodology.

This transactional approach between the government and the military presupposes that having an efficient accession process will attain the required measure of effectiveness—a representative army for the defense of the democratic nation. Why the transactional approach is perpetuated in opposition to effective representative accessions is explored further in Chapter 5. In pursuit of efficient recruiting, the increasingly professional military has produced an ever increasingly complex recruiting apparatus. However, if the vertices of the paradoxical trinity are not used to validate both the measures of recruiting performance and effectiveness, then the professional recruiting enterprise may reach a point of diminishing returns (i.e., insufficient accessions). Chapter 6 delves deeper into the behavior of the Army's recruiting enterprise.

Counter Argument

Some dismiss the 2nd order effects of an unrepresentative military by counter-arguing that the competitive labor market is the cause of the recruiting problem because servicemember wages and compensation have not kept pace. This counterargument offers that a thriving economy with low unemployment has given young people more lucrative alternatives to military service, especially the small percentage that are qualified for military service.[42] Two assumptions must hold to make this claim: a) that recruiting was not a problem during poor economic times, and b) that an increase in the market-competitive compensation package for military service could induce sufficient young people to join. History and data do not support these two assumptions.

While it is true that during years with high employment, the Army is more likely to fail in its accession mission, the inverse is not true. The years when the Army achieved its accession goals are relatively evenly spread across the unemployment scale during the 50 years of the AVF (see Table 5). Since 1973, the unemployment rate has risen and fallen in a manner that is not congruent with the overall declining propensity of youth to serve in the military. Unemployment may partially explain part of the variance in enlistments for the AVF, but it cannot be considered the primary cause. Regarding the second assumption of this counterargument—the need to offer increased compensation, the Commandant of the Marine Corps, General Berger, dismisses it when he states:

> The most frequently cited factor affecting military recruiting is the strength of the U.S. job market. Indeed, the joint force is subject to the laws of labor supply and demand just like any other large organization. Yet, some of our deepest challenges are chronic, indicating that the strength of the economy may be less critical than commonly thought...

---

42. Asch, Navigating Current and Emerging Army Recruiting Challenges, 12. See also John T Warner, "The Effect of the Civilian Economy on Recruiting and Retention," 72. See also Kapp, "Recruiting and Retention in the Active Component Military," 2.

. Throwing increasingly large sums of money at the problem is unsustainable and has a record of failure.[43]

Moreover, the magnitude of increasing compensation sufficiently to guarantee required accessions is economically infeasible (see Chapters 1 and 2).

Table 5. Unemployment Rate during Failed and Achieved Recruiting Years

Unemployment Rate	Failed Accession Years	Achieved Accession Years
3.9 – 4.9	1973, 1997, 1999, 2000 2006, 2016, 2017, 2018, 2019, 2022	1998, 2001, 2007
5.0 – 5.9	1979, 1995, 1996, 2002 2005, 2021	1974, 1988, 1989, 1990 2004, 2008, 2015
6.0 – 6.9	1978, 1991, 1994, 2003 2014	1987, 1993
7.0 – 7.9	1997, 2013	1976, 1980, 1981, 1984, 1985, 1986, 1992
8.0 – 8.9	2011, 2020	1975, 2012
9.0 – 9.9	2010	1982, 1983, 2009

Source: Unemployment data from the Bureau of Labor Statistics. Data for accession failed and achieved for 1974-1989 from the United States Army Recruiting Command, and for 1990-2022 from the Department of Defense.

Beyond the precarious nature of the two required assumptions necessary for this counterargument, the thesis obscures the larger point. If Army recruiting continues in the most efficient manner possible, it risks increasing the Army's disassociation from society. This pattern not only antagonizes the recruiting problem by concentrating the applicant pool but also increases the civil-military divide and further erodes an American democracy founded upon the belief that shared military service is a civic virtue.

CONCLUSION

While citizens' military service in a democracy has long been considered a civic duty and virtuous, the declining willingness of youth to

---

43. Berger, "Recruiting Requires Bold Changes," 1437-1445.

serve in the military calls into question whether this belief still exists in America today and fuels the debate of a growing civil-military divide. The recent record-setting recruiting failure begs the question of whether this condition has now reached a point of critical mass that endangers the AVF. For 50 years, Army recruiting has grown significantly and assumed the unprecedented function of securing personnel for a large force. The Army's apparent success at recruiting was largely enabled by a smaller requirement due to a shrinking force size. Because the Army generally met its manpower requirements in the early years of the AVF, the components of America's Paradoxical Trinity (military, government, and the people) have not had to engage on this topic. The absence of an accession crisis (until recently) has precluded consideration of necessary changes to *AVF 3.0*'s status quo. This missing dialogue, while allowing the recruiting problem to grow, has simultaneously contributed to the civil-military divide because the government has not conveyed to society an understanding of the military's personnel needs.

The unrepresentative accessions identified here identify a twofold problem confronting America's Paradoxical Trinity. First, young people today do not participate in the military out of a sense of duty but instead consider military service as a value proposition measured against personal objectives. Second, this shift in perception has largely gone unnoticed and without comment or action by the government and society. The former leaves the armed forces vulnerable due to poor oversight and resourcing, while the latter risks denying the military its most essential resource—citizen validation and participation. The recruiting problem and associated system failures require systematic redress rather than just an increase in servicemember compensation. There is precedent for this wider system approach. In 1946, the National School Lunch Program was enacted in response to the number of malnourished youths excluded from military service during World War II. Today, the vast disqualification of youth from the option for military service is accepted, and there is no larger social or political debate to address the root causes that limit youth participation in the military and the devaluation of this civic virtue.

As a minimum, the findings of a New Warrior Caste call for additional research. First, a similar analysis of the other services would validate whether the Army is a benchmark for the DOD regarding the long-term effect of service branch recruiting autonomy on accessions and civil-military relations. Second, other dimensions of social representation (e.g., race, gender, education, ethnicity) within the military should be explored to understand the degree to which a new warrior caste has emerged. The geographical disparities in accessions identified by this research raises the question of whether service recruiting has created other disparities in the AVF. The current standards for enlistment exclude the vast majority of youth and, in doing so, further exacerbate the recruiting problem. Lastly, further research is almost an imperative to determine the changes needed to restore the connection between the military and society, necessary to reestablish the civic virtue of military service.

CHAPTER 4
THE RESIDUAL CHALLENGE: RACE, GENDER, AND THE CHANGED DEMOGRAPHICS OF THE ALL-VOLUNTEER FORCE

THE AMERICAN SPIRIT SPEAKS:
To the Judge of Right and Wrong
With Whom fulfillment lies
Our purpose and our power belong,
Our faith and sacrifice.

Let Freedom's land rejoice!
Our ancient bonds are riven;
Once more to us the eternal choice
Of good or ill is given.

–Rudyard Kipling, *The Choice*

As an institution, the U.S. military's responsibilities and effects go far beyond its mandate to provide for the nation's defense. Not surprisingly, the recruiting crisis that has persisted since September 11, 2001, has raised several concerns as to the institution's role and performance. For the history of the republic, the military was intended as a manifestation of the republican virtue to share in the obligation of protecting the State. In this manner, republicanism as a civic virtue would serve as a means to integrate diverse populations and forge a common or shared national identity.[1] While a common identity among servicemembers is undoubtedly present, this does not guarantee that society is connected to its servicemembers since the latter is not a geographic representation of the former.[2] As a result, the civil-military divide has worsened over time as the subsequent veteran population has become increasingly less representative and thus less broadly connected to society. Today, the All-Volunteer Force (AVF) is over fifty years old and has struggled to meet personnel requirements for both the Global War on Terrorism (GWOT) and during peacetime—missing its accession targets 11 times in the 30 years before the 9/11 attacks and 15 times in the subsequent 20 years (see Figure 3 in Chapter 3). This persistent problem has led some to question the AVF's design and its role in a civil-military divide.

The 1970 "Report on the President's Commission on an All-Volunteer Force" (known commonly as the Gates Report) used an economic argument to justify the end of conscription in America and a return to a volunteer force, albeit with 2.5 million servicemembers it would be one that was much larger than at any time previous.[3] The report affirmed the importance of republicanism as a civic virtue by citing it as the principal reason for youth joining the military as "true volunteers."[4] The Gates Commission's report focused primarily on the Army as the service of greatest concern and concluded that sufficient volunteers would be available for a large volunteer "force in being." It argued that better compensation would enable more young people to volunteer for a variety of reasons to include patriotism, an expression of republican civic virtue.[5] Moreover, a volunteer military would be

---

1. See Chapter 2, "A Place for Virtue: The Role of Civic Duty in the All-Volunteer Force."
2. See Chapter 3, "The Crooked Smile: How Technology Made Recruiting for the All-Volunteer Force a Commodity."
3. "Commission on an All-Volunteer Armed Force," 49-67, 135.
4. "Commission on an All-Volunteer Armed Force," 6, 13, 16, 49. See also Table 2 in Chapter 2.
5. "Commission on an All-Volunteer Armed Force," 133, 136.

enabled by better-educated volunteers (who could now afford to serve because of the improved compensation) and by the participation of minorities and women.[6] Sensitive to the social concerns of the 1970s, the report explained: a) the need to make sure a volunteer force would not be over-represented by minorities, b) how increased enlistments by women (and transitioning some military jobs to civilians) could offset the accessions previously provided by the draft, and c) possible actions the military could take to secure sufficiently educated volunteers for a quality force. In this manner, the pursuit of volunteers for the AVF would meet the requirements of what was considered of central importance—having a representative force. Thirty years later analysts predicted that by 2025, the civilian labor force would comprise 48% women and 36% minorities.[7] As a result, the quality of the relations between society and the military (m-s vertex) in America's Paradoxical Trinity will reflect the degree to which minorities and women are part of the military accessions that provide representative service branches.

The post-conscription transformation of Army recruiting focused on efficiently achieving the required accessions for the new AVF. The result is a New Warrior Caste that is separated from society by a lack of geographic representation, and an overreliance on descendants of veterans in accessions (see Figure 9 and Figure 10 in Chapter 3). What is not known is whether other deviations from the Gates Commission's report specifications are present and contribute to a civil-military divide. This chapter argues that the AVF, as a New Warrior Caste, is also separated from society by accessions that underrepresented minorities and women. The analysis also shows that the effects of market-based recruiting on Black and female accessions by 2022 had become concentrated in the same geographic region despite their distinct patterns of geographic origins in 1990. The exception to the adverse effects of market-based recruiting is the education level of new recruits—a topic with consistent government engagement—which saw little change by geography, race, or gender. The chapter concludes with

---

6. "Commission on an All-Volunteer Armed Force," 49-67, 129-157.
7. Segal and Bourg, "Professional Leadership and Diversity," 706.

a discussion of the significance of these findings to the American Paradoxical Trinity and recommendations for further research.

FOUNDATIONAL SCHOLARSHIP

The AVF is now fifty years old; over that time, it has responded and adapted to military, political, and social change. To understand these adaptations as they relate to recruiting, it is useful to use Carter's categorization of the AVF as four versions: *AVF 1.0* as post-Vietnam, *AVF 2.0* post-Cold War and peacekeeping, *AVF 3.0* the Global War on Terror, and *AVF 4.0* (see Table 3 in Chapter 3). At the inception of the AVF (*AVF 1.0*), the economist of the Gates Commission argued that better compensation, the widespread presence of republicanism in America, and an active military greater than 2 million would provide for a legitimate force that stood in sharp contrast to the then existing military that relied on "the draft as a tax" administered by the Selective Service System (SSS). Historically, by social convention and necessity, no U.S. military force has ever been entirely representative of society, whether a force design based on conscription or volunteers.[8] Under conscription, the U.S. Government, with the SSS as its agent, directed who from society could/would enter military service (*g-s* vertex). Today, with the AVF, the Government's method of engaging society regarding the fulfillment of civic duty through military service is not clear. Instead, recruiting oversight functions are episodically exercised through legislative acts of Congress that direct the military's actions. The heterogeneity of American society makes a government's engagement with society on republicanism both more complicated and essential to keeping the American Paradoxical Trinity (see Figure 2 in Chapter 2) in balance to provide for military accessions.

A range of cultures and social prejudices have been reflected in U.S.

---

8. U.S. Army, "The Army and Diversity," U.S. Army Center of Military History, accessed October 11, 2023, https://history.army.mil/faq/diversity.html. See also Government Accountability Office, "Military Personnel." See also Aline O. Quester and Robert F. Lockman, "The All-Volunteer Force: Outlook for the Eighties and Nineties" (Alexandria, VA: Center for Naval Analysis, March 1984), accessed January 05, 2023, https://apps.dtic.mil/sti/pdfs/ADA153703.pdf.

military accessions and, as a consequence, are reflected in the veteran community where those who are also a minority are discriminated against in their standing and benefits as veterans.[9] Beginning with World War I, the military has sought healthy white male youths, generally aged 18-24, who were not otherwise deemed necessary for other "higher" priorities (recognized by being granted draft deferments). As a reflection of historic socially embedded prejudice, these selection attributes were justified as necessary for an effective military. Contemporary scholarship has found no evidence that diversity of race, gender, or sexual orientation interferes with task cohesion—the ability to work together to accomplish the mission—either vertically (confidence in superiors' competence) or horizontally (confidence in peers' competence).[10] To the contrary, armies with group inequality are more likely to suffer from greater casualties, desertion, defections, and fratricide.[11] Consequently, today, the scope of participation in the armed forces has a much broader requirement of representativeness if military service is to be considered a civic duty where the burden of State security is shared.

In theory, the government provides a person with select entitlements as a right of citizenship in exchange for the sacrifices made to fulfill the civic obligation of military service. Which persons or groups within society are deemed eligible for service, and the scope of benefits they earn from service provides a structural embodiment of the society's culture and beliefs. The comparative opportunity to participate in this exchange relationship also indicates relative equality of the citizens within society.[12] Some argue that the absence of universal oppor-

---

9. Kinder and Higgins, *Service Denied*, 2-6.
10. Task cohesion is a greater predictor of group success than social cohesion. Additionally, some evidence indicates that task cohesion (and group success) contributes to improved social cohesion. See Mady Wechsler Segal et al., "The Role of Leadership and Peer Behaviors in the Performance and Well-Being of Women in Combat: Historical Perspectives, Unit Integration, and Family Issues," *Military Medicine* 181, no. Supplement (January 2016): 29-30. See also Mady Wechsler Segal and Chris Bourg, "Professional Leadership and Diversity in the Army," in *The Future of the Army Profession*, Revised and Expanded Second Edition, ed. Don Snider and Lloyd Matthews, 2nd ed. (Boston, MA: McGraw Hill-Education, 2005), 708.
11. Lyall, *Divided Armies*, 17-18, 404.
12. Krebs, *Fighting for Rights*, 3-6. See also Segal, Recruiting for Uncle Sam, 3.

tunity to fulfill a civic obligation through military service represents a form of institutional discrimination, where those denied the chance to serve are denied the benefits derived from having fulfilled a civic virtue.[13] In the U.S., marginalized groups have used military service as a fulcrum upon which to secure full recognition as citizens. They do this by making the case that their military service constitutes a sacrifice worthy of equal recognition or by leveraging their political clout to change the participation policies to infer equal recognition and opportunity to serve and, in turn, receive associated entitlement.[14] Their arguments rest on the validity of republicanism as a central virtue. At the same time, among those citizens who are allowed to serve, the fulfillment of republicanism can be both a benefit (compensation, increased opportunity, prestige) and a burden (personal deprivation, injury, or death). When these military service cost/benefits are in balance for all citizen categories, a healthy American Trinity exists (admittedly, attaining this balance is made more difficult as the cost-benefit-obligation of the citizen is defined differently among constituents). When there is an imbalance the legitimacy of the military and its operations suffer, as was the condition in the U.S. during Vietnam, with a corresponding effect on recruiting.

With the collapse of the Soviet Union in 1991, the threat of armed conflict receded, and the AVF shrank significantly, and transformed to *AVF 2.0*, as society called for a "Peace Dividend." In this new environment, the Army sold itself to the government and society as a provider of social good and an opportunity for all American citizens.[15] This approach had its roots in the emerging social movements of the 1960s, marked by President Johnson's "Great Society," which led to the formation of a "grant economy" where perceptions of citizenship began to shift from a perspective of obligation to one of entitlement. In this manner, society had a responsibility to move what was deemed politically an economic surplus to the less productive. The military, as a major government employer, became an institutional structure

---

13. Snyder, *Citizen-Soldiers and Manly Warriors*, 2-9.
14. Krebs, *Fighting for Rights*, 187.
15. Bailey, *America's Army*, 200-201.

within the social welfare system.[16] Given the absence of an existential threat and the DOD's significant budget, society demanded that *AVF 2.0*, in addition to providing national security, also serve the country as a mechanism of social change by providing personal advancement. In response to this changed social perceptions and the growing accessions (see Figure 6 in Chapter 3), the recruiting enterprise marketed the Army as a melting pot of multiculturalism and a path to the middle class.[17] The result is that the representativeness of the military became necessary for several reasons: a) to ensure a shared burden of national defense, b) battlefield effectiveness, c) national cultural integration, and d) to enable the personal advancement of the disadvantaged.

While the need for representativeness in the AVF increased, so did the need for more qualified servicemembers. As David Segal explained, "The complexity of military technology has forced the United States to move from the principle of equipping the man, to a principle of manning the equipment, and such a change of emphasis is consequential for the kinds of people who are needed for the armed forces."[18] As the first Gulf War validated the AVF as viable, it transitioned from version *AVF 1.0* to *2.0* with the need to access more qualified applicants capable of managing the new military technology. The military, while long discriminating to ensure the induction of healthy youth, now had the additional functional imperative to induct smarter people. In this new environment, a three-way tension emerged between: a) the military, which desired healthy and intelligent recruits, b) the traditionalists who hold a republican belief in sharing the burden of military service widely, and c) the social activists who advocated for the military to provide social advancement to the disadvantaged.

The adaptations required over the subsequent ten years led to *AVF 3.0* as several conditions converged. In this new structure, *AVF 3.0* became smaller, more professional, and increasingly reliant on a technological advantage in weapons as compensation for reduced mass. As

---

16. Segal, *Recruiting for Uncle Sam*, 78-79, 90-99.
17. Saucier, "Mobilizing the Imagination," 16-31, 150-164.
18. Segal, *Recruiting for Uncle Sam*, 5.

this happened, a tribal or fractured American society had come to expect the defense of the nation to be done by professional soldiers rather than citizen-soldiers, and the military had become dependent on the educated lower middle class with increasing participation of racial and ethnic minorities to fill its ranks.[19] While this proved efficient in peacetime, this professional standing in the eyes of the public did not insulate the AVF from social tensions when it was committed to war. Post 9/11, when the AVF was committed in mass to the Global War on Terror, allegations were made that Blacks were again bearing a disproportional number of casualties, gender disparities became more salient, and minimum education standards were lowered to make enlistment requirements—as had happened in Vietnam during conscription. Again, in times of U.S. involvement in war, the role of republicanism as a shared value returned as a social argument, as the State's unmet need for greater military accessions indicated an American Paradoxical Trinity out of balance.

While some demographics in the military do represent the larger society, others do not and have not done so since the formation of the AVF. Today, by omission, having a representative military is considered necessary but secondary to efficiently achieving the accession quantity requirement, as seen by USAREC's disproportionate pursuit of accessions in select southern states (see Figure 9 in Chapter 3). In the words of Mady Segal and Chris Bourg, "A volunteer military divergent from its own populists in a democratic society will face continued problems of recruitment, retention, and legitimacy."[20] Chapter 3 demonstrates that since 1973, the marketing of military service has compounded this non-representative problem by creating a new warrior caste that is disproportionally represented by accessions from veterans' families and the southeastern United States. This condition aggravates the civil-military divide by disassociating the military from society, and ironically makes readiness more costly as these recruits from the South have higher medical attrition from initial entry train-

---

19. Segal, *Recruiting for Uncle Sam*, 41, 64. See also Golding and Adedeji, "The All-Volunteer Military," 30.
20. Segal and Bourg, "Professional Leadership and Diversity," 705.

ing.[21] In response to problems during the Global Wars on Terror (GWOT) in Iraq and Afghanistan, a return to great power conflict in 2015, and increasing recruiting shortfalls have caused several pundits and civic leaders to call for significant change to the AVF, such that if the need is acted upon *AVF 4.0.* would emerge. In this new era, the military must balance competing organizational demands of battlefield effectiveness with the cultural tradition of republicanism as a shared duty with societal requirements to deliver opportunity to the less privileged. At various times, usually when forced by crisis, these three tensions are reconciled within the American Paradoxical Trinity (see Figure 2 in Chapter 1).

In 2009, concerned with the demographic imbalance of the U.S. military, Congress affirmed the need for a representative military and directed through the National Defense Authorization Act (NDAA), a Military Leadership Diversity Commission, to assess policies and means for the advancement of minorities. The subsequent report noted that the DOD's strategic plan does not outline recruiting targets based on demographic groups.[22] For the Army today, the method of pursuit for volunteers by USAREC provides the most cost-efficient means of obtaining accessions, resulting in a New Warrior Caste (see Chapter 3). What is unknown is whether the recruiting enterprise is also skewing the force composition in other ways that violate the Gates Commission's assumptions and conditions for a volunteer force. The Army tracks minority representation in its ranks, beginning with recruiting. The Office of Army Demographics (OAD) now provides Army-wide analytical and policy recommendations to support senior-level decisions about readiness and the Army community.[23] Further analysis is required to understand whether military recruiting, which is foremost concerned with efficiently meeting the FY's accession requirements,

---

21. Zamone Perez, "Poor Fitness among Recruits Is Costing the Army Millions, Study Says," *Army Times*, April 3, 2023, sec. Your Army, accessed April 04, 2023, https://www.armytimes.com/news/your-military/2023/04/03/poor-fitness-among-recruits-is-costing-the-army-millions-study-says/.
22. Kamarck, "Diversity, Inclusion, and Equal Opportunity," 5-7.
23. U.S. Army, "Army Demographics," Office of Army Demographics, 2022, accessed May 25, 2023, https://www.army.mil/article/219140/demographics.

provides the intended representative force regarding race and gender, and whether the military's entry education requirements influence these. The below, first reviews how those demographic characteristics were deemed necessary for creating a volunteer force, then examines their saliency today by the scope of representation in the Army. These three variables are analyzed using Army accession data to compare 1990 to 2022 (the 50th anniversary of the AVF) to identify possible change.

Racial Diversity and Recruiting

In contrast to World War II, where minorities (particularly Blacks) were denied the danger and opportunity of serving in combat formations, the Vietnam War had Black male enlisted servicemembers in all branches of the service, especially the Army. While Blacks were less likely to be qualified for military service, they were more likely to be drafted by virtue of being less likely to receive a deferment—especially to pursue advanced education, or enlistment in the reserves.[24] This led in part to a common perception that Blacks were overrepresented in the infantry, the branch with the highest casualty rate, and were therefore bearing the brunt of the State's Vietnam War policies. While subsequent scholarship demonstrated that this was not the case, this concern was nonetheless a central consideration in designing a post-Vietnam volunteer force.[25]

Responding to the significant social and racial tensions present in the 1970s, the Gates Commission noted several reasons why a volunteer force would achieve the necessary racial representation. The report did this to address the objections of those who thought the better pay in a volunteer force would disproportionally appeal to Blacks who were more likely to be economically disadvantaged. Some cautioned against over-representation of Blacks for three reasons. First, Blacks

---

24. Taylor, *Military Service and American Democracy*, 10.
25. Charles Moskos and John Sibley Butler, *All That We Can Be: Black Leadership and Racial Integration the Army Way* (New York, NY: Basic Books, 1997), 9. See also "Commission on an All-Volunteer Armed Force," 143. See also Kamarck, "Diversity, Inclusion, and Equal Opportunity," 17.

would bear a disproportionate share of the burden of defense. Second, Blacks would receive military training and then participate in disorders and riots. Third, over time, any over-representation of Blacks would increase through retention, leading to a predominantly black military and, in doing so, become less appealing to whites—thereby exacerbating the imbalance.[26] The Commission flatly rejected these race concerns in their report.

> Many of these questions and concerns cannot be answered rationally. Racial attitudes and fears are emotionally based. Solid facts and sound judgments are seldom cures for prejudice. For example, those who fear "domestic disorders" as a result of blacks serving in the military raise such unanswerable questions. To bar blacks from the military because of these fears will not solve the root causes behind domestic disorders. Black participation in the military will neither quiet nor aggravate domestic disorders.[27]

Additionally, the Commission made a quantitative argument that the over-representation of Blacks would not occur. It did this by using the Army as the basis of analysis since it would be the service most affected by a change to a volunteer force; the report explained that "the best estimates" put Black participation in a volunteer Army at 18.8%, in contrast to 16.6% present under the draft. For the DOD, "at a 2.5-million-man force level, only five to ten thousand more Blacks will serve in the enlisted component of a volunteer force than in a mixed force."[28] The report used historical data to argue that: a) there were twice as many whites as Blacks below the poverty line, b) increased pay would breach a threshold to attract more whites who would not otherwise volunteer, and c) that historical data on volunteers showed that Blacks have generally enlisted in proportion to the general population, despite having a lower percentage who were qualified.[29] The

---

26. "Commission on an All-Volunteer Armed Force," 15-16, 140-141.
27. "Commission on an All-Volunteer Armed Force," 142.
28. "Commission on an All-Volunteer Armed Force," 143.
29. "Commission on an All-Volunteer Armed Force," 142, 145. See also Bailey, *America's Army*, 122-126.

Army led American society in racial integration since 1948 and continued to do so by experimenting with policies of compensatory action through programs to make minorities more competitive rather than preferential treatment.[30] As a result of these and other efforts, the Army is now routinely acclaimed as the most ethnically diverse institution in American society.

By 1991, the organizational adaptation that accompanied the transition to a volunteer force stabilized as *AVF 2.0*; as a large formation (see Figure 3 in Chapter 2, and Figure 5 in Chapter 3) that was fully engaged in the Cold War and Peacekeeping Operations. The rate of Black accessions in 1990 was just 5.32% in 1990 (4,664 of 89,140 total), down from 16% in 1973 when the AVF was founded. Confronting increasingly difficult recruiting conditions, the AVF force became increasingly dependent on the educated lower middle class and educated minorities.[31] This success proved to be a two-edged sword as others attacked the AVF for using educational attainment as a new form of racism to deny the underprivileged the chance to use the military as a means of social and economic advancement.[32]

As predicted by the Gates Commission, Blacks' participation in the AVF did increase without delegitimizing the social status of military service. In 2022, educational attainment and socio-economic status (SES) became better predictors of who would volunteer to serve.[33] For the last two decades, the AVF has been under-representative of whites at 50% and under-representative of Hispanics at 9% (in comparison to 76% and 19%, respectively, in the civilian workforce).[34] As of 2023, in the second year of a historical recruiting crisis, both Black and Hispanic accessions increased to 24%.[35] The increased percentage of

---

30. Scott, De Angelis, and Segal, *Military Sociology*, 101. See also Moskos and Butler, *All That We Can Be*, 66-70.
31. Segal, *Recruiting for Uncle Sam*, 41.
32. Bailey, *America's Army*, 119-126, 200-201.
33. Asoni et al., "A Mercenary Army," 594-598.
34. Government Accountability Office, "Military Personnel: Reporting Additional Servicemember Demographics Could Enhance Congressional Oversight," 19.
35. Steve Beynon, "Army Sees Sharp Decline in White Recruits," *Military Times*, January 10, 2024, sec. Daily News, accessed January 11, 2024, https://www.military.com/daily-news/2024/01/10/army-sees-sharp-decline-white-recruits.html.

accessions for these two groups is inflated by a reduced end-strength and a more recent disproportional decline in white enlistments. Black and Hispanic accessions are above the density found in the general population and typically come from families with both a higher SES and better employment qualifications than those of white accessions, and above the mean level for their respective ethnic categories. Once in the military, Blacks' percentage of the force increases to 1.5 times more than the general population due to better retention—a condition attributed to better opportunities for minorities within the military as compared to civilian society.[36] Among minorities, the role of republicanism (i.e., patriotism, sense of civic duty motivation) was less prevalent when compared to whites when considering military service, but minorities are not more likely than whites to attribute military service as the employment option of last resort (e.g., an economic, transactional motivation).[37]

The increased participation and success of Blacks in the volunteer Army did not remove social concerns over the racial composition of the AVF. When the AVF was tested under recent wartime conditions, race again surfaced as tension in the civil-military divide, as emotional debates emerged on issues of fairness. In the early days of the Iraq War, Representative Charles Rangel (D-NY) proclaimed the GWOT "a 'death tax' that is levied disproportionately on the poor and the nonwhite."[38] The subsequent release by the DOD of casualty information proved this statement false, as Blacks were underrepresented in the casualty figures of Operation Iraqi Freedom (OIF) and Operation Enduring Freedom (OEF), but the sensitivity to the racial composition of the force remained.[39]

In juxtaposition to these claims of adverse effects from the over-

---

36. Choongsoo Kim et al., "The All-Volunteer Force: A 1979 Profile and Some Issues," Youth Knowledge Development Report (Washington, DC: U.S. Department of Labor, Employment and Training Administration, Office of Youth Programs, 1980), World-Cat.org, https://permanent.fdlp.gov/gpo61400/ED203059.pdf, vii, 12, 15.
37. Krebs and Ralston, "Patriotism or Paychecks," 42.
38. Askia Muhammad, "Rangel: The Iraq War Is a 'death Tax' on the Poor," Final Call News (blog), April 29, 2004, accessed November 15, 2023, https://new.finalcall.com/?p=4757.
39. Golding and Adedeji, "The All-Volunteer Military," 24-34.

representation of Blacks in the AVF, claims of structural racial discrimination against non-Blacks, and over-sensitivity to acceptance of political arguments claiming the presence of racism (i.e., "wokeness," acceptance of critical race theory) were cited by some as reasons for the recent failed recruiting of Whites.[40] While these claims lack rigorous evidentiary merit, the strong effect nonetheless persists. As an illustration of the lack of precision in these claims, Claire Snyder argues that the idea of "wokeness" is a demonstration of identity politics that actually enables extremism in the military as resistance to purposeful efforts to ensure equality gets credentialed as adhering to core values.[41] No modeling or substantive argument exists that places accessions as zero-sum-gain; whereas if one category increases (i.e., Blacks), the other categories must decrease.

While the 2001 political rhetoric on race in the military was inflammatory, it did not reflect the new trends in accessions that were causing non-representative accessions. In 2005, with the wars in Iraq and Afghanistan well underway, recruits from the south and west continued to be overrepresented, as well as Blacks and Hispanics. Additionally, enlistees from these groups were more likely to make it a career.[42] While some activists applauded these gains by Blacks, others cited this rate and type of participation as a form of structural racism in the AVF, as it disproportionally injured Blacks and removed those most qualified Blacks from a community where their civilian success would have enabled racial progress in business and politics.[43] Although not supported by the data, this modern sentiment echoed

---

40. Lolita Baldor, "Army Sees Safety." See also Daniel Johnson, "Op-Ed: Military Could Help Recruitment by Doing More to Resolve Disparities," January 4, 2023, accessed January 09, 2023https://www.chicagotribune.com/opinion/commentary.
41. Snyder, *Citizen-Soldiers and Manly Warriors*, 107-136.
42. Government Accountability Office, "Military Personnel: Reporting Additional Servicemember Demographics Could Enhance Congressional Oversight," 80.
43. Like in Vietnam (see Moskos and Butler, 1997), the casualty rates during the Global War on Terror did not vary significantly by race, see Department of Defense, "Defense Casualty Analysis System," 2022, https://dcas.dmdc.osd.mil/dcas/app/conflictCasualties. Black veteran unemployment rate is 3 times that of Whites and Hispanics, indicating that their military service and associated skills are less valued by their community, see Department of Labor, "Black Veterans Research," Black Veterans Research, December 5, 2024, https://www.dol.gov/agencies/vets/resources/black-veterans-research.

the 1970s, when the Gates Commission had identified that" there is strong evidence to suggest that the Black community, more than the White, looks at the 'male drain'"as extremely costly."[44] The continued concern regarding Blacks' participation in the AVF indicates that the salience of race, as a dimension of the shared burden of republicanism, remains important.

In summary, for varying reasons, race has consistently played a significant role in evaluating the personnel composition of the U.S. military. Prior to 1948, Blacks were excluded by policy from the opportunity to fully demonstrate republicanism. Since then, having a representative force with proportional minority participation has remained a goal shared by all components of the American Paradoxical Trinity, although it has only been achieved with Blacks. During the Vietnam War and Iraq-Afghanistan Wars, society remained sensitive to the risks of Blacks being overrepresented in the military and the associated risks of becoming a casualty; and during times of peace, society is sensitive to Blacks being underrepresented in the military and thereby denied the benefits of military service. An imbalance in either condition fuels a civil-military divide. Currently, the enlisted ranks of the AVF have an overrepresentation of Blacks, while other minorities are underrepresented. An analysis is required to know better whether AVF recruiting has provided representative accessions, where Blacks enlist proportionally from all 50 states. If not, do the accession patterns of Blacks follow the larger pattern of geographic over-representation?

Gender Diversity and Recruiting

In contrast to race, which has consistently been a consideration of military accessions for a variety of reasons, the role of women in the U.S. military has a more nuanced history, but no less storied. Tradition-

---

44. "Commission on an All-Volunteer Armed Force," 142. In the officer corps Blacks are inversely underrepresented so their participation is even more removed as a credible "brain drain" to minority communities See Detrick L. Briscoe, "The Black Community Perspective: Recruiting Blacks into Combat Arms:" (Carlisle, PA: Army War College, March 1, 2013), Defense Technical Information Center, https://doi.org/10.21236/ADA589048.

ally, U.S. society has viewed women as a protected class, righteously exempted from military service regardless of their preference. Until recently, deviations from this approach were driven out of necessity; in more recent times, the expansion of the roles of women has been augmented by recognition of the right of women to demonstrate republicanism and receive the full benefits of citizenship that come from being a veteran of military service.

In the initial military expansion that preceded World War II, women were exempt from conscription by federal law and excluded as volunteers from the four services. This changed when critical vacancies (i.e., nurses) forced a policy correction to allow them to participate as auxiliaries in select positions (i.e., medical and clerical) in order to free men from these jobs for other duties. Even in this federally recognized capacity, women served outside of the regular force and were relegated by public law to separate commands (e.g., Women's Army Corps–WACs in the Army, and Women Accepted for Voluntary Emergency Service—WAVES in the Navy).[45] When the personnel demand lessened, women were pushed out of the service.[46] Following World War II, Congress made women a permanent part of the military with the Women's Armed Services Integration Act of 1948, with caveats reflecting social norms.[47] Women remained excluded from combat formations, ships, and aircraft—and unlike Blacks, whose participation was limited to the percentage in the general population—their participation was seemingly arbitrarily capped at 2% of enlisted ranks and 10% of officer ranks, despite a presence of 30% in the civilian workforce.[48] Although women became part of the standing four service branches in non-combat positions, their status remained as subalterns. For example, after World War II, when the military was again confronted by a personnel demand that exceeded capacity, it was forced to stop deferments for married men and provide a monthly family allowance; the new policy did not apply to women. Married

---

45. Mittelstadt, "Military Demographics," 97. See also Scott, et al., *Military Sociology*, 108.
46. Morten Ender, *Army Spouses: Military Families during the Global War on Terror* (Charlottesville, VA: University of Virginia Press, 2023), 15.
47. Taylor, Military Service and American Democracy, 142.
48. Kamarck, "Diversity, Inclusion, and Equal," 18-19.

women continued to be barred from enlistment and subject to separation for pregnancy, marriage, or parenthood—this policy remained in effect until 1975.[49]

The shift from conscription to the AVF resulted in an explosion of opportunity for women, again out of necessity, but this time propelled by the political energy associated with Congress's passing of the Equal Rights Amendment in March 1972.[50] Upon transitioning to the AVF (*AVF 1.0*), Army manpower analysts, retaining their earlier reservations about the AVF, were concerned that sufficient young men with a propensity to join the Army might not exist in the numbers the Gate Commission envisioned. Moreover, they knew that in less than a decade, the number of 17 to 20-year-old men would decline by 10-15%.[51] In keeping with tradition, women were again seen as having an increased role in the military to compensate for the insufficient number of male personnel in the new AVF.[52]

The increased role of women in the services dovetailed with the Army's 1990s (*AVF 2.0*) marketing strategy as a provider of personal opportunity and social good.[53] In 1972, the DOD set a recruiting goal of 6% women; by 1984, it was striving for 12%.[54] Despite doubling, women's participation rate fell woefully short of their 56% participation rate in the civilian workforce.[55] Today, the percentage of women in the Army has tripled since the advent of the AVF from 2% in 1973 to greater than 16% today. At the same time, the composition of Black women serving shifted from 14% in 1973 to 31% in 2022.[56] Without

---

49. Rostker, *I Want You!*, 578.
50. Scott, De Angelis, and Segal, *Military Sociology*, 109. Subsequently, the ratified Congressional amendment proposal failed to achieve the required ratification by 35 states before the March 22, 1979 deadline and expired without becoming an amendment to the Constitution.
51. Bailey, *America's Army*, 136, 154.
52. Taylor, *The Advent of the All-Volunteer Force*, 147.
53. Bailey, *America's Army*, 200-201.
54. Scott, De Angelis, and Segal, *Military Sociology*, 109-113.
55. Department of Labor, "Labor Force Participation Rate by Sex, Race and Hispanic Ethnicity," DOL, 2022, accessed December 5, 2024, http://www.dol.gov/agencies/wb/data/latest-annual-data/working-women/Labor-Force-Participation-Rate-by-Sex-Race-Hispanic-Ethnicity.
56. Michael D. Gambone, *The New Praetorians: American Veterans, Society, and Service from Vietnam to the Forever War*, (Amherst, MA: University of Massachusetts Press, 2021), 136.

significant changes to recruiting methods, the participation rate of women is not expected to rise above 17% by 2040.[57] Social pressures continued to limit women's pursuit of combat roles, and racial attitudes further complicated their participation. From *AVF 2.0* through *AVF 3.0* Black women make up the largest percentage of female accessions, racially slightly above the general population but far below the 51% of their gender.[58] Once in the service, the opportunity for women's advancement is considered more egalitarian than in the civilian workforce,[59] but this does not fully explain their retention. The retention rate for white women is lower than for white males, while the promotion rates for those women who remain are seen as better than in the civilian sector.[60] As a consequence of less attrition during initial entrance training and greater retention, minority women are overrepresented in comparison to the rest of the force and the veteran population.[61] In summary, the increased demand for women in the AVF did not directly correlate with the accession of women, and of those who enlisted, other societal factors resulted in distinct rates of accession based on ethnicity.

Over time, while the requirements of the AVF increased the need for women in uniform, this demand did not make the accession practice more egalitarian. In 1980, President Carter reinstated the SSS as a Federal agency without initiating conscription; requiring all males to register when they turned 18, but women continued to be prohibited from registering—an exclusion sustained by the Supreme Court in

---

See also Brenda L. Moore, "African-American Women in the U.S. Military," *Armed Forces & Society (0095-327X)* 17, no. 3 (March 1, 1991): 363-384, accessed December 7, 2024, https://research.ebsco.com/linkprocessor/plink?id=b4a5a314-8d21-3ec0-ab8f-1112efe37991, 363.

57. Jonathan E. Vespa, "Those Who Served: America's Veterans From World War II to the War on Terror," American Community Survey Report (Washington D.C.: U.S. Department of Commerce, U.S. Census Bureau, 2020), WorldCat.org, https://purl.fdlp.gov/GPO/gpo140251, 2.

58. Golding and Adedeji, "The All-Volunteer Military," 20. See also Segal and Bourg, "Professional Leadership and Diversity," 710.

59. Kim et al., "The All-Volunteer Force," vii.

60. Kim et al., "The All-Volunteer Force," 71-75.

61. Asoni et al., "A Mercenary Army," 594.

1981 in *Rostker v. Goldberg*.[62] For those women who volunteered, other formidable barriers existed within the military as each Service applied a "combat exclusion" coding indicating "front line" status to deny select occupations and positions to women—this had the additive effect of denying women access to those billets of greatest prestige and essential to promotion to senior grades. In a pattern similar to the role of race in the AVF, social norms governing the role of women continued to limit their participation regardless of their mental and physical ability.

Changes in social norms and gender bias came slowly, with abrupt shifts. In 2016, after three years of Services' experimentation, Secretary of Defense Ash Carter lifted all exclusions to women by formally rescinding the "Risk Rule of 1988," but the unequal social status remained as women were barred from registering for the SSS by statute.[63] By August 01, 2019, all Brigade Combat Teams of the Army had women in their infantry, armor, and field artillery battalions.[64] Looking at the future design of *AVF 4.0*, experts predict the military will have to increasingly embrace women and minorities to remain viable.[65] Women are progressively surpassing men in education, and men's participation in the workforce is declining.[66] Army accessions from 2013-2023 have not mirrored this trend, as the number of female

---

62. Selective Service System, "Women," Government, Selective Service System, accessed November 6, 2023, https://www.sss.gov/register/women/.
63. Connie A. Buscha, "Overturning the 'Risk Rule' of 1988, Opting for New Risks: U.S. Women Servicemembers and the War in Afghanistan," *Armed Forces & Society* 49, no. 4 (October 2023): 1037, https://doi.org/10.1177/0095327X221103295.
64. Kyle Rempfer, "Army 'Ahead of Schedule' in Integrating Women in Combat Arms, Outgoing SMA Says as He Departs," *Army Times*, August 18, 2019, sec. Your Army, accessed January 07, 2023, https://www.armytimes.com/news/your-army/2019/08/16/army-ahead-of-schedule-in-integrating-women-in-combat-arms-outgoing-sma-says-as-he-departs/.
65. Jennifer Hlad, "Military Must Recruit More Women, Immigrants for the Future Force, Experts Say," Defense One, January 27, 2023, accessed February 01, 2023, https://www.defenseone.com/policy/2023/01/military-must-recruit-more-women-immigrants-future-force-experts-say/382317/.
66. Meghann Myers, "Experts, Data Point to Women as Best Military Recruiting Pool," *Military Times*, January 26, 2023, accessed January 27, 2023, sec. Your Military, https://www.militarytimes.com/news/your-military/2023/01/26/experts-data-point-to-women-as-best-military-recruiting-pool/.

enlistees has increased modestly by virtue of end-strength reductions (at roughly 10k annually), while male enlistments have dropped by 35%.[67]

Ideally, the opportunities afforded women in the military, and the republican need for a representative force would drive an increased accession of women from across the country until their representation was proportional by geography, ethnicity, education, and gender. However, the above history, coupled with a strong tradition of conservative values (see Table 4 in Chapter 3)—which manifested as political objections to women serving in combat roles—would predict a lower per capita recruiting propensity for women, and especially minority women, from the southern states. An analysis is required to determine whether military recruiting efforts reflect the recognized central importance of race and gender to the AVF's composition and have responded to overcome long-standing social attitudes and biases in order to provide representative accessions.

Educational Diversity and Recruiting

The education level of military accessions has long been considered a determinant of the military's representativeness, especially since educational attainment averages vary by race and gender. The supporters of a transition to a volunteer force in 1970 argued that while it would be a smaller force (with risks offset by a ready reserve and a stand-by draft), a better-quality force would result as a consequence of volunteers having a higher education level than those drafted because they could not secure a deferment. The required education qualifications of enlistees have long served as one of the "levers" used by the Services to increase enlistments when necessary.[68] Unlike race and

---

67. Steve Beynon and Kelsey Baker, "The Army's Recruiting Problem Is Male," *Military Times*, June 17, 2024, accessed June 17, 2024, https://www.military.com/daily-news/2024/06/14/armys-recruiting-problem-male.html?utm_campaign=dfn-ebb&utm_medium=email&utm_source=sailthru.

68. MG Thurman, as the commander that brought USAREC into the modern era (circa 1979), defined five levers at the Army's disposal to effect recruiting: 1. Youth Attitudinal Tracking Survey to identify target populations, 2. educational benefits, 3. bonuses, 4. number of recruiters, and 5. Advertising; identified in Rostker, I Want You!, 607.

gender, whose role in accessions often reflected social biases and subgroup contests for equality, education has been, and continues to be the lever in accessions that was/is pushed or pulled in response to the arguments of quality versus quantity.[69] Those who argued that quality required higher education standards argued that a recruit with high educational attainment most efficiently yielded a quality force. Opponents of high education standards for military accessions argued that using education as a means of discernment constitutes a "code for racism" because measuring a recruit's quality, especially regarding education, was more a reflection of social opportunity rather than inherent talent.[70] Congruent with the social welfare and civil rights arguments related to ethnicity previously discussed, many viewed military service as a broad social entitlement and a means for the disadvantaged to demonstrate republicanism. In this way, the military's largeness could be used by society to improve a minority or disadvantaged citizens by imparting skills or opening opportunities for them as veterans that would have otherwise been unattainable. What is not known is whether the social tension associated with the education level of military accessions has resulted in purposeful oversight or whether this aspect of the AVF has been allowed to atrophy in a manner similar to geographical, racial, and gender representativeness.

Today, when confronted with the expansive demands of a global foreign policy, there is a limit to the degree to which a *quality* force can compensate for the *quantity* of the force. The debate as to how big a discriminator education should serve in accessions has continued since World War II to the present, with various arguments achieving ascendancy for periods of time. One of the enduring lessons of the mass mobilization of World War II was the benefits of using aptitude and qualification assessments in determining suitability for military service. The military—especially the Army—understood the relationship between servicemembers' education and the quality of their work.

---

69. Other criteria used as metrics of a "quality force," such as physical and mental health, have varied over time under the authority of the service branches.
70. Bailey, *America's Army*, 119, 89.

Generally, smarter inductees (as measured by scores on a common induction aptitude test and the attainment of a high school diploma) required less supervision, had fewer disciplinary problems, had a higher survivability rate in combat, and were more likely to complete their term of enlistment satisfactorily.[71] Additionally, they required less training and could perform more complex tasks on advanced weapons. The battery of tests first used in World War II has evolved and continues to be used today in modified forms. Since the beginning of the AVF, the DOD has used two metrics of cognition for each recruit, educational attainment and score on the Armed Forces Qualification Test (AFQT), to qualify potential recruits for service and assign them to an occupation. Educational attainment has three tiers: Tier 1—high school graduate or at least 15 credit hours of college, Tier 2—alternative credentials such as GED, and Tier 3—no educational credentials. AFQT scores place an applicant in one of six categories (see Table 6).

Table 6. Armed Forces Qualification Test Percentile Ranges

AFQT Category	Percentile Score Range
I	93-99
II	65-92
III A	50-64
III B	31-49
IV	10-30
V	1-9

Source: Information from Department of Defense Report on Social Representation in the U.S. Military Services, 2000.

In 1966, the Army, in an attempt to normalize accessions and fulfill its institutional requirement to society by providing an opportunity to more citizens, initiated Project 100,000. In the two-year experiment, 100,000 men who were otherwise not qualified for Army service by

---

71. Golding and Adedeji, "The All-Volunteer Military," 14. See also Office of the Assistant Secretary of Defense (Force Management Policy), "Chapter 2: The Recruiting Process," Population Representation in the Military Services (Washington, DC: Department of Defense, 2000), https://prhome.defense.gov/portals/52/Documents/POPREP/poprep99/html/chapter2/c2_recruiting.html. See also Rostker, *I Want You!*, 493. See also Bailey, *America's Army*, 107.

education were inducted and given extended training so that they might improve sufficiently to meet performance standards. The results were debatable, with parsed references to the data depending on what type of conclusions were necessary for the respective arguments. The proponents of the Army as a means for increased social opportunity proclaimed the experiment a success and cited the participants' achievements as evidence of bias that had previously deemed the participants unqualified. Conversely, opponents of this experimental training method made a pragmatic rebuttal against lowering recruiting standards (to those of the 100,000 participants) by citing the additional costs of increased training and a greater attrition rate.[72] Regardless of how the experiment is judged, it showed that as military service became increasingly marketed as a form of social advancement, the effect was to decrease the salience of military service as a republican civic duty.

During the Vietnam War, the accession standards for mental aptitude were comparatively low—with all but the bottom 10% deemed cognitively qualified for service—and this metric formed the basis for predicting the manpower available for a volunteer force.[73] Prior to 1973, the performance and casualty risks arising from a less educated force were partially offset by the draft, which inducted men with a wide range of education—albeit not proportionally inducted. As part of this process, the SSS also granted an increasing number of deferments from the draft to pursue post-secondary education. Since the pursuit of higher education covaried closely with SES, these deferments exacerbated the racial inequality of the draft.[74] One of the reservations from the Service Branches to ending the draft was that without the draft's induction of personnel of higher mental aptitude, the mean

---

72. Bailey, *America's Army*, 107. See also Morris Janowitz, "Characteristics of the Military Environment," in *The Military and American Society - Essays and Readings*, ed. Stephen E. Ambrose and James Alden Barber, Jr., 1st edition (New York, NY: Free Press, 1973), 166–76. See also Segal, *Recruiting for Uncle Sam*, 91.
73. "Commission on an All-Volunteer Armed Force," 146.
74. James Allen Barber, "The Draft and Alternatives to the Draft," in *The Military and American Society - Essays and Readings*, ed. Stephen E. Ambrose and James Alden Barber, Jr., 1st edition (New York, NY: Free Press, 1973), 212. See also Taylor, Military Service and American Democracy, 97.

education level of the volunteer force would decline, potentially to an unmanageable level.[75]

Throughout this debate on education, the Army as an institution has long prided itself on offering a second chance at having a career to those who had underachieved in society.[76] Recruiting campaigns of the 1980s deliberately portrayed the Army as the place where one could "Be All You Can Be." While the long-term benefits might not be as grand as touted, research has shown that military service does provide some long-term benefits for veterans and does, in fact, have a mild effect on social attitudes as a form of a melting pot.[77]

As part of the political conversion and the reduction in force structure that formed *AVF 2.0*, the Army restructured its recruiting objective. While the Army disregarded achieving geographic representation, it did seek to raise quality. By 1991, less than 1% of recruits were from Category IV, and almost 98% were Tier 1 with a high school (HS) diploma.[78]

In 2006, when *AVF 3.0* was nearly subsumed by the growing wars in Iraq and Afghanistan, the Army needed to expand to meet the requirements, without mobilization of the individual reserve or activation of a stand-by draft, and so lowered the education requirement by expanding the number of Category IV enlistees permitted from 2% to 4%.[79] This change, along with increased use of waivers for medical conditions and misconduct, saw Army accessions increase, where one in five recruits required a waiver.[80] In 2022, with consecutive years of

---

75. "Commission on an All-Volunteer Armed Force," 3-14.
76. Stephen E. Ambrose and James Alden Barber, Jr., eds., *The Military and American Society - Essays and Readings*, 1st edition (New York, NY: Free Press, 1973), 10-15.
77. James Allen Barber, "The Social Effects of Military Service," in *The Military and American Society - Essays and Readings*, ed. Stephen E. Ambrose and James Alden Barber, Jr., 1st edition (New York, NY: Free Press, 1973), 160-164.
78. Bailey, *America's Army*, 190, 200-203.
79. Lawrence. Kapp and Charles A. Henning, "Recruiting and Retention: An Overview of FY2006 and FY2007 Results for Active and Reserve Component Enlisted Personnel" (Washington, DC: Congressional Research Service, February 7, 2008), Defense Technical Information Center, https://apps.dtic.mil/sti/pdfs/ADA480780.pdf, 3.
80. Kapp and Henning, "Recruiting and Retention," 3. See also Davis Winkie, "Exclusive: The inside Story of How the Army Rethought Recruiting," *Army Times*, October 9, 2023, accessed October 10, 2023, sec. Your Army, https://www.armytimes.com/news/

failing to meet accession targets and Congressional opposition to a further reduction of accession standards, the Army expanded the recruiting pool by initiating a "Future Soldier Preparatory Course" to develop those otherwise unqualified based on education/AFQT scores or weight.[81] The Army reports initial results as positive and plans to continue the program. These claims are too new to include in this analysis, but do demonstrate a structural change to the *m-s* vertex; distinct from the implementation of the school lunch program and Project 100,000, both of which exercised the g-s vertex.

For the last three decades, in contrast to World War II (during a period of national mobilization that incentivized enlistment), the propensity to enlist has declined with education level.[82] Whereas one in four enlistees had college experience in 1942, today, this characteristic is "almost extinct" at less than 1 in 20 enlist with a college degree.[83] Counterintuitively, the Secretary of the Army announced in 2023 that one of the ways the service would seek to resolve its recruiting problem was to increase its pursuit of those with some college experience. Also, the Army's current statement on diversity acknowledges its past shortcomings resulting from social norms, and its need to deliberately discriminate against those it deems medically and mentally (encompassing mental illness and intelligence) "insufficient."[84] In this statement, the Army declares its intent to seek greater social diversity and affirms that its medical and mental accession criteria are absolute and valid metrics for determining suitability.

---

your-army/2023/10/09/exclusive-the-inside-story-of-how-the-army-rethought-recruiting/.
81. U.S. Army Public Affairs, "Army Announces Creation of Future Soldier Preparatory Course" (United States Army, June 25, 2022), accessed January 07, 2024, https://www.army.mil/article/258758/army_announces_creation_of_future_soldier_preparatory_course.
82. Government Accountability Office, "Military Personnel: Reporting Additional Servicemember Demographics Could Enhance Congressional Oversight," Report to Congressional Requesters (Washington, DC: U.S. Government, September 2005), https://www.gao.gov/assets/gao-05-952.pdf, 80. See also Krebs and Ralston, "Patriotism or Paychecks, 42.
83. David Kieran and Edwin A. Martini, *At War: The Military and American Culture in the Twentieth Century and Beyond, War Culture* (New Brunswick, NJ: Rutgers University Press, 2018), 4-8.
84. U.S. Army, "The Army and Diversity."

When the 1980s are contrasted with the 2020s, it is clear that in modern times, mental acuity as an enlistment criterion has varied.

When faced with an existential threat and personnel shortages, the DOD (through the granting of waivers) and Congress (through statute changes in the annual NDAA) have lowered education and other qualifications, then returned to the military to higher standards when achievement of the accession targets became easier.[85] In this way, Congress exercises the g-s vertex. As the State shapes AVF *4.0*, the DOD's accession benchmarks for education (in compliance with Congressional directives) are 90% Tier 1, 10% Tier 2, and none from Tier 3 unless granted a waiver or exception. The AFQT benchmark for accessions is 60% in Category IIIA or higher, no more than 4% from Category IV, and none from Category 5.[86] The services retain the authority to impose more restrictive standards. Further analysis is required to determine whether the established minimum education standards—approved by Congress—are enacted by military recruiting to provide a geographic, gender, and minority representative force through accessions.

METHOD AND DATA

Since the founding of America, the representativeness of the military has been of central concern based on society's commitment to republicanism—where the requirements of the state are a burden shared by all. Since the founding of the AVF, the representativeness of the military regarding race, gender, and education has remained a central concern for this and other reasons. The representativeness of the U.S. military results from two factors: accession of recruits and retention of current servicemembers. To further understand the stratification of the New Warrior Caste, race, gender, and education level of Army accessions are examined by state of residence at the time of enlistment. As

---

85. Under Secretary of Defense for Personnel and Readiness, "Department of Defense Instruction on Qualitative Distribution of Military Manpower, with Change 2" (Department of Defense, May 4, 2020).
86. Under Secretary of Defense for Personnel and Readiness, "Distribution of Military Manpower."

per Chapters 1 and 3, the Army appropriately serves as the exemplar of the AVF. As in Chapter 3, the subsequent analysis compares Army accession data regarding race, gender, and education from 1990 (*AVF 1.0*, pre-peace dividend drawdown) to 2022 (*AVF 3.0*, post-GWOT, and current recruiting crisis).

Race as a social construct is a set of categories, often aligned with physical characteristics, that serve as "a basis for social inequality and discrimination."[87] As a result, the actualization and implementation of identifying "race" have different consequences that change over time. The role of race, Black race in particular, was specifically cited by the Gates Commission in its study of the viability of a volunteer force. For coding accession data, the DOD uses six categories for race; in addition to Black, there are—American Indian/Alaskan Native, Asian/Pacific Islander, white, Hispanic, and Other. In 1990, the U.S. Census Bureau used ten racial categories, the preceding six, plus four more that refer to Asian and Pacific origins (i.e., Fijian). By 2020, the Census Bureau's conceptualization of race had expanded to include 31 categories, with each further stratified as Hispanic or non-Hispanic. For this analysis, the variable Black reflects self-identification as a person that the DOD's categorization as "Black," or reflects the U.S. Census Bureau's categorization of "Black" (for 1990 data) or "Black or African American alone" (for 2022 data). The variable Gender is coded for analysis as dichotomous, as defined at the point of military induction or census data collection, referred to as male/men and female/women, at 49% and 51% of the population, respectively. Similarly, education is coded for analysis as a dichotomous variable, indicating whether the enlistee had a high school diploma at the time of accession or not. Unless otherwise shown, numbers are rounded to the closest integer (i.e., 99.56% shown as 100%, 4.3% shown as 4%).

ANALYSIS

The analysis of recruiting in Chapter 3 identified that since 1990, there has been a decline in geographic representation in Army accessions; by

---

87. Johnson, *The Blackwell Dictionary*, 223.

2022, a representative force was largely absent. What is not known is whether this AVF military recruiting pattern has compounded the imbalanced problem with disproportional race, gender, and education accessions—the three conditions evaluated by the Gates Commission to inform its recommendation for creating a volunteer force. The following analysis looks at each of these three variables and how they interact with each other by comparing the geographic distribution of accessions in 1990 and 2022 to determine if military recruiting has changed the demographic composition of the AVF in ways other than geographic.

Blacks' Participation in the AVF

In 1990, Blacks comprised 12% of the population from the 50 U.S. states and 5% of Army accessions (N=29,986,000 and n=4,664), at a rate of 16 per 100k Blacks. Then, the distribution of Black enlistments by state per 100k shows an almost bimodal distribution with a much higher rate in the west (particularly the central western states) compared to a much lower rate in the plains and eastern states—NH and VT as the exception (see Figure 11). This geographic distribution pattern for Black accessions is distinct from the aggregate 1990 accession distribution pattern (see Figure 9 in Chapter 3). The locations with the greatest accession of Blacks are generally the inverse of the state's ranking of Blacks as a percentage of the overall population; states with lower percentages of Blacks have higher rates of Black accessions (see Figure 12). The covariance is not exact, so the low Black population density in 1990 is a strong predictor but does not explain all the variance.

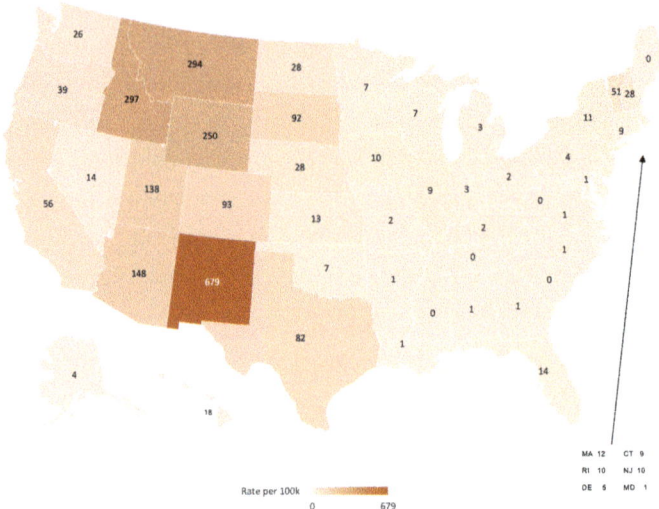

Figure 11. Army Black Enlistments, by State, per 100k, 1990
Source: Data from Freedom of Information Division, Department of Defense. For clarity, enlistments from U.S. territories, districts, overseas, and unknown locations were excluded, n=4,664; and the United States Census Bureau, "1990 Census of Population: General Population Characteristics."

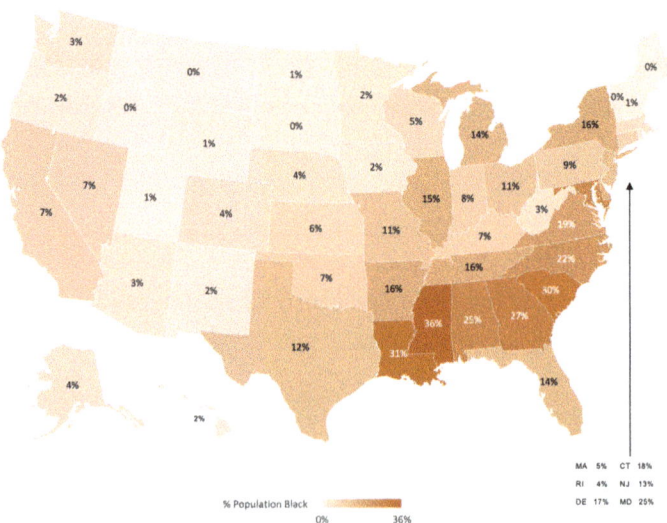

Figure 12. Blacks as Percentage of State Population, 1990
Source: Data from the United States Census Bureau, "1990 Census of Population: General Population Characteristics." * Percentages rounded to the nearest integer—thus, 0% is shown for VT and ID, although Blacks populate all states.

In 2022, Blacks comprised 13% of the population from the 50 U.S.

CHAPTER 4

states, and their participation rate had risen to 23% of Army accessions (N=44,087,000 and n=10,224), at a rate of 23 per 100k. By 2022, a significant change had occurred regarding Army accessions of Blacks; all but one state (VT) had Black residents enlist in the Army (see Figure 13). While the West continued to over-contribute to Black enlistments—but to a lesser degree than in 1990—the Southeastern states emerged with Black accessions above the mean. This increased concentration of Black accessions from the southeast region between 1990 and 2022 is similar to the regional shift of aggregate enlistments but not identical. Although the 1990 aggregate and Black accession concentrations were from different areas of the U.S., by 2022, a very similar—but not exact—crooked smile pattern emerged for both, indicating that military recruiting's pursuit of efficiency significantly changed pre-existing socio-cultural patterns. A comparison of the aggregate and Black accessions by the top and bottom 10% of the state's per capita contribution identifies that while a regional shift is taking place, the two categories do not precisely covary by state (see Table 7).

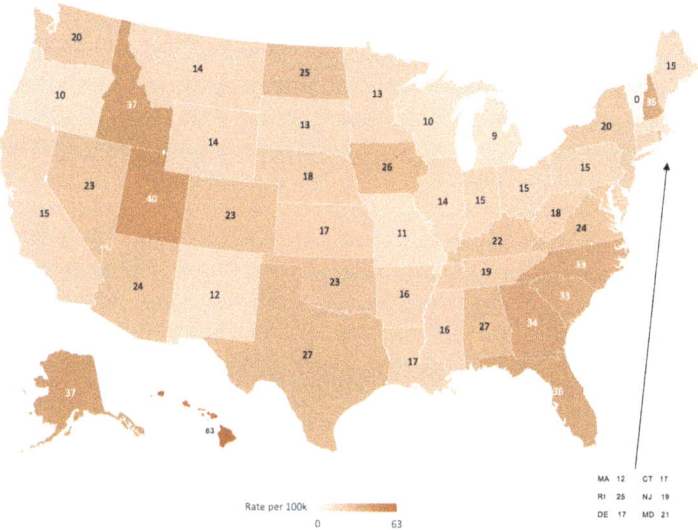

Figure 13. Army Black Enlistments, per 100k, by State, 2022
Source: Data from Freedom of Information Division, Department of Defense. For clarity, enlistments from U.S. territories, districts, overseas, and unknown locations were excluded, n=10,224; and the United States Census Bureau, "2020-2022 State Population Totals and Components of Change."

Table 7. State Rankings of All and Black Accessions in 1990 and 2022

Rank (per 100k)	1990		2022	
	General	Black	General	Black
1	WY	AZ	GA	HI
2	AR	ID	NC	ID, AK*
3	WV	MT	FL	
4	ID	NM	SC, TX*	NH, FL*
5	MT	UT		
46	UT	MN, MS, SC, TN, WV *, **	NJ	MO
47	MA		RI, CT*	OR, WI*
48	HI			
49	CT		VT	MI
50	NJ		MA	VT**

* Tied rankings of accessions per 100k.
** Ranking of 0 accessions per 100k resulting from no Black accessions.

Women's Participation in the AVF

In 1990, women, while just over half the population of the U.S., comprised 14.5% of Army accessions (n=12,930) at a rate of 10 per 100k women. The per capita geographic distribution of women volunteers during this time is shared across the 50 states, as the range variance has a nearly normal distribution with identical mean and median values of 11. The small geographic variance present identifies an over-representation of women enlistees from the Northwest and the Southeast (see Figure 14). Generally, the geographic pattern of women enlistments in 1990 mirrors the aggregate distribution of accessions in 1990 (see Figure 8 in Chapter 3).

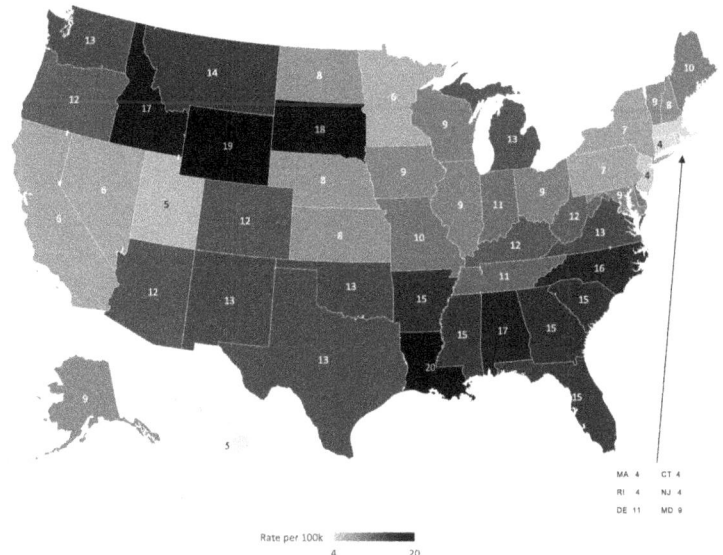

Figure 14. Army Women Enlistments, per 100k, by State, 1990
Source: Data from Freedom of Information Division, Department of Defense. For clarity, enlistments from U.S. territories, districts, overseas, and unknown locations were excluded, n=12,930; and the United States Census Bureau, "1990 Census of Population: General Population Characteristics."

Three decades later, the effects of military recruiting on women's accessions are clear. In 2000, the Army's accession of women as a percentage of the total active component peaked at 20% (n=14,665 and N=72,203). While women obviously remain the same percentage of the U.S. population, their Army accession rate had stabilized at 16% (n=7,001), while the rate per 100k women had declined by more than half to 4. Given that the total percentage of women accessed in 2022 had fallen by 6%, concurrent with the removal of combat exclusion codes that truncated career opportunities, this indicates that several factors besides military recruiting continue to significantly affect their participation. This contrasts with Black's increased total participation over the same period, which was accompanied by an increased percentage of Blacks in the force and an increased accession rate per 100k Blacks. A noteworthy indicator of the effect of military recruiting for the AVF is that by 2022, women who enlisted in the Army were predominantly from the Southeast (see Figure 15), replicating the same crooked smile pattern identified for 2022 aggregate enlistments (see

Figure 9 in Chapter 3). The influence of military recruiting is evident when considering female accessions, where it has caused even fewer states to overproduce to a greater degree when compared to aggregate accessions.

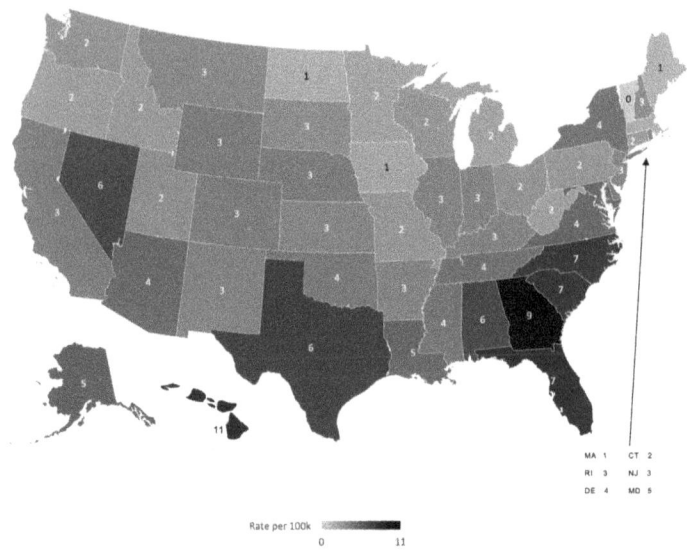

Figure 15. Army Women Enlistments, per 100k, by State, 2022
Source: Data from Freedom of Information Division, Department of Defense. For clarity, enlistments from U.S. territories, districts, overseas, and unknown locations were excluded, n=7001; and the United States Census Bureau, "2020-2022 State Population Totals and Components of Change."

When race is considered in conjunction with women's accession to the Army, the pattern is similar but exhibited with much lower numbers. In 1990, Black women comprised 6% of the U.S. population but less than 1% of Army accessions (n=592) at a rate of 4 per 100k Black women. The source of Black women's Army enlistments in 1990 demonstrates a clear geographic pattern of over-representation from the West (see Figure 16). This pattern generally aligns with the pattern of the aggregate Black enlistees—comprised primarily of males (see Figure 11)—but not aligned with the pattern of aggregate women enlistees—comprised primarily of white females (see Figure 14) whose proportion is in decline.

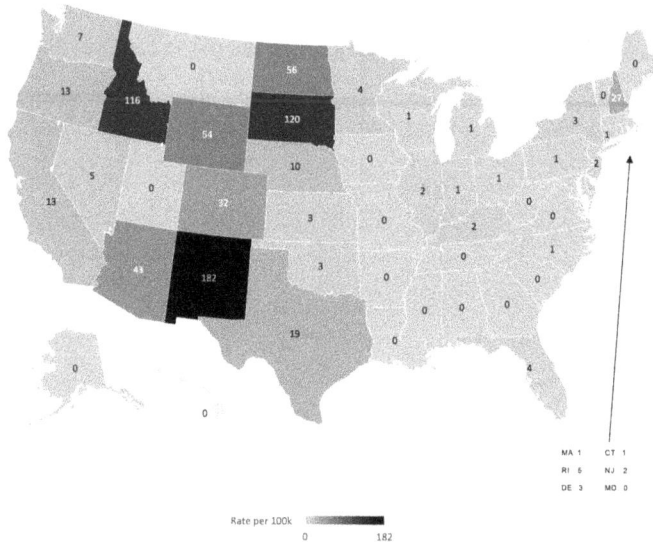

Figure 16. Army Black Women Enlistments per 100k, by State, 1990
Source: Data from Freedom of Information Division, Department of Defense. For clarity, enlistments from U.S. territories, districts, overseas, and unknown locations were excluded, n=592; and the United States Census Bureau, "1990 Census of Population: General Population Characteristics."

By 2022, Black women comprised 7% of the population, and their accessions had increased to 5% of the Army (n=2,373) with an accession rate of 10 per 100k Black women. The number of states considered as outliers for Black women's accession declined from 1990 to 2022, a pattern reversed from the findings for all women, where the number of outliers increased. In keeping with the trend of all Black accessions discussed above, Black women enlistments became much more geographically dispersed, but still show the effects of military recruiting's selective engagement. While Western states continued to overrepresent Black women's accessions, their rate fell markedly, whereas the Southeast became the region providing the highest rate of enlistments for Black women (see Figure 17). Like the preceding aggregate accession analysis and focused analysis of Blacks and women, AVF recruiting had changed Black women's accession pattern to the "crooked smile" of the Southeast.

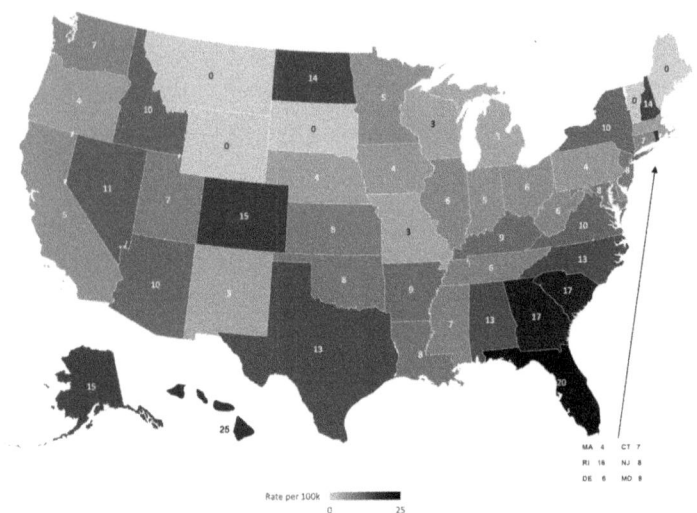

Figure 17. Army Black Women Enlistments per 100k, by State, 2022
Source: Data from Freedom of Information Division, Department of Defense. For clarity, enlistments from U.S. territories, districts, overseas, and unknown locations were excluded, n=2,373; and the United States Census Bureau, "2020-2022 State Population Totals and Components of Change."

Education Level and Accessions for the AVF

The third critical variable in the formation of the AVF was the role of education as a determinant of the force's quality and capability to employ technology. In 1990, 96.99% of Army accessions from the 50 states had graduated with at least a High School (HS) diploma. During this time there was no clear geographic accession pattern for those with a HS diploma (see Figure 18) in 1990; the variation in education from state to state compared to the Army's mean for education was slight and evenly distributed.

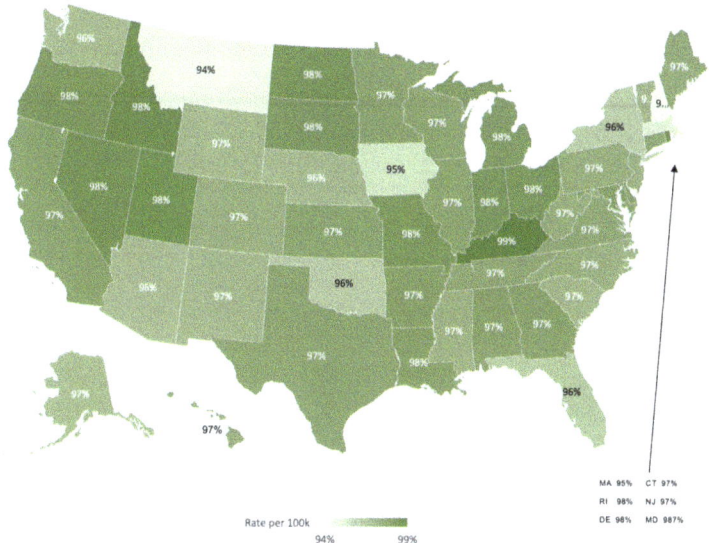

Figure 18. Army HS Diploma Enlistments, per 100k, by State, 1990
Source: Data from Freedom of Information Division, Department of Defense. For clarity, enlistments from U.S. territories, districts, overseas, and unknown locations were excluded, n=86,458.

By 2022, the Army's accession rate for those with a high school diploma had risen to 99.78%. In the intervening 32 years, the recruiting methods did not induce a change in geographic pattern for those with a high school diploma. As in 1990, the variation in education from state to state, compared to the Army's mean for education, was slightly increased and evenly distributed across the 50 states. (see Figure 19).

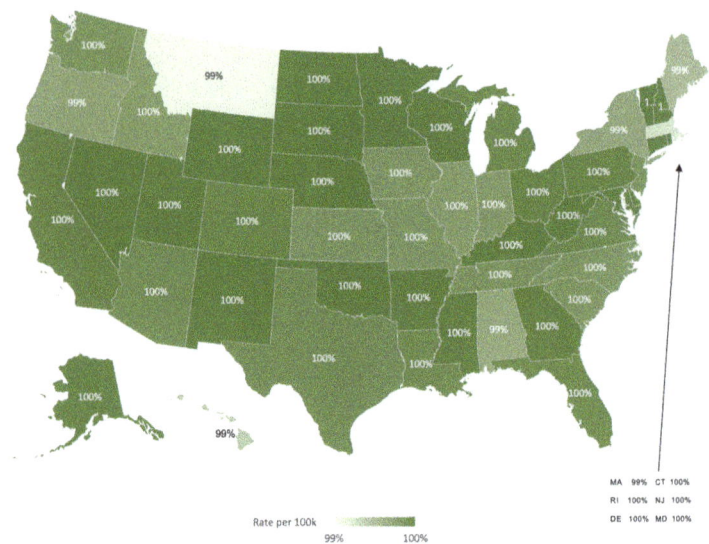

Figure 19. Army HS Diploma Enlistments, per 100k, by State, 2022
Source: Data from Freedom of Information Division, Department of Defense. For clarity, enlistments from U.S. territories, districts, overseas, and unknown locations were excluded, n=43,782.

Similarly, the 50 states show little variation from the Army's mean for education when HS graduate accessions are examined by race. Among Blacks who enlisted in the Army in 1990, 97.11 % had a high school diploma. Except for a few outlier states that had had zero Blacks enlist from that state in 1990, the percentage of HS graduates varied little from state to state, with no geographic pattern (see Figure 20). The small sample size of some states can appear as outsized scores; as an example, consider WA state, where the accession of four non-HS graduates dropped the state's percentage by 10%.

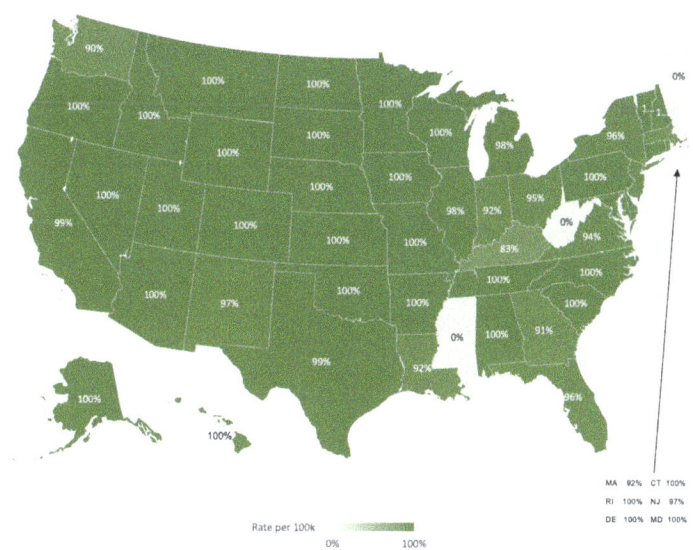

Figure 20. Army HS Diploma Black Enlistments, %, by State, 1990
Source: Data from Freedom of Information Division, Department of Defense. For clarity, enlistments from U.S. territories, districts, overseas, and unknown locations were excluded, n=4,579.
* States with a 0% coefficient (e.g., WV, AL) result from no Black enlistments to measure.

By 2022, the percentage of Blacks who enlisted in the Army with a high school diploma rose to 99.83% (slightly above the aggregate average), and each state's mean rose accordingly. Beyond this, there was little change other than the number of outlier states with no Black accessions dropping to 1—VT (see Figure 21).

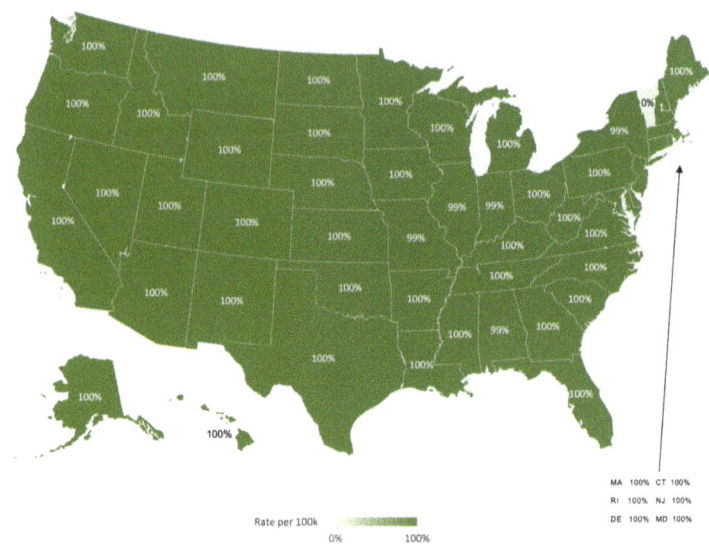

Figure 21. Army HS Diploma Black Enlistments, %, by State, 2022
Source: Data from Freedom of Information Division, Department of Defense. For clarity, enlistments from U.S. territories, districts, overseas, and unknown locations were excluded, n=10,207.
* States with a 0% coefficient (e.g., VT) result from no Black enlistments to measure.

When gender is considered in the Army's accessions of HS graduates, some change is evident over time. In 1990, 94.95% of women enlistees had a HS diploma. Like accessions of aggregate and Blacks with HS diploma, the rate is generally equal from state to state; the four exceptions—not geographically aligned—are IA, WV, VT, and NH (see Figure 22).

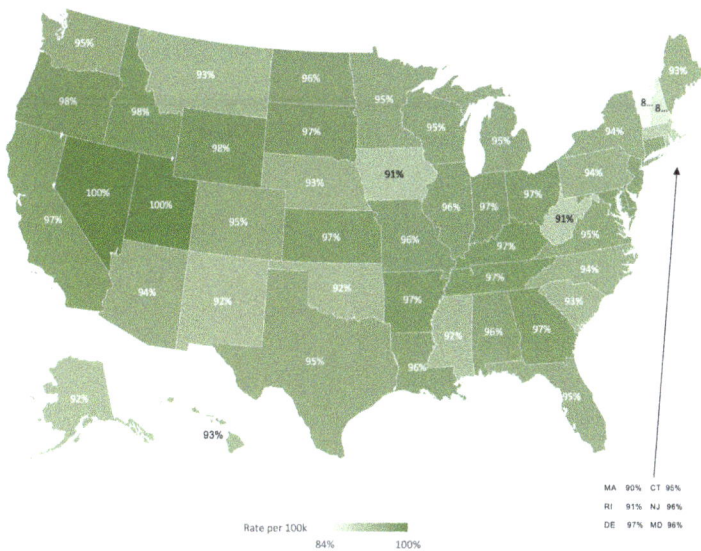

Figure 22. Army HS Diploma Women Enlistments, %, by State, 1990
Source: Data from Freedom of Information Division, Department of Defense. For clarity, enlistments from U.S. territories, districts, overseas, and unknown locations were excluded, n=12,298.

By 2022, the percentage of women with a HS diploma had risen to 99.76% (above the aggregate average), in keeping with the larger trend of increased percentage of HS graduate accessions. With this higher percentage, no geographic pattern is evident (see Figure 23), like the findings from the aggregate, and race comparisons of HS graduate accessions. MT, which seems to be a clear exception in the figure, has only a 5% deviation from the mean.

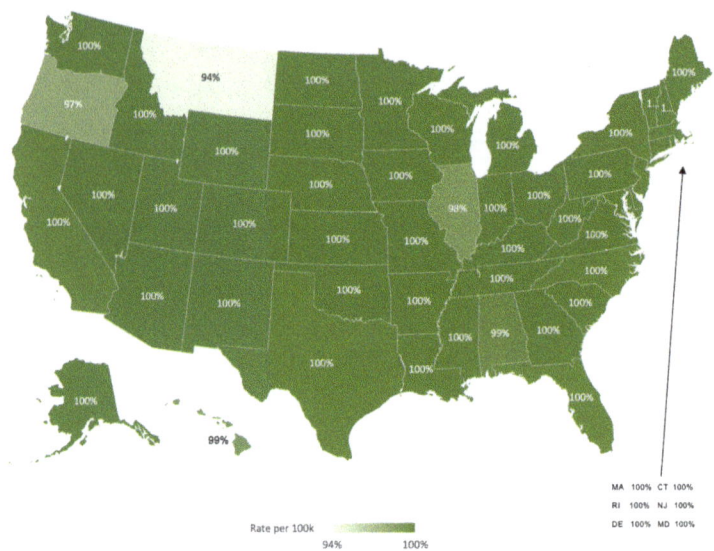

Figure 23. Army HS Diploma Women Enlistments, %, by State, 2022
Source: Data from Freedom of Information Division, Department of Defense. For clarity, enlistments from U.S. territories, districts, overseas, and unknown locations were excluded, n=6,986.

The small differences in Army accessions of women become evident when HS graduate women accessions are further stratified by race. Of the Black women who enlisted in the Army from the 50 states in 1990, 94.81% had a high school diploma; a rate lower than the aggregate total accessions of all Blacks and women. By small amounts, the Western states had a higher percentage of Black women HS graduates compared to the eastern half of the U.S. (see Figure 24), similar to the pattern seen for Black accessions in 1990 (see Figure 13, previous). Ten states (MT, UT, IA, AR, MS, WV, VA, SC, NH, ME) have 0% of Black women with HS diplomas enlisting because these states had zero Black women accessions that year.

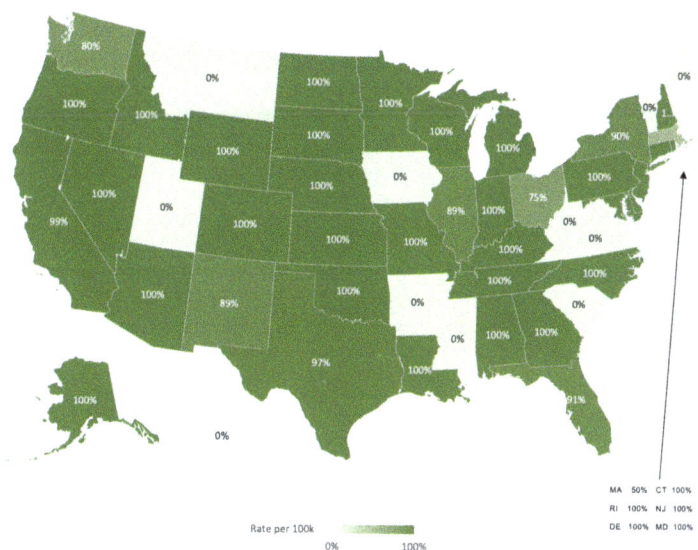

Figure 24. Army HS Diploma Black Women Enlistments, %, by State, 1990
Source: Data from Freedom of Information Division, Department of Defense. For clarity, enlistments from U.S. territories, districts, overseas, and unknown locations were excluded, n=592.
* States with a 0% coefficient (e.g., MT, SC) result from no Black women enlistments to measure.

By 2022, with 99.83% of Black women accessions with a HS diploma (slightly above the Army's average percentage), the geographical accession difference between West and East had disappeared (see Figure 25). Four states (WY, SD, VT, ME) had 0% of Black women with a HS diploma enlist because these states had zero Black women accessions to the Army in that year.

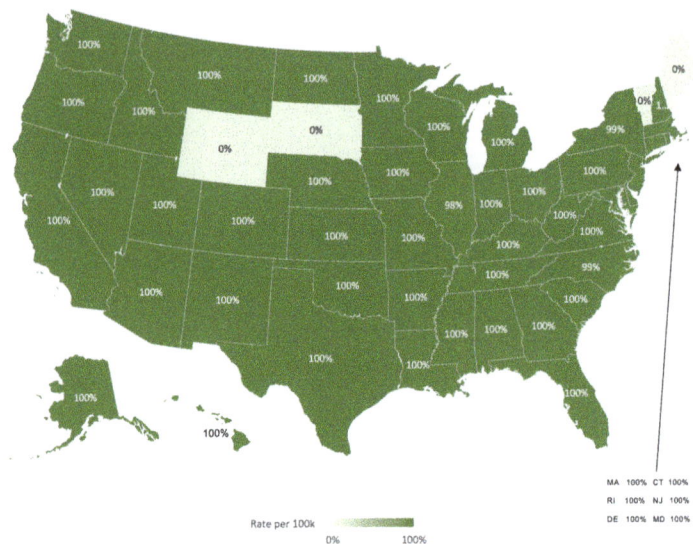

Figure 25. Army HS Diploma Black Women Enlistments, %, by State, 2022
Source: Data from Freedom of Information Division, Department of Defense. For clarity, enlistments from U.S. territories, districts, overseas, and unknown locations were excluded, n=2,373.
* States with a 0% coefficient (e.g., WY, ME) result from no Black women enlistments to measure.

FINDINGS

Race (particularly Blacks), female participation, and education level were of central consideration for the Gates Commission in explaining the feasibility of sustaining a large military with a volunteer force. The above analysis identifies that the New Warrior Caste, which is over-represented by children of veterans and under-represented by geography, is further stratified from society by these three variables. In the near term, the New Warrior Caste accessions profile defines the subsequent veteran population and, in doing so, causes a recruiting problem by making the applicant pool narrower and ever smaller. The changes in accession characteristics from 1990 to 2022 regarding race and gender, but not education, point to three significant findings that speak to the consequences of market-based recruiting on America's Paradoxical Trinity (see Figure 2 in Chapter 2).

First, the geographic source of accessions for race and gender were distinct from each other and the larger national pattern in 1990, then by

2022 had coalesced to the same geographic area, "the crooked smile," identified in Chapter 3. This quantifies the robustness effect of a market-based military recruiting driven foremost by short-term efficiency (e.g., meeting the FY's enlistment quotas). The rate of accessions per 100k has declined from 1990 to 2022, primarily because the reduced end-strength requires fewer recruits. However, the rate and direction of change per 100k are inconsistent across the analyzed demographics (see Table 8). The variance would indicate intervening effects on military recruiting (i.e., demographic targeting in advertising) and potentially exogenous social variables (i.e., a decline in republicanism). Blacks' confidence in the military peaked in 1986, and since then has lagged behind whites by 3% to 16%.[88] Despite this, the Army has achieved the worthy goal of eliminating the underrepresentation of Blacks in its accessions. For this to occur, the accession percentage of other groups (in this case, the majority—white males) must shrink. However, when the increased accession of Blacks from 1990 to 2022 is overlaid against an almost 40% end-strength reduction, then the increased participation of Blacks is accelerating disproportionally to the general population; military recruiting is increasingly underperforming in white male and female accessions while improving slightly with Blacks (male and female) and Hispanics. Put differently, current AVF recruiting methods increasingly isolate the geographic breadth of Americans from serving in their military, but the increased participation rate of Blacks and Black women demonstrates that the success that initially served as an initial justification for the military's recruiting methods has perpetuated without mitigation to become a liability through over-representation that risks the legitimacy of the AVF in peace and war. This condition was a central concern of the Gates Commission in 1973.

---

88. Feaver, *Thanks for Your Service*, 17-19.

Table 8. Demographic Accession Rates, per 100k, in 1990 and 2022

Characteristic	1990	2022	Change	
End Strength*	732,403	461,246	(-)	37%
Aggregate	36	13	(-)	64%
Black	16	23	(+)	77%
Women	10	4	(-)	60%
Black Women	4	10	(+)	150%

* End strength provided as a reference: it is a total number, not a rate per 100k

Second, unlike Black accessions, which have increased as a percentage, women's accessions have declined slightly from their peak in 2000 and, in the process, have become concentrated in the Southeastern U.S.—as have other accessions. The increased opportunities for women in the Army have not correlated with an increased participation rate. While not necessarily causal, the declining participation rate of women covaries with women's confidence in the military.[89] The exception to this finding is Black women, whose accession rate has increased. The comparison of 1990 women's accession to aggregate Black and Black women's accessions illustrates that race, more than gender, is better determined by which states Black women enlist from. By 2022, the covariance of these groups in accessions supports the argument that military recruiting methods are a strong force capable of overwriting social norms (both good and bad) related to race and gender. The increasing influence of military recruiting on civil-military relations and as an exogenous factor on America's Paradoxical Trinity is discussed further in Chapter 6.

Finally, the education level of enlistees did not appear to be affected by the military recruiting's quest for efficiency. From 1990 to 2022, little variance was seen in the percentage of HS graduates entering the Army, either by quantity or geography. The temporary authority granted to the Army by Congress to waive education requirements during the peak of the Iraq and Afghanistan wars was not captured in the periods of this analysis. When the educational level was measured by race and gender, no geographic concentration was evident. When

---

89. Feaver, *Thanks for Your Service*, 17.

the education level of recruits is considered, the recruiting enterprise does not appear to favor any one group (i.e., geography, race, or gender) over the other in its accessions. The maximum percentages of non-HS graduates permitted in each year's accessions are stipulated by law in the NDAA, and compliance is closely monitored by Congress and publicly reviewed in the annual Service's Posture hearing. In this way, the government specifically states and enforces accession criteria. While done to a lesser degree than the SSS, this method purposefully exercises the *g-s* vertex of the American Paradoxical Trinity. Conversely, in the absence of oversight, the military recruiting's drive to efficiently meet near-term induction requirements can, over time, create a New Warrior Caste, which can degrade civil-military relations, ultimately forcing the American Paradoxical Trinity to rebalance. The increasing influence of military recruiting is examined further in Chapter 5.

CONCLUSION

As Carl von Clausewitz explained, the State's military power is inherently shaped by the interaction and balance between its armed forces, society, and government. As these three parts of the American Paradoxical Trinity change, so too does their relationship with each other on the respective vertices (e.g., *m-g*, *m-s*, and *g-s*). When properly balanced, the State's military potential is realized; the problem of obtaining sufficient citizens from society for the armed forces indicates a Trinity out of balance. The current U.S. recruiting problem partly results from market-based recruiting that has created a New Warrior Caste. Chapter 3 identified that over the last 30 years, the Army's recruiting enterprise has resulted in a force disproportionately recruited from the "crooked smile" region of the southeast. While this has proven to be an efficient way to meet near-term accession requirements, the pattern has, over the long term, concentrated the very veteran pool that both influences youth's decision to join the military and models republicanism across the nation.

Beyond America's geographic dispersion and associated cultural differences, its society has always been heterogeneous (and arguably increasingly tribal and, as a result, is stratified across multiple categories—with race and gender featuring prominently. Consequently, the more representative the U.S. military is, the more equitably: a) the burden of defense is shared across society, b) the benefits of military service are shared across society, and c) the greater citizen efficacy in the military affairs of the state. This chapter's analysis shows that AVF recruiting results in accessions of Blacks and Women that are not geographically representative, limiting the nation's military capacity, the military's legitimacy, and depriving society of the benefit of veterans' military service. The fact that the geographic area that provides the disproportionate number of Black and Female enlistments is the same area as the total accessions makes the "success" of military recruiting more divisive. Military recruiting is not evil; rather, it is necessary but requires deliberate application reflecting the decisions resulting from the efforts to balance America's Paradoxical Trinity. Congress's deliberate specification of the minimum education level for accessions demonstrates that when purposeful control of military recruiting is exercised (via the g-s vertex), a desired outcome is possible.

The validity of republicanism, a duty of the individual to serve the State, as a civic virtue rests on its acceptance by society as demonstrated through such action by its members in each community. Put simply, if citizens do not serve, then republicanism is only an aspirational virtue, not a shared belief. The status of "veteran" identifies those who have demonstrated republicanism. USAREC reports that veterans are the most influential factor in determining whether a young person enlists (in order of precedence, veteran; parent, extended family, focal leader—i.e., teacher, coach, scoutmaster). In this way, they are the seed-corn for the future of the military and the perpetuation of a belief in duty to the State—republicanism. Where and whom the military recruits today determine who becomes a veteran and where they are likely to be located. Recruiting methods that provide accessions that fail to represent society (i.e., geography, race, gender) result in a veteran population that cannot span the breadth of society to influence the next generation to fulfill the civic duty of republicanism.

The effects of cost-efficient military recruiting methods explain part, but not all, of the current problems with American youth's propensity to serve. A richer understanding of the problem would be well-informed by further research, and the above analysis identifies several areas for exploration. First, as in Chapter 3, are the patterns identified here with the Army evident in the other services? Second, why is military recruiting successful in attracting more Blacks but not other minorities? Does socioeconomic status co-vary with the ethnicity of accessions? Third, why has military recruiting not been able to capitalize on the increased opportunities for women in the military? Fourth, given the success of the government in shaping the military through specifying accessions by education level, are there other ways the *g-s* vertex should be exercised? This last question opens another area of inquiry. The military had been supportive of the educational standards imposed by Congress, as both currently favor a smarter force. Should the military similarly favor a representative force, as they proclaim, then one could expect the senior military leaders to request similar assistance from the government as an additional means to exercise the *g-s* vertex. Chapter 5 examines the behavior of military leadership to understand why such action has not happened, and Chapter 6 examines how the cost-efficient recruiting approach was enabled to dysfunction.

CHAPTER 5
INSULAR OVERSIGHT: THE MILITARY PROFESSION, GOVERNMENT, AND THEIR ROLE IN RECRUITING

> *It is the greatest evil of the volunteer system that it slays or maims those who are most energetic and enterprising, who have the highest courage and the warmest devotion to their country, while it spares the inert, the timid, and the selfish.*
>
> – Munroe Smith, *Columbia University*

AS THE MILITARY'S RECRUITING SHORTFALL PERPETUATES TO SPAN MULTIPLE years, it is apparent to those involved and the concerned observer that this condition is neither an anomaly nor a problem that is self-correcting and thus cannot be ignored. Under Secretary of Defense Kathleen Hicks stated that at 50 years of age, the All-Volunteer Force (AVF) was the finest in the world, but civil-military relations and recruiting "require constant attention."[1] The permeations of blame for

---

1. John Tirpak, "Military Growing More Distant from Most Americans, Hicks Says," *Air & Space Forces Magazine*, November 7, 2023, accessed November 09, 2023, https://www.airandspaceforces.com/hicks-military-growing-distant-americans/. See also Rachel Cohen, "Air Force Recruiting Rebounds While Army, Navy Still Struggle," Military

current recruiting problems vary by source. Social advocates and researchers cite the marked decline of prestige in the institution as a bellwether of systemic problems with civil-military relations.[2] Concurrently, some political leaders seek recruiting solutions through broader social inclusion, while opposing political leaders decry such actions as examples of "woke" pandering, and a form of social engineering that has divided America and reduced the military's prestige in the process.[3] The military, as the principal agent for accessions, under the guise of remaining politically neutral, sidesteps debates and points to structural factors such as low unemployment and low exposure to the Department of Defense (DOD) as the principal cause of recruiting problems.[4] Additionally, social scientists offer that with the end of the draft and the dissolution of the Selective Service System (SSS) that included local draft boards, the responsibility and method of the government's involvement with society on military accessions has become episodic, informal, and ill-defined.[5] There is validity in each of these arguments; their respective coefficient or recursive effects on the problem are unknown.

As the AVF adapted over the last 50 years, organized here as version *1.0* to *4.0* (see Table 3 in Chapter 2)[6], the military's role has

---

Times, February 17, 2024, sec. Your Military, accessed February 20. 2024, https://www.militarytimes.com/news/your-air-force/2024/02/17/air-force-recruiting-rebounds-while-army-navy-still-struggle/.

2. For example, see Jonathan Lehrfeld, "Poll Says Confidence in US Military Lowest in 25 Years," *Military Times*, July 31, 2023, sec. Your Military, accessed August 01, 2023, https://www.militarytimes.com/news/your-military/2023/07/31/poll-says-confidence-in-us-military-lowest-in-25-years/.

3. For example, see Corey Dickstein, "Republicans Blame 'Woke' Policies for Recruiting Sag; Military Claims It's More Complicated than That," *Stars and Stripes*, December 13, 2023, https://www.stripes.com/theaters/us/2023-12-13/military-recruiting-diversity-pentagon-republicans-12350995.html. See also Jonathan Lehrfeld, "Poll Says Confidence."

4. Leo Shane III, "Political Fights Aren't Discouraging Recruits, Military Recruiters Say," *Military Times*, December 6, 2023, sec. Pentagon & Congress, https://www.militarytimes.com/news/pentagon-congress/2023/12/06/political-fights-arent-discouraging-recruits-military-recruiters-say/.

5. For example, see Kori N. Schake and Jim Mattis, "Ensuring a Civil-Military Connection," in *Warriors and Citizens: American Views of Our Military*, ed. Kori N. Schake and Jim Mattis (Stanford, California: Hoover Institution Press, 2016), 302.

6. See also Carter et al., "AVF 4.0."

expanded beyond the boundaries of preparing for and conducting warfighting. Concurrent with the evolution of the All-Volunteer Force (AVF), the military's authority has expanded to include responsibility for the accession process. The acceptance of this increased jurisdiction over recruiting was tacitly based on functional expediency and a shared belief that senior military leaders will be guided by a professional ethos to remain subservient to civil authorities. Until recently, perceived recruiting adequacy has provided sufficient legitimacy to preclude a detailed external/oversight review of the accession process. However, the long dwell of the current recruiting problem and the lack of a representative force beg for additional research. Why has the military not been the catalyst for a rebalancing of America's Paradoxical Trinity? What was the role of the military profession in allowing the emergence of a New Warrior Caste? Applying Clausewitz to these questions identifies that in its current form, the military profession, over time, operates with increasing autonomy in a manner that indicates an unbalanced American Paradoxical Trinity. This chapter argues that in the absence of engaged political oversight, a condition required for a balanced American Paradoxical Trinity, the military profession cannot manage the adverse and second-order effects of the AVF market-based recruiting enterprise. When confronted with accession shortages, the military profession has quietly accepted both a reduction in the armed forces' end-strength and the use of contractors (modern mercenaries) rather than risk its autonomy by confronting the government or society with the divisive efficiency of its current recruiting methods.

FOUNDATIONAL SCHOLARSHIP

The military's behavior as a hierarchical institution is well informed by associated scholarship of the military profession, although its application to recruiting and accessions is limited. While Clausewitz originally defined the armed forces as comprised of a standing military and its commanders, in modern times, the personality originating from the commander is insufficient to guide the military institution. Today, the chain of command in the various components of the services—enabled by their supporting staff and technical systems—represents the evolution of the once truncated role of command referenced by Clausewitz. This group acts as a hierarchical profession that shares a core ethic to serve and guide the military forces and the institution.[7] Sociologists generally define a profession as an occupation that has mastery of specialized knowledge that is of service or demand to the larger society. The fulfillment of these functions garners the profession's social credentials and unique authority. With this authority granted by society, the profession refines and develops new expert knowledge, inducts and trains new members into the profession, and disciplines its standing members.[8] The professional ethos manifests as the behavior (embodied in various ethics) that serves society in the absence of clear guidance or direction.[9] In application, the military profession serves society by molding an institution—capable of managing violence toward policy ends—that ensures the members maintain technical currency, doctrinal relevance, with an ethos of absolute deference to civilian authority, and a culture that reflects civilian values.[10] Concurrent with the rise of the nation-state in Western civilization, the military has become—like doctors and jurists—recognized as members of a profession with an expectation to fulfill an ethos of functional civil-military relations.

The scholarship on the military profession and civil-military relations generally derives from or falls within four widely cited theoretical paradigms (Objective Control, Subjective Control, Principal-Agent, and Systems). Of central concern to the four categories of civil-military relations scholars is understanding how to ensure that the military profession remains subordinate to the civilian leadership of the State, and the composition of the military features prominently as a component of their research, and in doing so proves useful for understanding the role of the military profession in the creation of the New Warrior Caste. For the same reasons that the Gates Commission concerned itself foremost with the Army, accepting that how goes the Army in

---

7. Snider, Once Again, 3.
8. Johnson, *The Blackwell Dictionary*, 216-217.
9. Finney and Mayfield, eds., *Redefining the Modern Military*, 4.
10. Efflandt, "Military Professionalism & Private Military Contractors," 50.

personnel matters is how goes the Department of Defense, so too does the predominance of civil-miliary relations scholars. These four paradigms, as they relate to military accessions and recruiting, are summarized below, grouped as either functional or system-based behavior.

Functional Paradigms of the Military Profession

As the United States came to terms with its new expanded role in a post-World War II system and the effect of advances in technology, two social scientists, Samuel Huntington and Morris Janowitz, theorized as to how best to maintain healthy civil-military relations in a democracy, where the military remained subordinate to its civilian masters. Their work used functional paradigms, where "professionals were thought to be social trustees, acting in a judiciary capacity to ensure the public good by developing needed expert knowledge."[11] Later, Feaver expanded the functional approach by explaining how the military profession's role in civil-military relations, while being unquestionably deferential, was one of degrees.[12] The military profession's compliance with the direction from civilian authorities is based on assessing the degree to which the civilian desired outcome correlates with the profession's goals. At different times, all three scholars had identified that the historical pattern of civil-military relations in the U.S. had been upended by the rapid proliferation of technology for military purposes. This necessitated a military profession and, at the same time, changed its relationship with society.[13]

For Huntington, the best way to protect civil-military relations was through "objective" military control. In this way, the profession would remain separate from politics and thus free of special interest contami-

---

11. James Burk, "Expertise, Jurisdiction, and the Legitimacy of the Military Profession," in *The Future of the Army Profession*, Revised and Expanded 2d Edition, ed. Don Snider and Lloyd Matthews, 2nd ed. (Boston, MA: Learning Solutions, 2005), 47. See also Williams, Cimbala, and Sarkesian, *US National Security*, 303.
12. Feaver, *Armed Servants: Agency*, 3.
13. Regarding the expansion of technology and the military profession see Janowitz, The Professional Soldier, 258-266. See also Huntington, *The Soldier and the State*, 345-346. See also Feaver, "Foreword," ix.

nation.[14] Such separation would allow for a stronger ethic of deference to civilian control.[15] The argument for Huntington's "objective control" of the military assumes: a) civil-military relations consist of a system of interdependent elements, and b) that the security function of the military profession is reduced by the unmitigated application of liberal values. To address these potential detractors, he called for a professional military with a warrant granted by society that exempts it from select liberal responsibilities so that the armed forces may pursue martial matters with limited political intervention. In return, the military profession honors its authority over its portfolio by divorcing itself from all affairs of a political nature—in this way, the military profession remains objective. This apolitical nature was to be achieved through focused education on the military art and inculcation of the military commitment to serve the state in a non-partisan fashion. Today, this model continues to dominate discussions on civil-military relations, aided greatly by its endorsement from the U.S. military officer corps, where it has long been the foundational theory in its leadership doctrine.[16]

While Huntington advocated for a military profession with a degree of insularity from society and its liberal ideas, Janowitz called for greater permeation of the military profession's distinct culture through greater connection to society and its liberal ideas. Janowitz argued that democracy is best served by a military professional derived from a citizen-soldier who is clearly a member of a society that establishes its democratic identity and legitimacy from a common military experience to achieve "subjective" military control. Janowitz stated that the military professional officer "is subject to civilian control, not only because of the 'rule of law' and tradition but also because of self-imposed professional standards and meaningful integration with civilian values."[17]

---

14. Huntington, *The Soldier and the State*, 82-85.
15. Williams, Cimbala, and Sarkesian, *US National Security*, 304.
16. Feaver, Armed Servants, 7-8. See also Will Atkins, "Who Lost Afghanistan? Samuel Huntington and the Decline of Strategic Thinking," *Armed Forces & Society* 49, no. 4 (October 2023): 966, https://doi.org/10.1177/0095327X221116129.
17. Janowitz, The Professional Soldier, 421.

When written, both the objective and subjective models of civil-military relations were prescriptive, an argument for how military leaders could serve the State through an enduring relationship as a profession. Since then, subjective control has remained aspirational with varying degrees of success—such as the increased participation of Blacks in the enlisted force. At the same time, objective control, marked by a high degree of professional identity and social distinctness, was embraced by the military and has long served as the counterargument to criticism that the U.S. military is not representative of society—since, by design, the profession is authorized to be distinct. Based on a review of post-World War II civil-military relations, where neither objective nor subjective models adequately explained the behavior of the military profession, Feaver argues for an application of agency theory to understand the control political leaders (principals) have over the military (agents). In this model, the agent will decide whether to fully comply (work) with the principal's instructions or do less than requested (shirk) based on both the degree of alignment between the principal's and agent's objectives, and the level of control and monitoring exercised by the principal.[18] Military shirking, in pursuit of its preferred outcome, usually takes one of three forms: a) giving inflated estimates of costs, b) making an end run (leaks to the press or others protesting the decision), c) bureaucratic foot-dragging, slow rolling (also exhibited by tying the hands of the principal as responsible for structural impediments).[19]

System Paradigm of the Military Profession

The study of the military profession expanded significantly with the introduction of Andrew Abbott's systems approach. He argued that professions form a complex and dynamic social system in a competitive environment where they will adapt or disappear based on their relative work performance and the ability to fulfill the demands

---

18. Feaver, *Armed Servants*, 54-60.
19. Feaver, *Armed Servants*, 58.

levied by society.[20] In the macro, each profession's ability to garner resources and control a body of knowledge to meet client demand determines whether it will endure in an environment defined by competing, established, and emerging professions. The entry of new technologies presents a challenge to existing professions' jurisdictions. According to Abbott, "the major shift in the legitimization of professions [in the last quarter of the 20th century] has thus been a shift from a reliance on social origins and character values to a reliance on scientization or rationalization of technique and the efficiency of service."[21] In a systems approach, the profession's survival is influenced not only by its processes but also by larger social forces and other professions that also change commensurate to the same macro social forces. If there is too much work, "non-professionals do it and compete to be part of the profession. This can result in boundary-blurring in the workplace or assimilation into the profession."[22] The outcomes are not absolute but mediated by culture; for example, "a few professions [e.g., English lawyers and American military] resolutely ground their work on fading values, in particular character rather than technique."[23] In this way, if another profession does not contest the military's jurisdiction because its jurisdiction is protected by the state or society's endorsement of its traditional values, then the military may feel justified in the misapplication of traditional techniques or the denial of emerging technologies, or the need to change.

Abbott, when referencing the military as an exemplar, described the profession's jurisdiction as influenced by factors outside the give and take of civil-military relations; these included its history and the actions of its members. Abbott's brief explanation of the military profession as a system was explored in greater detail by Don Snider and Lloyd Mathews in an edited volume that applied Abbott's paradigm to a contemporary analysis of the Army profession based on the premise that the Army should remain a vocational profession

---

20. Abbott, *The System of Profession*, 16.
21. Abbott, *The System of Profession*, 195.
22. Abbott, *The System of Profession*, 65.
23. Abbott, *The System of Profession*, 192.

where its members feel called to serve.[24] In a testament to the dynamic nature of professions, Snider concluded in 2005, before the peak demand for the Iraq and Afghanistan wars, that the Army military profession was much improved from a post 9-11 low point—when the Army was doctrinally unprepared (i.e., had failed to develop requisite expert knowledge) for the enduring wars in Iraq and Afghanistan—because the Army leaders (officers and senior NCO's) saw themselves as professionals and not bureaucrats.[25]

Today, the AVF's market-based recruiting has produced a New Warrior Caste that is perpetuated unchallenged by the military profession and unaddressed by the other two parts of America's Paradoxical Trinity. The result is fewer accessions with less diversity and geographical representation, producing a more geographically concentrated and homogeneous veteran pool to model republicanism to civilian society and influence youth to volunteer for military service.

METHODOLOGY FOR UNDERSTANDING THE MILITARY PROFESSION

Before the current recruiting crisis, using a modern form of Clausewitz's Paradoxical Trinity, William Rapp argued that the most significant problem confronting elected officials and citizens was how the military should be "manned and resourced."[26] Most scholarship on the military profession's role and effectiveness frames the analysis within a generally binary civil-military framework.[27] However, for the 50-year history of the AVF, this approach is not adequate. To understand how the military profession responded to the responsibility of recruiting the AVF, this analysis applies Clausewitz as an American Paradoxical

---

24. Don Snider and Lloyd Matthews, eds., *The Future of the Army Profession*, Revised and Expanded Second Edition, 2nd ed. (Boston, MA: McGraw Hill-Education, 2005).
25. Don Snider, "The U.S. Army as Profession," in *The Future of the Army Profession*, by Don Snider and Lloyd J. Matthews, 2nd Edition (Boston, MA: McGraw-Hill Education, 2002), 3.
26. William E. Rapp, "Crisis in the Civil-Military Triangle?," in *Reconsidering American Civil-Military Relations: The Military, Society, Politics, and Modern War*, ed. Lionel Beehner, Risa Brooks, and Daniel Maurer (New York: Oxford University Press, 2020), 191.
27. Yuengert, "America's All-Volunteer Force," 62-65.

Trinity (see Figure 2 in Chapter 2) to understand the role of the military profession in governing recruiting methods and accessions. In this way, the civilian aspect of civil-military relations is expanded into two groups of the paradoxical trinity: the government (comprised of the executive branch and Congress) and society (comprised of all its subcultures and tribes). As the relationships with these actors changed within America's Paradoxical Trinity, so too did the AVF; as part of this the military profession had to adapt.

The military aspect of civil-military relations is considered to be under the direction of the military profession, represented here by the Army. Tony Ingesson applied four models of a profession to the military (one of which was Huntington's) and concluded that the requirement to implement policy, as described by Clausewitz, placed the military profession outside any universal model. He concluded that "while the U.S. Army can claim to have created a profession of its own, this profession only has tentative links to traditional professions."[28] The analysis of the military profession's role in recruiting used here accepts Ingesson's findings that the military profession cannot self-define, nor can any single military profession paradigm explain its behavior. Given this, the following proposes a broader "autonomy and demand" model to understand how the military profession's motives (the reasoning that justifies the behavior and relationship with society and civil authority can vary in response to external forces, with second-order effects on recruiting and accessions.

The "autonomy and demand" model combines the functional and system models of professions to understand the military profession's behavior when faced with 30 years of increasing recruiting difficulties and declining representativeness in accessions. This model accepts that the military profession's status rests on the authority granted by the government and society to manage the institution and its warrant to apply lethal force, both of which are derived from the government and society. These two conditions, as independent variables, are repre-

---

28. Tony Ingesson, "When the Military Profession Isn't," in *Redefining the Modern Military: The Intersection of Profession and Ethics*, ed. Nathan Finney and Tyrell Mayfield (Annapolis, MD: Naval Institute Press, 2021), 82.

sented within the "autonomy and demand" model as the degree of autonomy the military profession enjoys and the demand for military forces by the State.

The first force, labeled as "autonomy," is represented on a vertical axis. It ranges from low to high, where the less active the government is in military affairs (the *g-m* vertex), the greater the military profession's autonomy to exercise and expand its jurisdiction. The second force, labeled as "demand," is represented on a horizontal axis. It ranges from low to high, to indicate the relative operational demand for military services in relation to the size of the force. This axis represents the degree or percentage of the ground force that is committed to military operations. It shows how "busy" the force is conducting non-routine activities or deployments (the military term of art is "operational tempo" or OPTEMPO). The greater the OPTEMPO, the greater the need for the military to engage society (the *m-s* vertex) regarding increased accessions: to grow the force, compensate for increased attrition, and solicit the utilization of reserve forces (see Figure 26). The military profession's motives and associated behavior, the dependent variable, *are determined by* the intersection of these two forces.

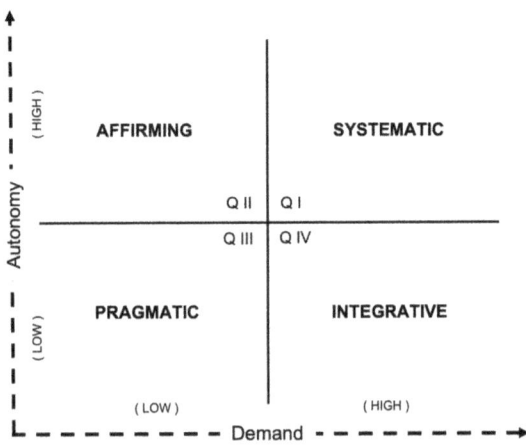

Figure 26. Autonomy and Demand's Effect on the Military Professional Ethic

The two forces presented on their respective axes are theoretical, not quantifiable, and intended for relative comparison. As an example of these forces, two dates during the AVF's history illustrate the variability of autonomy and demand as influential conditions. Consider that in the years following the fall of the Berlin Wall and the subsequent collapse of the USSR, the U.S. military got smaller while becoming increasingly deployed in peacekeeping operations—the force of "demand" increased.[29] Regarding autonomy, likewise consider that Peter Feaver noted that Congressional oversight of the military increased dramatically following Vietnam (during *AVF 1.0*) and remained high until the end of the Cold War in 1989 (*AVF 2.0*), then declined significantly (*AVF 3.0*)—autonomy of the military profession increased.[30] These examples do not mean that the forces of "autonomy" and "demand" are chronologically or teleologically determined. Instead, over time, there are +/- variances in each force, which have second-order effects on the military profession. The variance, which results from changed relationships in the American Paradoxical Trinity, causes a change in the military profession's behavior, oscillating to resemble one of the four military profession models. For this analysis, each of the four types represents a Weberian "ideal type" of the military profession. The types expand the above models of the military profession to explain the profession's behavior towards recruiting as an *outcome* shaped by government oversight and mission requirements. The four types of behaviors are arranged in a 2 x 2 matrix, with each quadrant representing recruiting behavior/motive described as follows (see Table 9).

---

29. Michael Ryan, "Military Readiness, Operations Tempo," 2-3.
30. Feaver, *Armed Servants*, 127. For a summary of AVF 1.0 to AVF 4.0 see Table 3, in Chapter 2, "A Place for Virtue: The Role of Civic Duty in the All-Volunteer Force."

Table 9. Behavioral Characteristics of the Military Professional

Behaviors / Factors	Affirming	Pragmatic	Integrative	Systemic
Demographic Composition	Indifferent	Compliant	Representative	Homogeneous
Relation w/ Government	Objective Control	Principle - Agent	Subjective Control	Economic Control
Recruiting Technology	Embracing	Status quo	Managed	Embracing
Professional Autonomy	High	Low	Low	High
Demand for Forces	Low	Low	High	High
Quadrant	II	III	IV	I

Affirming Behavior

The "affirming" form of military professional behavior (upper left, in Quadrant II, or Q-II) results from a high degree of autonomy (relatively low political oversight) and a low demand for military services that are capable of being met with existing human capital. Under these conditions, the military profession is conducting its preferred method of civil-military relations per Huntington's "objective control." With this high level of autonomy, the profession pursues actions it deems appropriate to *affirm* and secure (or expand) its prestige and jurisdiction to maintain the required supporting systems. In this quadrant, the profession already considers itself distinct from civilian society; a lack of representativeness, while not considered favorable, is not considered a problem. The "affirming" Army profession defends its lack of social inclusion and under-representation and resists change on the grounds that its personnel actions are merit-based and that its distinct social standing allows it to buffer and interdict social biases from its merit-based assessments. This sense of acceptable social difference is manifested in recruiting slogans such as, "Marines, the few, the proud" or "There's strong, and then there is Army strong." In this quadrant, because the Army meets the demand for personnel, any recruiting oversight by society or the government happens by exception as a form of periodic maintenance. The few oversight-directed tweaks are not sufficient to change the nature of how it interacts with society (the *m-s* vertex), which further protects its "objective" status. In this environment/quadrant, recruiting technology is embraced by the profession and flourishes. It operates in the background, justified by its efficiency, which frees resources for the profession's priorities. The result is that successful accessions create social consciousness unconcerned with the need for societal representation as a precursor to having a veteran population that demonstrates civic duty.

Pragmatic Behavior

Under conditions of low "autonomy" and low "demand" (moving counterclockwise, down to Q-III), the Army profession's approach to increased political oversight is to respond to the degree necessary to reduce the political pressure and intrusion into its autonomy and risk an enduring change to its jurisdiction. The Army profession is *pragmatic* and feels it must change to preserve its social standing and remaining autonomy, so it steers the institution to the minimum necessary change to keep the status quo functioning rather than pursue systemic change. In keeping with Feaver's principal-agent theory, the Army as the agent "shirks" or performs to a minimally acceptable standard to comply with what the government (the principal) requested and then uses its remaining political capital and influence to focus remaining resources on what it considers important. Pete Feaver's classic example of shirking is when post-Vietnam military leaders' conclusion that it must have public support before military commitment moved select essential battlefield functions to the Reserves so that civilian leaders wishing to take military action would have to garner sufficient public support to justify mobilizing Reserve forces.[31] As for accessions and having a representative force, Army professional "functional" behavior can take two forms. First, the profession's actions to achieve greater representation are proportional to the government's specified requirements and oversight. Second, if the government's request does not involve accessions, the profession

---

31. Feaver, *Armed Servants*, 67.

will provide a functional response to the principal's specific intrusion to prevent further oversight into what the profession considers its jurisdiction (a reduction of autonomy). In either case, recruiting changes would not provide for increased prestige or jurisdiction, so the profession will pursue a minimal response (i.e., accepting undeclared homosexuals rather than dismissing this behavior as exclusionary) rather than delay compliance or seek alternative solutions. The functional Army profession seeks to comply and return to Q-I (Affirming) with revised behavior; in the absence of unfulfilled demand for forces or social demand for change, there is not a compelling reason in government or society to further curtail autonomy and force the Army profession to Q-IV (Integrative). In this environment, recruiting technology continues to advance as the status quo, delivering a commodity —recruits—adapting slightly when directly required by the principal.

Integrative Behavior

When the Army's professional autonomy is low by virtue of active and sustained government oversight, and the Army cannot meet the high demand for forces, then conditions exist for the Army profession to pursue "Integrative" accession behavior (Q-IV). The legitimacy of the profession's jurisdiction is questioned for two reasons: a) it has not provided a representative force—a condition is required to ensure republicanism and to share the largeness of the republic; b) it has left unfulfilled its duty to provide sufficient armed forces as required by the state. Confronted with high demand, the government may change its policies to reduce demand (g-m vertex), and the profession will shirk until it can return to Q-III and then Q-IV. However, if the high demand cannot be satisfied and the profession is not seen by society as legitimate (the g-s vertex), then the profession will respond by becoming more *integrated* with society by seeking the change required to garner personnel from a bigger candidate pool and, in doing so, become more representative of society. The military's response to President Truman's desegregation order is an example.[32] Because existing

---

32. Taylor, *Military Service and American Democracy*, 59-69.

recruiting methods have proven inadequate, recruiting technology will have active oversight that directs change to include more of society (the *m-s* vertex). Military recruiting will depart from a model of accessing who it wants to accessing who it needs and, in doing so, become more integrative. This provides for Janowitz's "subjective" control, and if the profession remains in an integrative state over time, these actions can create a dispersed and representative veteran population that sows the seeds of republicanism.

Systemic Behavior

When the Army profession is confronted with a high demand that exceeds its capabilities but can retain a high degree of autonomy, then it will pursue and adapt its accession practices to those ways that are least disruptive to its jurisdiction and autonomy while seeking to lessen demand. This is a "systematic" approach (Q-I). The central task of the profession is defined within a system, and when faced with insufficient capacity and an inability to expand sufficiently, the military profession accepts a change in the *system* by divesting itself from select ancillary tasks (i.e., increased hiring of civilians). For warfighting tasks, the military profession can outsource more functions to contractors, and/or partners and allies can assume a greater role (aided and enticed by U.S. weapons technology). Because the military profession operates within a system of professions, for those times when coalition and recruiting expansion prove insufficient, the government allows for select tasks to be "outsourced" to auxiliaries and contractors. The professional groups are typically homogeneous due to their own selection process, with greater heterogeneity between groups.[33] Under these conditions, the military profession shares the authority for the use of lethal force on behalf of the state with other organizations. For example, consider Vladimir Putin's addition of the commercial Wagner Group to accompany the Russian army in the war against Ukraine.[34]

---

33. In this instance, homogeneity is not limited to ethnicity or gender; it may be defined by personality type, geography, education source, military service association, or similar social network.
34. Amy Mackinnon, "What Is Russia's Wagner Group?," *Foreign Policy*, July 6, 2021,

The U.S. military profession leverages the government to the extent necessary to prevent a permanent incursion into its jurisdiction and protect its ability to return to QII.

ANALYSIS OF POST-1990 AMERICAN PARADOXICAL TRINITY

With the collapse of the Soviet Union and the accompanying adjustment of the AVF to version 2.0 in 1990, a marked shift in civil-military relations occurred, with a decrease in understanding between the three parties of the Trinity. A series of changes with each actor resonated with the other two actors on the respective vertices. The smaller military in *AVF 2.0*, especially the Army, resulted in significant changes to the military profession and increased isolation that led to society and the government's atrophy in their understanding of the norms that formed the historical bedrock of American civil-military relations. Then GWOT, fought by *AVF 3.0*, exposed these changes.[35] The following qualitative analysis will identify the key conditions affecting the three parts of the American Paradoxical Trinity to identify the behaviors that led to the current problem of inadequate accessions and a non-representative force.

Society Behavior

After World War II, the U.S. operated with an expanded definition of Globalism that manifested itself in the Korean and Vietnam wars. The advent of the AVF in 1973 expanded the definition of globalism.[36] The end of the draft and the integration of technology allowed the military, primarily the Army, to operate with fewer people (see Figure 3 in Chapter 2). The second-order effect was that fewer and fewer

---

accessed January 07, 2024, https://foreignpolicy.com/2021/07/06/what-is-wagner-group-russia-mercenaries-military-contractor/.
35. Ulrich, "Civil-Military Relations Norms," 42, 57.
36. David Fitzgerald, David Ryan, and John M. Thompson, *Not Even Past: How the United States Ends Wars* (New York, NY: Berghahn, 2020), 3-7.

people were exposed to the military, either through direct participation or association with a veteran.

When the Berlin Wall fell and the Soviet Union's implosion circa 1990, the Army began a significant reduction in end-strength (see Figure 5 in Chapter 3); concurrently, the general public's trust in their civilian leadership began to decline.[37] At the beginning of this period of increasing Peacekeeping Operations, scholars erroneously predicted that the resulting postmodern military (*AVF 2.0*) would suffer from public indifference.[38] While this condition did manifest initially for a few years, it did not hold for long as a consequence of several factors, not the least of which was the terrorist attacks on 9/11 and military victories.

The military's success in the first Iraq war in 1991 vindicated it from the legacy of Vietnam and saw the emergence of "vicarious sacrifice" as a form of civic duty.[39] In this manner, a citizen's giving to the troops—via personal offering or support of public recognition—legitimizes one's patriotism as republican behavior. Duty and sacrifice to the state were becoming redefined: "The practice of citizenship had been turned into a mere 'simulation,' a sign with no reference."[40] Purposeful direct involvement with the military took the form of "neoliberal capitalism" as society was distrustful of institutions and professions, and demanded increased social value in exchange for monetary support.[41] Following the 9/11 attacks on the U.S., the AVF achieved initial success in the Afghanistan and Iraq invasions (while transforming to *AVF 3.0*) and enjoyed widespread societal support for the military profession, the institution, and servicemembers. This support was expressed as an amplification of the pattern that emerged during

---

37. James Golby, Lindsay P. Cohn, and Peter D. Feaver, "Thanks for Your Service: Civilian and Veteran Attitudes after Fifteen Years of War," in *Warriors and Citizens: American Views of Our Military*, ed. Kori N. Schake and Jim Mattis (Stanford, California: Hoover Institution Press, 2016), 110.
38. Moskos and Burk, "The Postmodern Military," 14-31.
39. Fitzgerald, Ryan, and Thompson, *Not Even Past*, 108.
40. Moskos and Burk, "The Postmodern Military," 167.
41. Christopher Dandecker, "A Farewell to Arms? The Military and the Nation-State in a Changing World," in *The Adaptive Military: Armed Forces in a Turbulent World*, ed. James Burk, 2nd ed. (New Brunswick, NJ: Transaction Publishers, 1998), 151.

Desert Storm. As David Fitzgerald explained, "Aside from these acts of gratitude and occasional crises, the general public is free to ignore these unending wars. Despite good intentions, they [the acts] have not served in any meaningful way to close the gap between the all-volunteer force and the society it serves."[42]

Over time, with the routinization of the Iraq and Afghanistan wars, society's distrust of institutions—including the military—returned, but its support of servicemembers remained strong. In 2015, American society still had a close affinity with its military members, but not the leadership, leading to a false sense of connectedness. When questioned about the military, few civilians could provide any factual, accurate information. Typically, they overstate its size and capabilities, a reflection of America's overly optimistic view of the results capable of technology.[43] As a result, Americans do not appreciate either the degree to which the military is isolated from society and government and the associated adverse effects this has on civil-military relations.

The increase in civilian ignorance or apathy about military issues also proves problematic for changing civil-military relations. The willingness of "the American people to acquiesce to the military" has given the military an outsized and unintended influence on national strategy and security matters.[44] This separation of society from the military precludes the public from developing stable issues about policy or military standards, at times "asking it to be all things to all people at all times."[45] This manifests as civilian deference to the military in the conduct of wars. Knowing that the military is technologically well equipped, society is "happy to send them off to foreign wars with little thought or concern."[46] Moreover, an increasing number of non-political elites outside the military think that military officers

---

42. Fitzgerald, Ryan, and Thompson, *Not Even Past*, 246.
43. Benjamin Wittes and Cody Poplin, "Public Opinion, Military Justice, and the Fight against Terrorism Overseas," in *Warriors and Citizens: American Views of Our Military*, ed. Kori N. Schake and Jim Mattis (Stanford, California: Hoover Institution Press, 2016), 145-149. See also Gambone, The New Praetorians, 35.
44. Donald S. Travis, "Why the U.S. Military Lost Afghanistan," *Armed Forces & Society* 49, no. 4 (October 2023): 939–52, https://doi.org/10.1177/0095327X221100584, 9487.
45. Wittes and Poplin, "Public Opinion, Military Justice," 145, 148-149.
46. Inbody and Shields, "Perspectives on the Afghanistan War," 886.

ought to resist direct orders from civilian authorities if the officer thinks these orders are unwise.[47] The vacuum created by an absence of societal engagement in military affairs allows those who are self-described as "very liberal" (comprising less than 5% of Americans) to hold a skeptical view of our military and wield a disproportional cultural influence that can alienate civilians unfamiliar with the military.[48]

In short, the American public (society) has a high degree of confidence in its technologically superior military. This results in strong vicarious support for the military that neither compels personal participation nor provides a consistent opinion on what authorities the military profession should have. Because of social disengagement and a lack of trust in political institutions (expressed as apathy), society does not pressure the government on military matters. The exception is "liberals," who episodically pursue their objectives by leveraging the military.

Government and Political Behavior

While the President and the Secretary of Defense are explicitly at the top of the military's chain of command, Congress shares constitutional oversight of the military with the Executive branch—an implicit part of the chain of command. By design, the authorities of the three branches of the government are not discreet. As John Williams, et al. explain, "The popular notion that the US government has three separate branches with distinct powers, has a corollary: The branches also share power, which also allows each to influence or intervene in the affairs of others."[49] While Congress typically fulfills its duties by specifying force size, equipment, and organization, and as needed or indirectly on matters of doctrine and personnel, it remains part of the chain

---

47. Golby, Cohn, and Feaver, "Thanks for Your Service," 132, 115. See also Wittes and Poplin, "Public Opinion, Military Justice," 145, 152.
48. Todd Lindberg, "The 'Very Liberal' View of the US Military," in *Warriors and Citizens: American Views of Our Military*, ed. Kori N. Schake and Jim Mattis (Stanford, California: Hoover Institution Press, 2016), 238-239.
49. Williams, Cimbala, and Sarkesian, *US National Security*, 124.

of command, except during times of crisis. Military officers, by tradition, support the president on budget requests to Congress and the use of force; they have a duty to provide their alternative views to Congress.[50] While there is debate as to the degree to which the military profession fulfills its obligation to Congress, that matter is moot if the government (both the Executive and Legislative branches) does not provide the required oversight of the military. Since 1990, Americans have become less accepting of institutions and have put little consistent pressure on the government to manage the country's other institutions. The military and political institutions' elites struggle to resolve complex problems framed by an insidious knowledge gap between them; where politicians do not appreciate the complexity of managing the technology of warfare, while the military is suspicious of the long-term motives and commitment of politicians.[51] Consequently, the government is less involved with the breadth of routine military matters, except for episodic Congressional oversight related to politically sensitive issues (e.g., egregious conduct, or greater inclusion of a minority demographic, or expenditure of funds in a district).[52] An uninformed public gives political leaders wide latitude to impose the "transmutation" of progressive cultural values over the functional imperatives of the military for success on the battlefield.[53]

The presence of a New Warrior Caste and the enduring recruiting problem indicate an American Paradoxical Trinity out of balance. Historically, an unbalanced trinity is aligned when either: a) military failure on the battlefield, the loss of blood and treasure forces accountability—as was case with the U.S. in Vietnam after the Tet offensive, or b) when operational demands on the military escalate beyond its resources (to include personnel)—as was the case with U.S. naval expansion under President McKinley in 1897. The rebalancing of the paradoxical trinity to secure more personnel typically involves

---

50. Owens, "What Military Officers Need," 71-72.
51. Brooks, "Civil-Military Paradoxes," 39.
52. Bacevich, "Tradition Abandoned," 16–25. See also Feaver, *Armed Servants*, 195.
53. Mackubin Thomas Owens, "Is Civilian Control of the Military Still an Issue?," in *Warriors and Citizens: American Views of Our Military*, ed. Kori N. Schake and Jim Mattis (Stanford, California: Hoover Institution Press, 2016), 87.

increased military interaction with the government for society to enable greater accessions, and the increased government oversight of the military to provide legitimacy to the increased demand placed on society.[54] Recently, in America, during the GWOT, neither has been the case. Regarding the latter, political leaders are increasingly shying away from their responsibilities to shape public attitudes on civic duty and military service. The enduring GWOT created a high demand for forces, while the services were granted high autonomy.

The power of the military within the policy process has been growing steadily since the 1960s.[55] As Adam Barsuhn explains, "Huntington's objective control has created an environment in which questioning operational and tactical decisions has become taboo. Military leaders chafe against civilian meddling while wanting to avoid discussions of strategic goals in their bid to remain apolitical."[56] Rather than question the assumptions and conclusions of the military profession, political leaders have developed a tendency to rely on the credibility of the military commanders as justification to support their recommended policies.[57] Congress initially addressed the unmet personnel needs of the AVF during the GWOT with substantial increases in recruiting and retention budgets and by authorizing and funding the military's expanded use of contractors.[58] Through these actions,

---

54. Eliot Cohen's *Supreme Command: Soldiers, Statesmen, and Leadership in Wartime* (New York, NY: Free Press, 2002) provides four excellent examples of culturally distinct democratic governments' executive conducting close military oversight, rather than deferring to the military profession's judgement.

55. Richard H. Kohn, "The Erosion of Civilian Control of the Military in the United States Today," *Naval War College Review* 55, no. 3 (Summer 2002): 16, https://ez-salve.idm.oclc.org/login?url=https://search.ebscohost.com/login.aspx?direct=true&db=a9h&AN=7498206&site=ehost-live. See also Williams, Cimbala, and Sarkesian, *US National Security*, 195.

56. Adam Barsuhn, "'We Don't Negotiate with Terrorists'—Afghanistan, Bargaining, and American Civil–Military Relations," *Armed Forces & Society* 49, no. 4 (October 2023): 953–64, https://doi.org/10.1177/0095327X221077299, 956.

57. Schake and Mattis, "Ensuring a Civil-Military Connection," 302.

58. For recruiting response, see Kapp, "Recruiting and Retention," 13. For contractor responses, see Gambone, *The New Praetorian*, 44. See also Deborah Avant, "The Mobilization of Private Forces after 9/11: Ad Hoc Response to Inadequate Planning," in *How 9/11 Changed Our Ways of War*, ed. James Burk (Palo Alto, CA: Stanford University Press, 2013), 215.

Congress deferred to the military's recommendations by electing to provide additional resources to the military rather than conduct a more extensive oversight of the military accession problem.

When confronted with the recent post-GWOT recruiting shortfalls, the Government has increasingly abdicated oversight of accession by instead reducing the demand for accessions by reducing end-strength (see Figure 5 and Figure 6 in Chapter 3). More recently, the reduction in active-duty Army end-strength by 24,000 Soldiers from 2020-2022 equates to a loss of combat power for an Army that most of its leaders and external experts already believe is stretched too thin for the nation's needs.[59] As Tom Spoehr points out, "the last three Army Chiefs of Staff have testified to Congress that their service is too small to meet the needs of the National Defense Strategy."[60]

Awareness of the military's lack of ethnic and geographic representation is explicitly known by the government, but has not driven substantive change. For example, the Senate Armed Services Committee scheduled a non-standard hearing in 2015 to pursue generational change to the AVF in a manner intended to be as sweeping as the Goldwater-Nichols Act of 1986. Invited witnesses included two former Under Secretaries of Defense for Personnel and Readiness (one of whom had been involved with AVF policy since Nixon), a former OSD comptroller, and a former CNO. While all recognized the problem of the AVF's increased cost, neither the statements, questions, nor recommendations revisited the AVF's foundational economic or socially representative premises. Proposed solutions largely centered on cost savings from controlling healthcare costs, lengthening the service member career model, and increasing the utilization and pay for the civilian workforce. An absence of accountability over Defense contractors (including Private Military Security Companies—PMSCs) emerged during follow-up questioning.[61] Similarly, in 2017, Congress

---

59. Davis Winkie, "Exclusive: Army Secretary Talks."
60. Thomas Spoehr, "The Incredible Shrinking Army: NDAA End-Strength Levels Are a Mistake," Breaking Defense (blog), December 20, 2022, https://breakingdefense.sites.breakingmedia.com/2022/12/the-incredible-shrinking-army-ndaa-end-strength-levels-are-a-mistake/.
61. "Department of Defense Personnel," 5-95.

noted the lack of minority and gender integration in the military, as well as the role of veterans in recruiting. It also noted that in 2009, the same problem had been identified. The result was the Congressional affirmation of its commitment to diversity and the formation of a Military Leadership Diversity Commission.[62] On balance, the government's role in engaging society on military matters is minimal, while its oversight of the armed forces of the military has produced little directed change to the military profession's preferred behavior and methods.

In summary, the result of the government's changed role in America's Paradoxical Trinity manifested as less oversight of the military and less government engagement with society on military matters. This has allowed the profession to: a) pursue accessions without consideration of long-term consequences, and b) become distant from the larger society. By circumventing the need for more personnel to serve in the military with the increased use of contractors, the veteran pool in society is reduced. By allowing the military to lack social representation, some classes or types of veterans remain "marginalized" while other social classes remain absent from the veteran population.[63]

Military Profession Behavior

Advances in technology have led to increased specialization that both defines the boundaries of the profession and redefines membership—often into new derivative professions. According to Janowitz, "The vast proliferation of the military establishments of the major industrialized nations is a direct consequence of the continuous development of the technology of warfare," which both enabled and required armed forces to exist as a force in being.[64] The military profession expanded as the means to manage the number of standing formations that employed technology as a means of warfare and institutional management. Not surprisingly, Chief of Staff of the Army (CSA),

---

62. Kamarck, "Diversity, Inclusion, and Equal Opportunity," 4-54.
63. Kinder and Higgins, *Service Denied*, 2-3.
64. Janowitz, *On Social Organization and Social Control*, 103.

General Westmorland led the Army to expand the military profession from a class-based distinction associated with officers to include warrant officers and non-commissioned officers.[65] In this way—as a counter to the increased specialization driven by technology—the military profession, based on an ethic of what best serves the state, served as a governing mechanism across an immense force.

History has shown that resource and force reduction periods have resulted in an Army profession with reduced capabilities that is not ready for the next war.[66] True to form, in the 1990s, as the Army implemented significant reductions in end-strength and transitioned to *AVF 2.0*, the Pentagon became increasingly more bureaucratic with the expanded use of business models and practices—a trend that pleased civilian leadership. These methods, justified by efficiency, gained prominence over measures of effectiveness.[67] Not surprisingly, advice from the military profession—ill-prepared for such arguments—as to what it thought was best for the republic (i.e., base closures and force structure) lacked external validity and fell on deaf ears.

Ten years later, the limited wars in Iraq and Afghanistan (as opposed to total or large-scale wars required for foes such as Russia or China) identified significant problems with the AVF that would likely be catastrophic if tested at the scale of a major war. As a point of comparison, Karl Eikenberry points out that in 1968 (the height of the Vietnam War) defense spending accounted for 45% of federal outlays; in 2008 (the year marking the maximum combined level of effort in the Iraq and Afghanistan Wars) defense spending was only 20% of the federal budget, a percentage exceeded by Health and Human Services (24%), and Social Security (22%). In 1968, defense spending stood at 9%

---

65. Kasey Landru, "Evolution of Defining the Army Profession," in Redefining the Modern Military: The Intersection of Profession and Ethics, ed. Nathan Finney and Tyrell Mayfield (Annapolis, MD: Naval Institute Press, 2021), 50. See also Pauline Shanks-Kaurin, "Questioning Military Professionalism," in Redefining the Modern Military: The Intersection of Profession and Ethics, ed. Nathan Finney and Tyrell Mayfield (Annapolis, MD: Naval Institute Press, 2021), 18.
66. Snider, *Once Again*, 1.
67. Milan Vego, "Is the Conduct of War a Business?," *Joint Forces Quarterly*, no. 59 (2010): 61, ndupress.ndu.edu.

of GDP, whereas in 2009, it was 5% percent.[68] Scholars argued that the military profession had a firmly established false sense of separation between politics and military affairs, which led to negative outcomes from the strategic to the tactical level and its doctrine.[69] In the absence of other stimuli for change from the government or society, the military profession pursued typical adjustments to the AVF, only slightly varying from the status quo. As Rosa Brooks explains, while overall, the military had become more professional as the AVF matured, "its internal structures—from recruiting, training, and education to personal policies—lag badly behind those in most civilian workplaces, making it difficult for the military to change within."[70] As a result of the GWOT demands, recruiting technology, which was much more cost-efficient in the short term, was expanded rather than seeking different long-term methods to achieve a sufficiently sized and representative force.

Ultimately, war is the crucible upon which an army is judged by the state. Assuming the latter survives, if the former is found wanting, change results. During the GWOT, the AVF (particularly the Army) was found wanting, "while the military was arguably more cost-efficient, the reduced force structure proved inadequate for the military to train itself and coalition partners, or provide required security on the modern noncontiguous battlefield."[71] In response, the military profession pursued adaptation—not change—in two areas that are germane to understanding the current problem with accessions. The first adaptation of the AVF that the Army profession pursued was the traditional modifications to its accession and personnel system. In the near term, the Army profession endorsed temporary fixes such as waivers to established enlistment criteria and stop-loss personnel policies to

---

68. Karl W. Eikenberry, "Reassessing the All-Volunteer Force," *Washington Quarterly* 36, no. 1 (Winter2012/2013): 7–24, https://doi.org/10.1080/0163660X.2013.751647, 12.
69. Risa Brooks, "The Best They Could Do? Assessing U.S. Military Effectiveness in the Afghanistan War," *Armed Forces & Society* (0095327X) 49, no. 4 (October 2023): 913–22, https://doi.org/10.1177/0095327X221116876, 916.
70. Rosa Brooks, "Civil-Military Paradoxes," in *Warriors and Citizens: American Views of Our Military*, ed. Kori N. Schake and Jim Mattis (Stanford, California: Hoover Institution Press, 2016), 21, 56.
71. Efflandt, "Military Professionalism & Private Military Contractors," 52.

retain those whose enlistment was about to expire.[72] Additionally, the profession changed the role of the reserves to one outside that envisioned by the Gates Commission and CSA General Abrams. Rather than functioning as an operational force that filled gaps until a strategic reserve could be called up (or a stand-by draft enacted), it was iteratively deployed at the expense of unit integrity and accessions. It did not serve as the envisioned "tripwire" to ensure political and societal support as a counter to executive adventurism.[73] The heavy reliance on the same active and reserve servicemembers to serve repeated deployments without the AVF's intended mobilization of a strategic reserve isolated them from society. Then, as veterans, these servicemembers have become a subculture distinct from society, leaving civil-military relations as "brittle and fragile."[74]

These measures alone were insufficient to sustain the AVF personnel requirements for the GWOT. As a matter of mitigation, the military profession obtained contracting and oversight authority from Congress to begin unprecedented outsourcing of key military functions to contractors, including heavy reliance on PMSCs that comprised 25% of the services contracted.[75] Those used in Iraq and Afghanistan numbered in the tens of thousands for each country. As a point of comparison, in Operation Desert Storm (1991), the contractor-to-military ratio was 1:50. When Operation Iraqi Freedom and Operation Enduring Freedom first overlapped in 2003, the ratio went to 1:10.[76] By 2015, in Afghanistan, the ratio peaked at 4:1, with four

---

72. Taylor, *The Advent of the All-Volunteer Force*, 88.
73. Jessica D. Blankshain, "Who Has 'Skin in the Game'?," in *Reconsidering American Civil-Military Relations: The Military, Society, Politics, and Modern War*, ed. Lionel Beehner, Risa Brooks, and Daniel Maurer (New York: Oxford University Press, 2020), 98-104. See also Eikenberry, "Reassessing the All-Volunteer Force," 10.
74. Gambone, *The New Praetorian*, 1-5.
75. Scott, De Angelis, and Segal, *Military Sociology*, 68. See also Ori Swed, "The Afghanistan War's Legacy: The Reimagining of the Outsourcing of War and Security," *Armed Forces & Society* 49, no. 4 (October 2023): 1030, https://doi.org/10.1177/0095327X221101340.
76. David Isenburg, "A Government in Search of Cover: Private Military Companies in Iraq," in *From Mercenaries to Market: The Rise and Regulation of Private Military Companies*, ed. Simon Chesterman and Chia Lehnardt, 1st edition (Oxford; New York: Oxford University Press, 2007), 83.

contractors for every service member.[77] They were used initially to compensate for an AVF that was too small and then to allow a reduction of troops for political reasons.[78]

In a transnational study of PMSCs, Christopher Spearin offers that while the use of contractors is not new, the large number is without precedent. They are a descendant of the third oldest profession—mercenaries—and have been a concern that predates Machiavelli's warnings in *The Prince*. He notes that PMSCs today have helped compensate for technologically fixated state militaries that are quantitatively and doctrinally limited when they are confronted with contemporary land operations.[79] While their use solves an immediate problem, it masks larger problems. As Ambassador Karl Eikenberry explains, the large-scale use of PMSCs "in support of our volunteer armed forces conceals the real scope of conflict from the American people. It also reduces pressure on the military's leadership either to recommend strategies that can be implemented by the extant force, or alternatively to request a large expansion of the AVF."[80] Questions of accountability remain as each PMSC develops its own level of competence and corporate culture—one that lies outside the influence of public institutions and their associated social values.[81] Today, PMSCs are not an existential threat to U.S. civil-military relations, but they are subversive to the relationship as their paid role does little to reinforce republicanism as a civic virtue or force the dialogue necessary to balance the American Trinity.

The second adaptation to the AVF pursued by the military profession was to capitalize on its standing with the government and society. In the wake of the post-1990 public support and endorsement for the military, the military nurtured the idea that this sentiment was appro-

---

77. Swed, "The Afghanistan War's Legacy," 1028.
78. Taylor, *Military Service and American Democracy*, 169, 171-174. See also Efflandt, "Military Professionalism & Private Military Contractors," 54.
79. Spearin, *Private Military and Security Companies*, 88.
80. Eikenberry, "Reassessing the All-Volunteer Force," 12.
81. Anna Leander, "Regulating the Role of Private Military Companies in Shaping Security and Politics," in *From Mercenaries to Market: The Rise and Regulation of Private Military Companies*, ed. Simon Chesterman and Chia Lehnardt, 1st edition (Oxford; New York: Oxford University Press, 2007), 60-62.

priate and came to see themselves as elite. The Pentagon cooperated with public displays, such as sporting events and "hometown hero" news, and in some instances, paid for the events as promotional opportunities.[82] In 2013, this author explained that "the trust relationship between the military and the public is now so strong that tactical success is taken for granted, with little regard by civilian leaders or the public for the profession's requirements beyond having sufficient resources."[83] This belief is so strong that polling showed that an increasing number of non-veterans and civilian elites considered it appropriate for military leaders to violate civilian orders if the professional thought adherence was unwise.[84] In this environment, politicians did not exercise governmental oversight and allowed officers to use their influence to pursue institutional interests at the expense of ensuring rigor in national policy.[85] The military profession, under the auspices of being apolitical, focused its energies on developing technological expertise and remaining autonomous.[86] The result, per Mac Owens, is that a "strategic black hole exists largely because the military has focused its professional attention on the apolitical operational level of war, abdicating its role in strategy making."[87] The military profession, unchecked by the media and sometimes encouraged by politicians, does overreach and has expanded its jurisdiction beyond traditional warfighting matters, assuming control over policy matters.[88] In this environment, when confronted with accession problems with strategic implications, there is no impetus for the military profession to validate its assumptions, consider systemic problems with its actions, and identify the long-term adverse effects of its methods.

The organizational culture of a Service branch can exert a strong influence on civil-military relations, frequently constraining what

---

82. Fitzgerald, Ryan, and Thompson, *Not Even Past*, 243.
83. Efflandt, "Military Professionalism & Private Military Contractors," 56.
84. Golby, Cohn, and Feaver, "Thanks for Your Service," 115, 134.
85. Bacevich, "Tradition Abandoned," 3-10.
86. Atkins, "Who Lost Afghanistan," 969.
87. Mackubin Thomas Owens, "Military Officers: Political without Partisanship," *Strategic Studies Quarterly* 9, no. 3 (Fall 2015): 91.
88. Eikenberry, "Reassessing the All-Volunteer Force," 13.

civilian leaders can do and often constituting an obstacle to change and innovation.[89] Today, the strength of culture within the military profession continues to resist fundamental change, opting instead for traditional adaptation. For example, in response to the current multi-year recruiting problem, the U.S. Army stated it will reform its accession process by returning to a historical pattern of marketing and organization. The Army will reintroduce the 1980s "Be All You Can Be" advertising slogan, and it will reorganize the United States Army Recruiting Command (USAREC) in 2024 as a 3-star command to closely resemble the former Accessions Command (which was deactivated in 2014 as an effort to de-layer and streamline recruiting and marketing within the Army).[90] In this way, the Army states it hopes to garner efficiencies by combining assets of Army Marketing, Cadet Command, and Recruiting Command under a single headquarters, similar to the arrangement that existed up until 2014, the last time the Army easily met accession requirements.[91] While this may make the *m-s* vertex more appealing, it does not increase or make this relationship more robust. More importantly, since the advertising campaign and the restructuring will happen under the initiative and supervision of the Army, these actions are unlikely to exercise the *g-m* or *g-s* vertices.

In summary, in the post-Cold War world (with *AVF 2.0* and then *3.0*), the role of the military professional has expanded its jurisdiction beyond that envisioned by either the Gates Commission, Huntington, or Janowitz. As a consequence of a lack of familiarity with the military and the increasing technology of warfare, political leaders have granted greater deference to the military on matters of national strategy and policy. In this new role of connecting policy to operations, the military profession has been found wanting. The Army recognizes

---

89. Owens, "What Military Officers Need," 83.
90. U.S. Army, "New Army Brand Redefines 'Be All You Can Be' for a New Generation," www.army.mil, March 8, 2023, accessed January 03, 2024, https://www.army.mil/article/264594/new_army_brand_redefines_be_all_you_can_be_for_a_new_generation.
91. Davis Winkie, "Army Recruiting Reforms Go 'Back to the Future' to Fix Ongoing Crisis," *Army Times*, November 8, 2023, sec. Army Recruiting, accessed November 09, 2023, https://www.armytimes.com/news/recruiting/2023/11/08/army-recruiting-reforms-go-back-to-the-future-to-fix-ongoing-crisis/.

this. In a 2024 article to the force, GEN Gary Brito, the commander of the Army Training and Doctrine Command (TRADOC) states,

> The Army profession isn't broken; it simply needs to be stewarded more thoroughly. While it is important to note shortfalls such as soldier and leader misconduct, lack of fitness, harmful behaviors, and more, we — as a total team — are obligated to embrace the profession to build soldiers and leaders of character, competence, and commitment, and to foster positive organizational cultures. To do so, we will continuously improve and refine our professional systems to ensure focus, prioritization, and accountability.[92]

The military, by clinging to a culture of "objective" control where there is a clear line of separation between politics and war, has produced a strategic perspective of warfighting and an institution that has often been characterized as dated or absent.[93] As Richard Kohn explains, "American officers have, over the course of the Cold War and in reaction to certain aspects of it, forgotten or abandoned their historical stewardship of civilian control, their awareness of the requirement to maintain it, and their understanding of the proper boundaries and behaviors that make it work properly and effectively."[94] The result of the current relationship between the government and the military (g-m vertex) has been battlefield and institutional failures and changes in civil-military relations.

FINDINGS

Three forces determine how the military profession will act: the autonomy granted by the government, the demand for military

---

92. TRADOC is the Army's proponent for the "Military Profession" and the Army's Professional Military Education (PME) program. Quotation from Gary Brito, "Professionalism Is the Foundation of the Army and We Will Strengthen It," *War on the Rocks*, March 18, 2024, (accessed March 18, 2024, https://warontherocks.com/2024/03/professionalism-is-the-foundation-of-the-army-and-we-will-strengthen-it/.
93. Owens, "What Military Officers Need," 81-83.
94. Kohn, "The Erosion of Civilian Control," 33.

services created by the government and accepted by society, and the military profession's preferred type of behavior. Having withdrawn from Iraq in 2011 and Afghanistan in 2021, the demands on the Army have decreased, but not to pre-1990 levels.[95] With fewer combat requirements and less end-strength, the demand for accessions decreased. From 1990 onward, society has largely admired the armed forces, applying minimal pressure for political intervention in military affairs, the net result being a large degree of autonomy granted to military leaders. Under these conditions, per the "autonomy and demand" model, the Army profession's behavior is "Affirming" (Q-II). While the Army profession has maintained an ethos of deference to civilian authority on explicit matters of warfighting, it has at the same time accepted the ethic that in an environment of high autonomy, it is appropriate to exercise its prestige to expand its jurisdiction and use its authority to protect its jurisdiction, as has occurred with recruiting and the resulting lack of representative accessions.

One of the foundational concerns noted by the Gates Commission was that volunteer forces would become isolated from civilian society and threaten civilian control.[96] While these concerns were mitigated with *AVF 1.0*, today, as America transitions to *AVF 4.0*, there is a threat to effective—albeit not total—control of the military by civilians. While the four descriptors of military professional behavior in the "autonomy and demand" model are treated as categorical, in a real-world application, there is behavior variance towards the other quadrants based on the significance of the external stimulus. The history of the AVF is marked with change and adaptation (notably in 1990 and the move to *AVF 2.0*), but there have been micro-oscillations of the military profession's ethics that correspond with similar short-duration changes to oversight and demand. Given that the AVF's recruiting problem and its second-order effects on civic virtue are not micro problems of short duration, then generalization to broad descriptors and trend lines is appropriate.

---

95. The PERSTEMPO of the Army remains elevated above pre-1990 levels with partnership activities in the European and Pacific theaters.
96. "Commission on an All-Volunteer Armed Force," 129.

A counterargument to the "oversight and demand" model's conclusions would be that during the GWOT, the military profession faced conditions of 'high demand" and "high autonomy." Per the autonomy and demand model, this condition would result in a "Systemic" profession (Q-I). The counterargument supports its conclusion by citing the use of PMSCs as proof of high demand and the presence of what Abbott would describe as a competing profession. This counterargument is incomplete because the U.S. military retained contracting authority for and over the majority of the PMSCs, but they were never in true competition (a condition of "Systematic" professional behavior) with the military profession. While the U.S. military would have preferred to expand to meet demand (a condition precluded by the effects of the previous 35 years of recruiting), it accepted the need for PMSCs under its control rather than risk its professional autonomy by engaging society and the government to find a solution to the limitations of the AVF and the current recruiting enterprise.

It is reasonable to conclude from this counterargument that the categorization of the military profession's behavior does not align cleanly with the "Affirming" ideal type. During the GWOT, the military professional ethic was probably close to the line of separation between Q-II and Q-I. With the military profession's cultural predisposition for "objective" civilian control (nurtured by its long-standing Professional Military Education doctrine), it tolerated "Systemic" behavior to the degree necessary to preserve its autonomy until demand declined sufficiently for it to return to "Affirmative" behavior. The duration of the GWOT was insufficient to change the military profession's culture. More troubling than the U.S. military profession's drift towards "Systematic" behavior (Q-I, where non-professionals would perform the coercive tasks of the state) is the absence of professional drift towards "Integrative" behavior (Q-IV). While all three actors of the American Trinity are aware of and endorse the benefits of a representative military, the absence of a force that represents America's geography, ethnicity, and gender has not curtailed the military profession's desire for autonomy sufficiently for it to supplant the efficiency of current recruiting by engaging externally and dealing with the consequences.

CHAPTER 5

CONCLUSION

Faced with a recruiting problem of such magnitude and duration that it threatens the AVF on its 50th anniversary, Congress has asked senior military leaders, specifically Army senior leaders, how it will correct the problem. Not asked, and equally important is why the military's recruiting methods have been allowed to create this recurring accession problem, and to what degree is the military profession capable of addressing it? Without knowing these answers, any corrective action risks aggravating rather than correcting the problem. This chapter argues why the AVF evolved into a warrior caste by explaining that the Army profession was, at best, indifferent to a recruiting enterprise that created an Army that did not represent American society and, at worst, was dependent on efficient recruiting to avoid government oversight that would have reduced its autonomy.

As explained by Clausewitz, the State's military power is inherently shaped by the interaction and balance between its armed forces, society, and government. As these three parts of the American Paradoxical Trinity change, so too does their relationship with each other (e.g., *m-g*, *m-s*, and *g-s* vertices, see Figure 2). When properly balanced, the State's military potential is realized. A problem obtaining sufficient personnel from society for the armed forces indicates a Paradoxical Trinity out of balance. Since 1990, America's Paradoxical Trinity has become increasingly out of balance as the profession gained increased autonomy. At the same time, the integration of technology has enabled the AVF's success on the battlefield and in the recruiting office…until recently when accessions could not meet demand. By integrating the behavior of society, government, and the military within the "autonomy and demand" model of the military profession, the analysis identified that under conditions of decreasing political oversight and little social pressure, the military profession has developed "Affirming" characteristics such that it would rather endorse the validity of the status quo that accepts the unwanted effects of recruiting methods rather than risk an erosion of its jurisdiction by clearly presenting the problem to the other two actors in the Trinity.

While the military profession remains subordinate to civilian authority, in those areas where the government does not exercise its authority, the military has expanded its jurisdiction by inferring its mastery of requisite technical knowledge. Since 1990, with declining oversight, the Army profession has increasingly made recruiting part of its jurisdiction and relied on market-driven efficiency to deliver necessary accessions for a shrinking Army, at the expense of providing a representative and adequately sized force. On the occasions that the recruiting enterprise failed to deliver adequate accessions, the military profession accepted the government's authority for end-strength cuts and/or the use of PMSCs rather than risk intrusion into its jurisdiction by engaging in a detailed discussion with the government. Society, because of its affinity for servicemembers and a lack of military understanding, has accepted force reductions and the use of contractors as an adequate solution. The second-order effect is a reduced *representative* veteran population to propel a sense of republicanism in future generations.

A democracy in general, and America in particular, needs a military profession. An effective military profession requires trust across the Paradoxical Trinity. If the trust evolves from an absence of conflicted discourse, then it will be shallow. If the American Trinity masks an imbalance by avoiding exploration of a possible resolution, then either the profession or the State will not endure when confronted with greater adversity. In an age of technology—discussed in Chapter 6, the military must do more than exercise discretion as part of its warrant to apply violence on behalf of the state and it must now also earn trust by informing the government (both executive and legislative branches) and society on the efficiency and effectiveness of a range of military affairs—not the least of which is recruiting. Further research on this topic is appropriate. The analysis in previous chapters identifies the AVF's change to a New Warrior Caste, the "what" happened to the AVF. This chapter explains professional behavior as the "why" the AVF changed. This analysis consistently identifies a non-linear rate that begs explanation; more analysis is needed on the "how" of the AVF's change was enabled in a manner that accelerated without drawing the attention of society or government. Additionally, further research should seek to affirm this pattern in other service branches or the militaries of other Western democracies. Lastly, assessing individual senior military leaders' professional behavior would provide fidelity to the macro patterns identified here, as that would identify senior leader preferences apart from system obstacles to correcting the problems associated with the New Warrior Caste.

CHAPTER 6
DECEIVED BY SUCCESS: HOW TECHNOLOGY MADE RECRUITS A COMMODITY FOR THE ALL-VOLUNTEER FORCE

> *It is, I think, particularly in periods of acknowledged crisis, that scientists turn to philosophical analysis as a device for unlocking the riddles of their field. Scientists have not generally needed or wanted to be philosophers. Indeed, normal science usually holds creative philosophy at arm's length, and probably for good reasons.*
>
> –Thomas S. Kuhn, *The Structure of Scientific Revolutions*

As the recruiting shortfalls continued into 2024 for the Army and Navy despite ongoing corrective efforts initiated in 2022, clarity on the cause and solution has become muddled. The Army reinstated a 1980s recruiting slogan to "Be All That You Can Be" in the hopes of attracting applicants who want to enter the new cyber and technology fields of the 21st century.[1] Concurrently, the Secretary of the Army Christine Wormuth—in a rhetorical sleight of hand—announced plans

---

1. Patty Nieberg, "Army Debuts New Recruiting Ads Aimed at High-Tech Civilians

to request force structure additions and larger reductions to offset accession shortfalls. In her words, "The service's recruiting challenges have left it with a "hollow force structure, so we needed to basically reduce 32,000 spaces to both shrink over-structure and make room for those 7,500 [spaces] of the new structure."[2] The Secretary's strategy on force structure affirms the pattern used for the last 30 years; first, it will reduce recruiting demand by having a smaller force, and second, it will modify what remains in the force structure to accommodate new personnel billets required by changes in battlefield technology. The reduction of end-strength below the minimum size specified by the Gates Commission to resolve recruiting problems mirrors the pattern for the last 30 years (see Figure 3 and 5 in Chapter 2), while the reorganization of the force in response to technology was a condition seen at the advent of the AVF.[3] Not discussed currently are considerations of previously unforeseen systemic causes to the current recruiting problem that necessitate other unprecedented actions.

In 1970 the Gates Commission advocated for the AVF to employ market-based recruiting in large cities that leveraged "advertising in mass media" to attract the necessary amount of "true volunteers" (i.e., motivated by a sense of republicanism).[4] At the time, this approach was not considered disruptive by the Gates Commission: "Because we [the Commission] do not expect major changes in the composition of the armed forces, we do not expect major changes in the relationship between the armed forces and the rest of society."[5] From the preceding chapters' analysis it is evident that: a) recruiting problems for the AVF increased drastically post 1990 (see Chapter 2); b) the Army is not representative of society by geography, family service history, or ethnic and gender demographics (see Chapters 3 & 4); c) the military profes-

---

Rather than Soldiers," *Task & Purpose*, May 9, 2024, https://taskandpurpose.com/military-life/army-commercial-open-civilian-jobs/.

2. Jen Judson, "Here Are the Winners and Losers in US Army's Force Structure Change," Defense News, February 27, 2024, accessed February 29, 2024, sec. Land, https://www.defensenews.com/land/2024/02/27/here-are-the-winners-and-losers-in-us-armys-force-structure-change/.
3. "Commission on an All-Volunteer Armed Force," 43.
4. "Commission on an All-Volunteer Armed Force," 85.
5. "Commission on an All-Volunteer Armed Force," 134.

sion has expanded its jurisdiction to fill a vacuum in the accessions system and in doing precluded a re-balancing of the America's Paradoxical Trinity (see Chapter 5).

Given these conditions another question emerges. How did the original AVF design become invalidated and result in a New Warrior Caste without a correction or re-balancing of the American Paradoxical Trinity? This chapter argues that the computer/technology revolution of the 1980s changed the process of military accessions in ways the Gates Commission had not foreseen when it advocated for an increased AVF recruiting enterprise in the cities and the use of advertising. The following analysis shows that military recruiting has become a technology that, in the current system, measures success by the volume of accessions without regard to the foundational conditions deemed necessary for an all-volunteer force. In this analysis, technology represents the purposeful application of artifacts, devices, machines, and systems in an ordered process for a deliberate purpose. Over time, military recruiting has become a technology that functions outside of public awareness. As technology changes at an increasingly faster rate, so too do the accession failures. The second-order effect is that the most recent accession failures are incorrectly assumed to be a by-product of environmental conditions rather than a manifestation of a systemic problem.

FOUNDATIONAL SCHOLARSHIP

The advocates for any given science compete for jurisdiction by arguing and demonstrating its utility. The application of science produces technology. In modern times, the three Industrial Revolutions have changed both society and the military. The 1st Industrial Revolution provided for the standardization of parts, which enabled the mass production of weapons. The 20th Century saw the 2nd Industrial Revolution, where power was harnessed within the factory, and the specialization of labor provided the means of the mass production of weapons. Ongoing is the 3rd Industrial Revolution with the proliferation of computing technology transforming the nature of work.⁶ The 3ʳᵈ Industrial Revolution also ignited predictions of a revolution in military affairs where precision munitions and networked forces would provide a decisive edge for those forces that acquired the most advanced technology.⁷ The challenge with the 3ʳᵈ Industrial Revolution regarding military accessions is that it began after the AVF was founded.

Fifty years ago, Gordon Moore—the founder of Intel Corporation, accurately predicted that the rate of growth of computing power would double every five years—this compounding rate of change has become colloquially labeled as Moore's Law" and is used to explain the rate of technology growth.⁸ Today, in matters of military affairs and national security, the rapid advance of technology has resulted in a truncated debate framed as a necessary weapons characteristic whose cost must be controlled, or used as a means to control such costs. In a review of emerging national security issues, John Williams et al. expanded consideration of the relationship between technology and the military by offering,

> One fear is that technology, whether civilian or military, increasingly tends to drive itself: that is, a technological culture may develop to a point that technology will be seen as a good in its own right, with little reference to its impact on the quality of life, values, and morals of society. In its extreme form, the fear is that technology will advance without recourse to its social utility, and society will blindly adapt to it rather than technologies adapting to society.⁹

---

6. Roy B. Helfgott, "America's Third Industrial Revolution," *Challenge* 29, no. 5 (December 1986): 41–46. See also Castells, *The Rise of the Network Society*, 30.
7. Donald M. Snow, "The Shifting Threat and American National Strategy: Sources and Consequences of Change," in *The Adaptive Military: Armed Forces in a Turbulent World*, Second Edition, ed. James Burk, 2nd ed. (New Jersey: Transaction Publishers, 1998), 115–138.. See also McKitrick et al., "Chapter 3." See also Eliot A. Cohen, "A Revolution in Warfare," *Foreign Affairs* 75, no. 2 (April 1996): 37–54.
8. John Sawers, "Technology, Security, Freedom," *Vital Speeches of the Day* 82, no. 2 (February 2016): 43.
9. Williams, Cimbala, Sarkesian, *US National Security*, 352.

Missing from the discussion is the broader effect of technology on military accessions and, by extension, its effect on the American Paradoxical Trinity. As noted by Feaver, technology serves as an exogenous factor in civil-military relations and will continue to redefine how it operates.[10] While the role of technology on the battlefield is well documented, the scholarship on the social effects of technology, as it relates to the military, is limited, summarized below in four categories, in declining abstraction. First, technology is considered a social object, a condition larger than any single technical innovation. Second, technology is considered a force of innovation that drives change, often in ways unforeseen. Third, the literature on how technology has affected the military profession is summarized. The last section reviews explanations of the role of technology on military accessions.

Technology as a Social Object

The application of Albert Borgmann's *Focal Things and Practices* paradigm to military recruiting for the AVF illustrates how it functions as a technology and, in doing so, has disconnected the American military from the democratic society it serves. His technology paradigm has three components: a *thing*, a *device*, and a *commodity*. First, a *thing* is defined by context; its full meaning is tied to the environment where it exists. A classic example of this is a fireplace as a focal point within the home; it provides heat, a meeting place for the family, and stratifies tasks for the household. In this way, one's experience with *things* is both a physical object and a social engagement.[11]

Second, a *device* is the physicality or demonstration of the process, organized and built around a purpose. Within a *device*, there are machines, and the number varies depending on the complexity of the technology, which increasingly disburdens people of the device's requirements. As a result, "[t]he machinery makes no demand on our skill, strength, or attention, and it is less demanding the less it makes

---

10. Feaver, "Foreword," vii–x.
11. Albert Borgmann, "Focal Things and Practices," in *Readings in the Philosophy of Technology*, ed. David M. Kaplan, 2nd edition (Lanham: Rowman & Littlefield Publishers, 2009), 56–75.

its presence felt. In the progress of technology, the machinery of a *device* has, therefore, a tendency to become concealed or to shrink."[12]

Third, a *commodity* is the output of a *device*, and it indicates what the *device* is for. The construct of the commodity is intentionally fluid, not necessarily material. It makes goods and services available for consumption and, in doing so, enables disengagement and distraction by the community (i.e., the consumption of fast food in contrast to all that is entailed in making a family meal). A *thing* can provide more than one *commodity*. Borgmann acknowledges that there are unavoidable ambiguities in the concepts of *devices* and *commodities*, but these can be "resolved through substantive analysis and methodological reflection."[13] Over time, the technology will grow to offer greater opportunities in the form of an increased *commodity*. The more these opportunities increase and the *commodity* is made available, the more meaningless they become to the community.

The existence of Army recruiting for the AVF as a technology rather than a deliberate activity is made evident when viewed as a *Focal Practice*. The interaction of the three components forms a technology that procures its own social standing and secures its continued use. Volunteer enlistment is a *thing*, defined by the context of the AVF. The sum of the parts and activities associated with securing voluntary personnel for Army service forms a *device*, labeled as Army recruiting. The output of a *device* is a *commodity*, and in this case, the *commodity* is an Army with adequate personnel accessions that make no further demands on society.

To arrest ungoverned technological change, Borgmann states that "the more strongly we sense and the more clearly we understand the coherence and the character of technology, the more evident it becomes to us that technology must be countered by an equally patterned and social commitment, that is by a practice."[14] According to Borgmann, protecting democracy and its values must be done in such a way (i.e., dialectic discourse) as to make the values meaningful but not proscrip-

---

12. Borgmann, "Focal Things and Practices," 55.
13. Borgmann, "Focal Things and Practices," 57.
14. Borgmann, "Focal Things and Practices," 66.

tive to "the good life" based on focal practices that illuminate what is true and important.[15] In this manner, political discourse, "forcefully reaches out to its listeners, takes account of their situation, and searches out the strongest existing bonds between the audience and the matter of concern. Thus, the discourse is more likely to create conditions of collective assent and the basis of common action."[16] Borgmann makes his argument about modern technology as a social object with simple examples such as running, cars, Big Macs, Coca-Cola, and family dinners. However, this is done for clarity, not as an inferred limitation of the paradigm's utility. He clearly believes the *Focal Things and Practices* paradigm is useful for understanding modern technology to resolve large society problems, as evidenced by his recommendations to use this approach to address wealth distribution, hunger, disease, confinement, and charity. In this way, the study of focal practice related to military accessions could protect the values of Western democracies by identifying the unintended effects of technology in recruiting.

Technology as a Social Function

While technology functions as an object, as stated above, it does not do so in isolation. As a human phenomenon, technology also has external interaction with dispersed second-order effects. Using two hermeneutic dimensions, Andrew Feenberg explains how modern technology and society function in a reciprocal relationship that determines the extent to which the former is controlled by the latter. The first dimension is *social meaning*, where a technical object has both a social role and enables a social pattern (lifestyle). Over its lifecycle, the technical object is a product of unpredictable social attitudes that, in turn, influence its later design. In this way, various social groups determine what the object is "for," which will ultimately determine what the object becomes over time. The second hermeneutic dimension is a *cultural horizon*, which Feenberg considers the basis of modern forms of

---

15. Borgmann, *Technology and the Character*, 177, 222-225.
16. Borgmann, *Technology and the Character*, 179.

social hegemony. This happens because the assumptions that underwrite a technology seem natural and obviously persist without conscious awareness—they lie far below the threshold that would engender societal questioning or review. The resulting shared understanding of social power and its application seems natural to all, perpetuating hegemonic structures. Consequently, when technology is introduced to society, it validates the *cultural horizon* under which it was designed to perform. In this way, technology is neither deterministic nor neutral but biased. Feenberg concludes that if choices to the technology are not identified, then "truth" remains hidden, and the uncontrolled technology, in turn, affirms the social factors it deems applicable.[17]

Andrew Feenberg explains that in democracies, the political process is "overshadowed by the enormous power wielded by masters of technical systems," which include military leaders.[18] He does not see technology as deterministic, as Marx argued, but as something that must be understood as an interactive social object rather than considered as something purely rational and functional. Social requirements are often portrayed as technological imperatives, and as such, these are often accepted without question.[19] Should democracy fail to expand to address modern technology, it risks falling victim to modern forms of control in such areas as "production, medicine, education, or the military."[20] In this manner, technology is both a product of and can be constrained by social factors. Given the behavior of technology, Borgmann states that when technology is known and seen as a social object, then the democratic processes and their institutions can adapt to manage how modern technology functions and, in turn, ensure the representation of the people as intended. Consequently, if military recruiting were seen as a technology, then it could be deliberately

---

17. Feenberg, "Democratic Rationalization," 142, 146-147.
18. Andrew Feenberg, "Democratic Rationalization: Technology, Power, and Freedom," in *Readings in the Philosophy of Technology*, ed. David M. Kaplan, 2nd Edition (Lanham, MD: Rowman & Littlefield Publishers, 2009), 139.
19. Andrew Feenberg, "The Ambivalence of Technology," *Sociological Perspectives* 33, no. 1 (Spring 1990): 35–50, https://doi.org/10.2307/1388976, 47.
20. Feenberg, "Democratic Rationalization: Technology, Power, and Freedom," 140.

employed, ideally by a balanced American Paradoxical Trinity, to function for the good of society (i.e., provide a representative force that models republicanism across the geography and demographics). In this way recruiting technology is not inherently bad, unless it is ungoverned.

Technology and the Military Profession

The growth of technology both caused and enabled the expansion of the military profession and bureaucracy. Traditionally, scholars apply a derivative of one of the above four paradigms to explain how the military profession should or did act, and the subsequent effect on civil-military relations. These scholars recognized that emergent technology would change the profession; their arguments assumed that the relevant technology would become part of the profession's expert knowledge, which in turn would drive purposeful organizational change. Recent scholarship has identified four technology-related threats to the Army profession. First, like other professions, the Army operated within a society increasingly skeptical of technical experts and objective science.[21] Second, the Global Wars on Terrorism (GWOT) in Iraq and Afghanistan included an unprecedented use of contractors that has led those inside and outside the Army to question whether a vocational commitment that requires technical mastery of warfare also requires a military profession marked by a sense of social obligation or republicanism.[22] Third, the 3rd Industrial Revolution (marked by the use of computers and information) would blur the lines of authority for lethal force and, in doing so, change the military profession's scope of duties.[23] Finally, the increasing application of technology in the management of the military institution risks changing

---

21. Burk, "Expertise, Jurisdiction," 39–60.
22. Deborah Avant, "Losing Control of the Profession Through Outsourcing?," in The Future of the Army Profession, Revised and Expanded Second Edition, ed. Don Snider and Lloyd Matthews, 2nd ed. (Boston, MA: McGraw Hill-Education, 2005), 271–90.
23. Snow, "The Shifting Threat," 125-127.

the profession into a compartmental plug-n-play bureaucracy, a condition contextualized as "MacDonaldization".[24]

Such scholarship considers the relationship between technology and the profession as recursive. In this way, the military profession can decide how it will respond (e.g., behavior) to technology (i.e., as it did with the advent of nuclear weapons), or technology can drive how the profession will respond to it (i.e., as happened with the recent growth of social media).

Technology and Military Recruiting

The relationship between the advancement of technology and the advancement of the military has long been inextricably linked. Since the 18th century, effective democracies have required the full participation of leaders and citizens. Until recently, the concept of civic duty, expressed as national service, has served American democracy and foreign affairs well. Benjamin Barber says, "Democracy can be reinforced by technology, and it can be corrupted by technology, but democracy's survival depends on human, not machine inspiration."[25] He argues that strong leaders have, over time, made American citizens politically weak, where foundational institutions enacted Michels' iron law of oligarchy—where authority is centralized to an elite few—and in doing so, separated the citizenry from their government.[26]

The scholarship on military change resulting from technology initially focused on how technology had enabled weapons and refashioned warfare. Later scholarship identified that the proliferation of computers would connect the military services with vast amounts of data that could profoundly affect society.[27] Since the return to a volunteer force in 1973, the four service branches have increasingly used a technology-enabled, market-based approach to recruiting to induce enough citizens to volunteer for service in exchange for personal compensation (see Chapter 3). Today, working in conjunction with the

---

24. Hajjar and Ender, "The McDonaldization in the U.S. Army, 215–30.
25. Benjamin R. Barber, *A Passion for Democracy* (Princeton University Press, 1998), 257.
26. Barber, *A Passion for Democracy*, 97.
27. Eliot A. Cohen, "A Revolution in Warfare," 43.

Army Marketing Enterprise Office and its $400 million annual advertising budget, Army recruiting uses big data to hyper-target potential applicants.[28] In the face of recent Army recruiting failures, some argue that Army recruiting advertising should deliberately change its approach, discarding the individual cost-benefit rationale and instead appealing to a sense of civic duty, as the Marine Corps does, to secure more accessions.[29] This argument assumes a high level of patriotism or "true volunteers" with a sense of republicanism, as assumed when the AVF was founded (see Chapter 2).

To summarize the literature, in the period following the fall of the Berlin Wall in 1989, the increasingly rapid rate of scientific advances profoundly affected society, the military, national security, and—by extension—civil-military relations. This would lead to *AVF 2.0*, but not in a linear or controlled fashion. Today, as *AVF 4.0* emerges, technology has arguably created a revolution in military affairs, but not as anticipated. Recent military operations have shown that technology moves in two dimensions: vertically—becoming increasingly more complicated, and horizontally—becoming simpler to use and available to more actors. In this manner, mobile phones wired as detonators to "dumb" munitions (e.g., low technology such as artillery shells or mines) destroyed modern battle tanks. At the same time, society has developed the perception that military technology has made combat operations so efficient that service requirements are limited to those with special skills, of which it is believed there are plenty of applicants.[30] The sum of this scholarship makes it plausible that military accessions, in the context of America's Paradoxical Trinity, are a result of a government that has not forced a reconning between society and the military on the role of technology. In this condition, the influence of

---

28. Jared Serbu, "Army Stands up Chicago-Based Marketing Operation to Help Bolster Recruitment," Federal News Network," August 22, 2019, accessed November 02, 2022, https://federalnewsnetwork.com/army/2019/08/army-stands-up-chicago-based-marketing-operation-to-help-bolster-recruitment/. See also Jeb Blount, *Fanatical Military Recruiting*, 92-97.
29. Theodore Camp, "The Military Depends on Virtues That Are Fading," *Public Discourse*, March 23, 2023, accessed March 26, 2023, https://www.thepublicdiscourse.com/2023/03/87979/.
30. Snow, "The Shifting Threat," 127-134.

technology on the military spreads of its own accord in unintended ways.

Accepting the logic, assumptions, and conditions of the Gates Commission, then once the AVF stabilized as AVF 2.0, any change in the factors influencing the accessions (e.g., compensation, republicanism present in "true volunteers") would result in a predictable adjustment to recruiting. If there was a reduction of Army end-strength, then there should be a proportional reduction of recruiting efforts as the requirement has lessened. However, if the recruiting has matured into a social technology (as described by the above literature), then the increased autonomy of the services, enabled by its improved professional standing (see Chapter 5), would allow the accessions to reflect market-based recruiting at the expense of the AVF's requirement for representativeness. In private, beyond public scrutiny, recruiting resources (e.g., advertising monies, location of recruiting stations, number of recruiters, etc.) would not be balanced to provide representativeness, but instead pursue efficiency at the expense of a balanced American Paradoxical Trinity.

METHOD FOR UNDERSTANDING RECRUITING AS A TECHNOLOGY

As an exploratory work into how the AVF became a New Warrior Caste and increasingly fails to secure necessary accessions, this analysis uses both qualitative and quantitative methods to identify the role of technology in the current recruiting problem. The hazard of modern technology to society is not merely a single manifestation—such as the saturation of mobile phones in the classroom—but the increasing pervasiveness of the technology that obscures society's drift from what it considers essential aspects of its humanity. Modern technology is neither a single period-specific phenomenon nor an object that demonstrates emergent engineering. The result of modern technology is that it has so permeated our lives that its role and effects often go unnoticed. Thus, a given society could have numerous technologies that, at times, may compete with each other.

As a theoretical argument, Albert Borgmann and Andrew Feenberg's social-technology behavior models are suitable for understanding technology as it relates to military recruiting. These are applied to the U.S. Army Recruiting Command to determine how it functions as a technology and pursues recruits to efficiently meet accession requirements at the expense of an effective representative force. Per the preceding chapters, for the same reasons, the Army is used as the population of record for analysis of the AVF for three reasons. First, it is the service with the largest personnel requirement. Second, it is the service most indicative of the recruiting environment for DOD writ large. Finally, the Army was the service of greatest concern when creating the AVF. In short, when it comes to personnel, how goes the Army is how goes the DOD.

The location of active component Army recruiting stations and recruiters in comparison to state populations is evaluated to measure and test the relationship between recruiting technology and AVF accessions. While the brick-and-mortar infrastructure of recruiting stations may seem antiquated and merely a portion of the larger recruiting activity, they remain central to the process and represent a significant commitment of resources. The location of recruiting centers provides a dynamic indicator of how and where the Services allocate recruiting resources. For example, in 2023, the Marine Corps—with its own significant and enduring recruiting problem—announced the closing of recruiting stations in "underperforming areas" across three states and the opening of additional ones in three other states identified to have "trendy urban areas."[31] Beyond their physical presence, recruiting stations are purposefully very visible on the internet and social media. Additionally, recruiting stations also represent the commitment of another finite resource, recruiters. The locations of active Army recruiting stations and the minimum number of recruiters assigned to each were determined from data acquired for the USAREC

---

31. Hope Hodge Seck, "Marines Move Some Recruiting Centers to Urban Hubs in Massive Realignment," *Marine Corps Times*, June 17, 2024, accessed August 6, 2024, https://www.marinecorpstimes.com/news/recruiting/2024/06/17/marines-move-some-recruiting-centers-to-urban-hubs-in-massive-realignment/?utm_campaign=dfn-ebb&utm_medium=email&utm_source=sailthru.

by a Freedom of Information Act Request (FOIA 24-0020).[32] The U.S. Census Bureau reports for 2022 provided the population numbers for the respective states.[33]

ANALYSIS OF TECHNOLOGY AND RECRUITING

When recent accession outcomes are overlaid on the expansion of recruiting technology, America's current and growing problem with accessions is better understood. The following analysis is conducted in two parts. First, the United States Army Recruiting Command (USAREC) is defined in scope and scale to explain it as a closed system —internal to the Army—that has grown in technological complexity concurrent with an increasingly smaller accession requirement. Second, the technology of Army recruiting is contextualized by the presence of recruiters assigned to recruiting stations as a quantitative indicator of the resources applied in pursuit of either a market-based or a representative force.

Technology of Military Recruiting

The effects of technology on the Army were not limited to the battlefield. The transition to the All-Volunteer Force in 1973 coincided with a broader democratization of technology. By *AVF 2.0*, the result was a seismic change, which affected the military more than the introduction of the stirrup and gunpowder.[34] The mobile phone and personal computer illustrate this rapid and profound change phenomenon. In 1973, Motorola unveiled the prototype personal cellular phone; by 1980, America had 120 thousand mobile phones, and by 2020, it had 277 million users.[35] Shortly following, the personal

---

32. USAREC, "Station Listing," PDF, July 11, 2024.
33. United States Census Bureau, "2020-2022 State Population."
34. Roland, *War and Technology*, 31, 69, 108-114.
35. Tom Farley, "The Cell-Phone Revolution," American Heritage, December 2011, accessed 02 September 2023, https://www.americanheritage.com/content/cell-phone-revolution. See also Calvin Wankhede, "The History of Cell Phones: A Decade-by-Decade Timeline," *Android Authority*, July 14, 2023, accessed 01 September 2023, https://www.androidauthority.com/history-of-cell-phones-timeline-3264425/. See also "Mobile

computer (PC) emerged with the release of the Apple II, PET 2001, and TRS-80, dubbed by *Byte* magazine "The 1977 Trinity."[36] That year, household PCs entered the market, selling 48 thousand units; by 2020, there were more than 121 million PCs just in U.S. homes.[37]

As part of the transition to the AVF, the Army created the United States Army Recruiting Command (USAREC), the successor to the General Recruiting Service. It was commanded by a Major General (MG, 2 stars), under the authority of the Department of the Army G1—a Lieutenant General (three-star)—for Personnel. The organization was comprised of 8,000 military and civilian personnel, and it fielded 3,000 Sergeant recruiters in 950 offices.[38] The marketing budget went from $3 million in 1969 to $35 million by 1974, when the Army overcame internal dissent to purchase its first TV advertisement.[39]

Since the creation of the USAREC in 1972, Army recruiting has evolved and grown more expensive while the size of the force shrank to almost half its former size. Army recruiting now employs an extensive array of advertising symbols, machines, and systems in an internally regulated process connected with the Department of Defense. USAREC, which coordinates with the Army Marketing Enterprise Office, employs over 12,000 Soldiers and civilians across the United States in over 1,400 offices. The cadre is trained in-house at "The Recruiting College," with some members funded to participate in a civilian internship or obtain an advanced degree at a civilian university.[40] The activity is still commanded by a MG, with eight regionally

---

Phone Users United States 2012-2020," Statista, February 23, 2017, accessed 25 August 2023, https://www-statista-com.ez-salve.idm.oclc.org/statistics/222306/forecast-of-smartphone-users-in-the-us/.
36. Michael Kanellos, "PCs: More than 1 Billion Served," *CNET*, March 18, 2009, accessed 24 August 2023, https://www.cnet.com/culture/pcs-more-than-1-billion-served/.
37. United States Census Bureau and Michael Martin, "Computer and Internet Use in the United States, 2018," American Community Survey Reports (Washington DC: United States Department of Commerce, April 2021), https://www.census.gov/library/publications/2021/acs/acs-49.html, 5.
38. Griffin, Jr, and Mountcastle, *The U.S. Army's Transition*, 115.
39. Saucier, "Mobilizing the Imagination," 15, 83.
40. Davis Winkie, "US Army to 'Overhaul' Recruiting School amid Personnel Shortage," Defense News, March 29, 2023, accessed March 30, 2023, https://www.defensenews.com/global/the-americas/2023/03/29/us-army-to-overhaul-recruiting-school-amid-personnel-shortage/.

CHAPTER 6

aligned direct reports (see Figure 27), and six special-purpose direct reports (medical recruiting, special operations recruiting, marketing and engagement, logistics, U.S. Army Parachute Team, and U.S. Army Marksmanship Team). After the inactivation of the U.S. Army Accessions Command in 2012,[41] Recruiting Command became subordinate to the U.S. Army Training and Doctrine Command (TRADOC)—a General (GEN, four-star) headquarters that reports to the Department of the Army—pending organizational changes that will have USAREC commanded by a LTG (3 star) and report directly to the CSA and the Secretary of the Army (SA).[42]

Figure 27. USAREC Recruiting Regions
Source: U.S. Army Recruiting Command -- About.

This nationally networked structure seeks to engage American youth ages 17-24 with a variety of methods. There remain recruiting advertisements on billboards and military displays at public events such as state fairs, but these recruiting tools have moved to the background. The traditional recruiter, who works from an office in a local strip mall, continues to connect through the high school guidance

---

41. . Department of Defense, "U.S. Army Recruiting Command History," Government, National Archives NextGen Catalog, accessed May 12, 2023, https://catalog.archives.gov/id/10677594.
42. U.S. Army, "U.S. Army Recruiting Command -- About," Government, U.S. Army Recruiting Command: Official Website, 2022, accessed November 02, 2022, https://recruiting.army.mil/aboutUSAREC/. See also, Department of Defense, "U.S. Army Recruiting Command History," Government, National Archives NextGen Catalog, accessed May 12, 2023, https://catalog.archives.gov/id/10677594.

counselor, but this is almost a secondary engagement.[43] In the foreground of Army recruiting today is a sophisticated, technology-enabled outreach process. The Army is active on social media with advertisements and virtual connections. By the 21st century, it licensed images to toymakers and paid for the commercial development of custom electronic games.[44] As an extension of this effort, the Army sponsored various gaming competitions, such as those held at the 14,500-square-foot, $12 million Army Experience Center (AEC) at the Franklin Mills Mall in Philadelphia, PA, where players develop an avatar as part of their engagement.[45] Working in conjunction with the Army Marketing Enterprise Office and its $400 million annual advertising budget, Army recruiting uses big data to hyper-target potential applicants.[46] The Army seeks to connect with youth likely to join the military by reaching them in an environment where they feel comfortable.

The USAREC employs the above system to enlist 55-75 thousand young adults annually, down from 198 thousand in 1974 when there was a much smaller population. The annual Congressionally authorized end-strength of the Army determines the annual accession requirement. When the Army fails to meet its recruiting mission, Congress typically responds by reducing the subsequent year's end-strength authorization.[47] Additionally, the Army typically responds to a failure to meet accession goals by increasing the resources made available to its recruiting apparatus for the subsequent year. These

---

43. U.S. Army, "U.S. Army Recruiting Command – About."
44. Saucier, "Mobilizing the Imagination," 339-342.
45. Jason Schapp, "ESports Team Ready for Today's CODE Bowl," Press Release (Fort Knox, KY: U.S. Army, December 11, 2020), accessed November 02, 2022, https://recruiting.army.mil/News/Article/2443775/esports-team-ready-for-todays-code-bowl/. For an example of an avatar experience, visit U.S. Army Recruiting. https://www.goarmy.com.
46. Serbu, "Army Stands up Chicago." See also Blount, *Fanatical Military Recruiting*, 92-97.
47. For an example of this cause-and-effect relationship, consider FY 23 accessions and FY 24 end-strength authorizations. Senate Committee on Armed Services, "Summary of the Fiscal Year 2023 National Defense Authorization Act" (Washington, DC, December 27, 202AD), and Todd South, "The Army Keeps Getting Smaller," *Army Times*, March 13, 2023, sec. Your Army, accessed March 15, 2023, https://www.armytimes.com/news/your-army/2023/03/13/the-army-keeps-getting-smaller/.

additional resources are made available by diverting what was otherwise planned for other activities (including the readiness of combat formations) to USAREC.[48] Response expenditure examples include manpower for additional recruiters, increased monies for marketing, and enlistment incentives (i.e., enlistment bonuses and student loan repayment).[49]

The increased use of technology on the battlefield drove the military to seek increasingly capable and smarter recruits, a stark difference from the characteristics of the rank and file before 1973—where military service provided an opportunity to the disadvantaged who might not otherwise have a means of social advancement and drafted more educated and wealthy elites. Since the 1990s, more strict induction standards have established the desired volunteer recruit as a citizen, 17-24 years of age, a high school graduate, capable of passing the entrance physical, with less than 30% body fat, no history of chronic or severe mental illness, no criminal record or regular drug use, and scores in the 50th percentile on the military aptitude test.[50] These individuals are most likely to come from families in the second quartile for income, with less minority representation than in 1973.[51]

Today, just 29% of American youth meet these criteria; half of this group will attend college following high school, leaving just 12% of the age-eligible population as potential future Soldiers, Sailors, Airmen, or Marines.[52] These discerning enlistment standards (in comparison to the lesser standards in place before 1973) have reduced the candidate pool in society, which in turn created an appetite for even more "efficient" recruiting technology. The vast array of material and activities involved in today's Army recruiting are codified and governed as a

---

48. Bruce R. Orvis et al., *Recruiting Strategies to Support the Army's All-Volunteer Force* (Santa Monica, Calif: RAND Corporation, 2016), 32-34.
49. For a recent example, see Lauren C. Williams, "More Money for Info Ops, Army Recruiting, Cyber In Omnibus," Defense One, December 22, 2022, accessed December 27, 2022, https://www.defenseone.com/defense-systems/2022/12/more-money-info-ops-army-recruiting-cyber-omnibus/381278/.
50. Office of the Under Secretary for Personnel and Readiness, "Military Personnel Policy for Active Component Enlisted Applicants and Accessions," (Department of Defense, 2022), https://prhome.defense.gov/M-RA/Inside-M-RA/MPP/.
51. Asoni et al., "A Mercenary Army," 591.
52. Office of People Analytics, "Official DOD Quality," 3.

system through Federal statutes, Army regulations, and policies that integrate a complex network.[53]

At the highest level, the Army's marketing instructions dictate that content delivery is a "critical component that relies on data analysis and a strong understanding of modern marketing capabilities, from search engine optimization and social media marketing to more creative and ill-defined emerging methods, and locally important considerations."[54] At each echelon, the USAREC chain of command closely monitors the attainment of subordinates' recruiting mission through detailed reporting and analysis that is scrutinized down to the individual recruiter's performance at each step (initial contacts, follow-up contacts, missed appointments, testing, contracting, etc.). Complex analytics identify varied and evolving opportunities to help secure the required enlistments. For example, in the Midwest, the data led one recruiting battalion to "focus more heavily on for-profit colleges since they contribute to over a third of all student loan defaults even though they represent less than 7% of the total college student population."[55]

Efficiency versus Effectiveness of Military Recruiting

The analysis of recruiting in Chapters 3 and 4 identified that since 1990, there has been a decline in geographic and racial representation (and little change in gender representation) in Army accessions such that by 2022, a representative force was largely absent, replaced by a

---

53. For example, see United States: Congress: "Enlistments: Recruiting Campaigns; Compilation of Directory Information. Sec. 503," Subtitle A-General Military Law PART II-PERSONNEL CHAPTER 31-ENLISTMENTS Title X, Armed Forces § 503 (2011), https://www.govinfo.gov/app/details/USCODE-2011-title10/USCODE-2011-title10-subtitleA-partII-chap31-sec503. See also US Army, "Army Regulation 601-208: The Army Marketing Program" (Headquarters Department of the Army, November 10, 2021), https://armypubs.army.mil/epubs/DR_pubs/DR_a/ARN32229-AR_601-208-000-WEB-1.pdf. See also US Army, "USAREC Manual 3-0: Recruiting Operations" (United States Army Recruiting Command, September 18, 2019), https://recruiting.army.mil/about USAREC/.
54. U.S. Army, "Army Pamphlet 601-208: Army Marketing" (Department of the Army, November 10, 2021), https://armypubs.army.mil/epubs/DR_pubs/DR_a/ARN31147-PAM_601-208-000-WEB-1.pdf, 2.
55. Battalion Commander - Cleveland, "3rd Recruiting Brigade 2QFY22 Operational Update Brief" (Quarterly Report. Fort Knox, KY, February 28, 2021), 8.

warrior caste. If USAREC's recruiting methodology was congruent with the founding principles of the AVF regarding republicanism and proportional representation, then the expenditure of resources would be, at best, used in a manner to correct ineffective representation or, as a minimum, expended evenly based on population. Should either of these conditions be true, then other socio-cultural and economic phenomena gain increased validity as explanatory variables for poor accessions and the creation of a warrior caste.

When the density of Army recruiting stations is considered per 100k persons by state (mean value = 0.4 per 100k), two clear patterns become evident. First, states with lower populations per square mile have a higher density of recruiting stations (i.e., Alaska and Wyoming). Second, the variance between states (controlling for Alaska and Wyoming as outliers) can be as high as 100% (see Figure 28). The "crooked smile" pattern does not emerge; the distribution of recruiting stations generally aligns with the 1990 accession (see Figure 8), with the highest density of recruiting stations in the central plains' states and the southeast.

A more fluid resource is the assignment of recruiters, as more can be assigned at any given time, and with a 100% turnover every three years, a reduction in the number of recruiters assigned at any given station is almost as easy to effect. When the density of Army recruiters (working at the stations in the above analysis) is considered per 100k persons by state (mean value = 2.6 per 100k), a familiar pattern is again evident. The location of the highest density of recruiters is in the southeast states, in a "crooked smile" pattern (see Figure 29). This distribution generally aligns with the state accession density of 2022 (see Figure 9). The two most populous states (CA, NY), which are underproducing in accessions, are resourced with fewer than the mean number of recruiters given the population of their respective states.

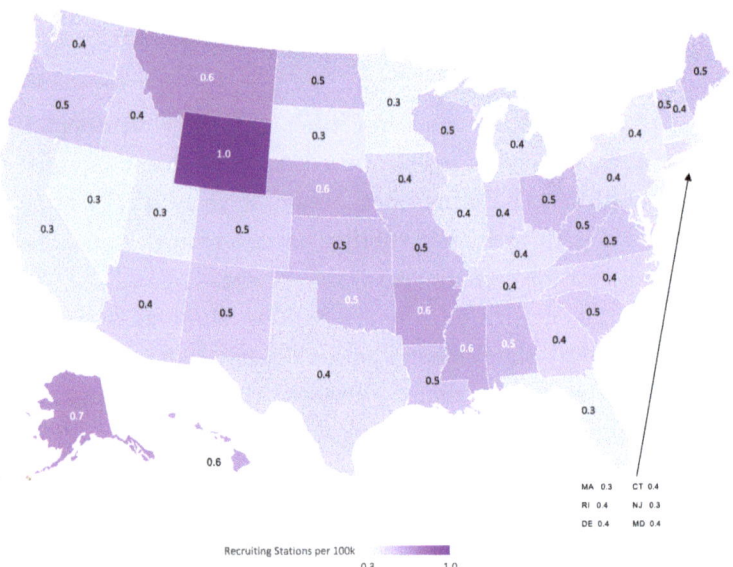

Figure 28. Army Recruiting Stations, by State, per 100k
Source: Data from U.S. Army Recruiting Command FOIA 24-0020, n=1355; and United States Census Bureau, "State Population Totals and Components of Change: 2020-2022."

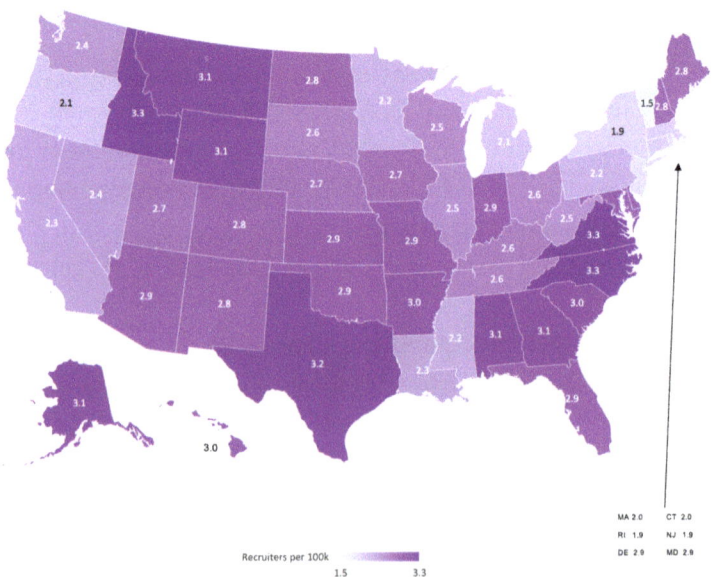

Figure 29. Army Recruiters by State, per 100k
Source: Data from U.S. Army Recruiting Command FOIA 24-0020, n=8638; and United States Census Bureau, "State Population Totals and Components of Change: 2020-2022."

FINDINGS

An examination of the Army's recruiting enterprise and how it has changed since the transition to the AVF shows that it is dynamic and growing increasingly complex. Rather than recruiting functioning as a bureaucratic institutional system, Army recruiting has grown while the force shrank, and in doing so, it increasingly fails to meet requirements. The above analysis identifies two significant findings that inform the understanding of the role of recruiting in the current recruiting crisis

First, A qualitative analysis identifies that Army recruiting functions as a technology and, in so doing, provides the vocabulary and paradigm to understand how America's Paradoxical Trinity remained out of balance long enough to enable a New Warrior Caste and an enduring recruiting crisis. The application of Borgman's "Focal Practice" paradigm and Feenberg's "Two Hermeneutic Dimensions" identifies the military recruiting technology as a perpetuating phenomenon that reverberates through other American institutions. In contrast to 1938, when the U.S. last had a voluntary army, the AVF in 1973 required a large force in being. To meet this great demand for volunteers the Army established—and over the subsequent 50 years increasingly resourced—the United States Army Recruiting Command, which adapted and integrated technology with unanticipated and unobserved second-order effects. In this manner, the U.S. Army's recruiting technology fulfills its stated purpose of resourcing the country with adequate personnel for its land force (i.e., a commodity). The sum of these recruiting efforts functions as a recruiting technology by being both an object (i.e., the recruiting enterprise) and a function (i.e., an accepted practice), as explained by Bormann and Freeman, respectively.

Per Borgmann, U.S. military service is considered a *thing*. From 1939 to 1973, military enlistment as a *thing* was an open and known activity in society via the SSS, an agency of the Executive branch. Congress, as the other arm of the government, approved and resourced its activities at the President's request. This civic interaction represented a *focal practice* that kept the expenditure of American youth in combat as a central social matter—a truth. In this manner, military service remained both a physical and societal event. Since 1973, the incipient growth of technology in recruiting has led to military recruiting to emerge as a technological phenomenon defined by the sum of its *artifacts, devices, machines,* and *systems*. The generally successful AVF accessions through most of the 1980s resulted in an erosion of military recruiting as a *focal practice*, accessions became a *commodity*. Volunteer enlistments (*thing*) were both a material input and provided a service to the state by enticing youths to serve in the Army without non-routine intervention by other actors. In this way, recruiting technology was reinforced, and an *artificial horizon* emerged where military recruiting technology (with its associated efficiency) became accepted as the status quo, thus seemingly negating the deliberate external evaluation of the recruiting enterprise's effectiveness. Put differently, in a prolonged period of peace in the 1980s and 90s, there was no public debate about who served. During this time the recruiting enterprise became as a technology (under supervised by the military profession and government) and delivered sufficient recruits as a commodity (without regard to representativeness) and in doing so removed the need for society to consider the 2nd order effects (such as a New Warrior Caste, reduced veteran dispersion, and shared citizen efficacy on military affairs) of this approach. This resulted in the recruiting crisis that began with the GWOT and continues today.

Second, a quantitative analysis indicates that Army recruiting—in an environment of a declining *focal practice* to serve in the military and an *artificial horizon* that obscures the need for representative accessions —functions efficiently as an imperative, at the expense of recognizing the need to rebalance America's Paradoxical Trinity. For example, the geographic footprint of the subordinate commands within USAREC is almost devoid of alignment with state boundaries. This indicates that USAREC considers the possible increased accessions effectiveness that could result from unity of command/purpose between both actors (and more likely to yield geographic representation) as secondary to the efficiency provided by the current arrangement's more uniform span of control (i.e., in size and distance). Considered alternately, had geographic representativeness in accessions been more important to the Army, then USAREC would have invested resources (i.e., recruiters and recruiting stations) in underperforming states. A purposeful pursuit of geographic representativeness would manifest as a recruiting station density greater than the mean of 0.4, and a recruiter density above the mean value of 2.6, in those states with a pattern of low accessions (i.e., California and New York). Instead, the states with the lowest population density or a history of over-producing accessions currently have the greatest density of stations and recruiters. Regarding recruiters—a more fungible resource, their distribution as a resource is roughly analogous to the 2022 aggregate "crooked smile" accession pattern, which failed to provide for geographic, ethnic, or gender representation.

CONCLUSION

Through the application of philosophy of technology to the recent recruiting crisis a plausible explanation emerges as to why America's Paradoxical Trinity regarding accessions could remain out of balance and allow the creation of a New Warrior Caste. Since 1973, the Army has reduced in size by almost 50%; concurrently, the technology of recruiting has grown as predicted by Moore's law. Until recently, these two trend lines allowed for the recruiting enterprise (*device*) to produce volunteer enlistments (*thing*) sufficiently to meet public expectations (*commodity*). This helped fuel the increasing autonomy of the Army profession, further enabling its isolation from society. In this manner, because the Army met its recruiting goals, there was no need for a broader engagement with the American public or government about the fulfillment of civic virtue or duty. The *commodity* increased in value; not necessarily in total numbers (as the Army declined in end-strength), but by increasingly unburdening society from having to think about providing youth for its Army. The cumulative effect is that recruiting for the AVF transformed from a form of social action to an object that acts in the background of society.

Since 1990, with declining oversight, the Army profession has increasingly made recruiting part of its jurisdiction and relied on recruiting technology to efficiently deliver necessary accessions at the expense of providing a representative and adequately sized force that enables the effectiveness of republican virtue. An analysis of the density of recruiting stations and recruiters shows that the Army does not invest its resources into the areas that would better provide representative accessions. Instead, recruiting resources are concentrated in the market areas that most efficiently provide new recruits. Those "areas" can be both a physical location correlated with the placement of recruiting stations, or a particular demographic correlated with hyper-targeted marketing on social media and internet applications. The second-order effect of this process manifests in an increasingly disproportionate veteran population; with a growing density in the high-accession areas and declining in the low-accession areas. As the environment has allowed recruiting technology to become increasingly pervasive, so too have the challenges of meeting annual accession requirements. Recall from Chapter 1 that the Department of Defense (DOD) failed to achieve its AVF accession targets 26 times in its 50-year history. These accession shortfalls have occurred with increasing frequency, as 9 of these failed recruiting missions occurred in the last 10 years.

Technology is neither good nor bad, but an outcome of an inevitable progression of science. The merit of the outcome is determined by the purposeful oversight of its application.[56] On the occasions that recruiting technology failed to deliver its commodity (adequate accessions), the military profession accepted the government's authority for end-strength cuts and/or the use of PMSCs rather than risk intrusion into its jurisdiction by engaging in a detailed discussion with the government on the resulting operational limitations and the structural problems with accessions. Society, because of its affinity for servicemembers and a lack of military understanding, has accepted force reductions and the continued application of recruiting technology as an adequate solution. This repeated solution spread across generations, achieved without confrontational discourse,

---

56. Martin Heidegger, "The Question Concerning Technology," in *Readings in the Philosophy of Technology*, ed. David M. Kaplan, Second Edition (Lanham, MD: Rowman & Littlefield Publishers, 2009), 22.

provided a sense of normalcy—an *artificial horizon* for society and the government, where the need for republicanism as a civic duty is replaced by the preeminence of personal liberty. The long-term structural result is an American Paradoxical Trinity out of balance and chronic accession problems. Army enlistments provide a service to the state by enticing youths to serve in the Army (*m-s* vertex), and in doing so, minimizes government engagement with the military (*g-m* vertex) and avoids the need for the government to become engaged with society (*g-s* vertex) regarding the importance of republicanism (see Figure 2). The "success" of Army recruiting technology, obtained by a pursuit of efficiency over effective representation, both enables and moves to social prominence a lifestyle of individual liberty without regard to its effect on civic duty.

As an exploratory argument as to how the New Warrior Caste arose in the AVF, the analysis of the role of technology in recruiting proves useful but not complete. Knowing how the problem arose helps determine how the problem needs to be resolved. The robustness and fidelity of the argument would be well served with additional research in three areas. First, additional research should quantify the "resource" variable of technology by means other than recruiting stations and recruiters (i.e., dollars spent, or algorithmic social media targeting). Second, other research should identify where the patterns seen here with the Army are also evident in the other services. Lastly, subsequent scholarship should seek to understand recruiting technology as applied to other demographics—such as race and gender—and whether the coefficient representing the rate of return produces similar results. The associated scholarship better informs how the New Warrior Caste arose and, in doing so, enables the correction to civil-military relations discussed in Chapter 7.

CHAPTER 7
CONCLUSION

> *Freedom is not procured by a full enjoyment of what is desired, but by controlling the desire.*
>
> – Epictetus, *Discourses*

THE UNITED STATES FACES A SIGNIFICANT AND SUSTAINED SHORTAGE OF citizens willing to serve as volunteers in the armed forces, indicating deteriorating civil-military relations. This problem has immediate implications for national security when considered in the context that recognizes: a) current accession requirements are the smallest since the advent of the All-Volunteer Force (AVF), b) servicemember compensation is at an all-time high, c) the AVF was unable to expand sufficiently to meet the requirements of the comparatively modest end-strength requirements of the Global War on Terrorism (GWOT). Since the AVF was founded in 1973, it has undergone significant structural change for physical, social, and political reasons. Again, the AVF is at an inflection point where social and political change necessitates an adaptation to the U.S. military's force structure and, potentially, its force design (e.g., a return to conscription). Planning and implementing any change to military forces' active and reserve force structure first requires understanding what happened and how this condition was allowed to grow over time until it became a crisis.

The AVF's subsequent adaptation in response to an increasingly difficult recruiting environment, resulting in a New Warrior Caste, did not happen in isolation. The process is understood as the forces and tensions embedded in America's Paradoxical Trinity (*military profession and forces, government comprised of Executive and Congress, the people and society*). The U.S. ended 34 years of conscription in 1973 and transitioned its military to a volunteer force design. When this happened, the Selective Service System- an agency of the executive branch— ceased to exist. With its dissolution, the government's principal means of communicating with society about military accessions ceased, without replacement.. Today, the American *people* (*society*) are fractionalized and distant from the Army for personal, physical, and sociostructural reasons. Without external oversight, the military's recruiting enterprise now accepts efficiency as its first principle, leading it to rely on market-based recruiting. In this manner, it does not concern itself with broadly connecting to society. In violation of America's republican tradition and a founding principle of the All-Volunteer Force, current military accessions are not effective in representing America by geography, ethnicity, gender, and education.

Today's recruits are tomorrow's veterans. They typically return to the state from which they came, where, as veterans, they become the most significant influence on the young people within their network to join the military. The consequence of decades of biased accessions is a non-representative, unevenly distributed veteran population that, for large segments of America, is not present to either model republican virtue or directly influence the next generation of young people to enlist. The State's military potential is realized when its Paradoxical Trinity is balanced. The analysis of the accessions from 1990 compared to 2022, using the Army as an exemplar for the DOD, identifies a New Warrior Caste; an indicator of an unbalanced American Paradoxical Trinity that calls into question the long-term viability of the AVF in its current form.

Since the advent of the AVF in 1973, the *military* has become much more professional—with greater political power—and more distant from society (*people*). The Army profession, while aware of recruiting technology's failures to provide representative accessions, has remained focused on efficiency, prioritizing achieving near-term recruiting success over effectively representing the breadth of society. The profession protects its legitimacy and jurisdiction by avoiding a likely contentious discourse on how to change this pattern. Concurrently, the *government* has had decreasing engagement with the *people* regarding the need to support the *military* with personal service. The result is that the *military* struggles with accessing sufficient personnel from *society*. By using the Army as an exemplar of the AVF, the analysis shows that the resulting estrangement of the *government* from *society* on military matters has increased the difficulty in connecting youth to the armed forces, despite the significant reduction in accession requirements for a smaller military. This has driven the Army's increased dependency on technology to meet accession requirements.

The 3rd Industrial Revolution—the computer age—began in parallel with the creation of the AVF, enabling more lethal weapons and better management. At the same time, it also changed military recruiting in ways not anticipated when the AVF was founded. Military technologies are typically viewed as discreet devices or activities, but technology is also a complex force that increasingly operates as an environmental condition that goes unnoticed by society (the consumer) who relies on it to meet its needs. The resulting recruiting technology focused on efficiently meeting requirements and grew at pace in keeping with Moore's law. This compounded the systemic faults of reduced government involvement and a shrinking military, resulting in the military profession minimizing the second-order effects to the other parts of the Paradoxical Trinity. Over time, the net result was increasingly frequent problems achieving required accessions and a smaller military, until 2022, when the scope of this problem became existential in the face of potential Great Power competition.

CHAPTER 7

FINDINGS

First, while a sense of individual liberty has always been a defining characteristic of Americans, the preeminence of republicanism in matters relating to military service has been at the forefront of the U.S. way of war. Historically, it has been expressed individually through volunteer military service or as a corporate virtue used to justify conscription. Until World War II, the government only compelled this virtue with conscription during times of war. Post-World War II geopolitics and advances in military technology necessitated a large standing peacetime force, so conscription continued. In the 1970s, demographics, politics, and dissatisfaction with the Vietnam War caused the ascendency of liberalism in politics, but it did not displace the role of, or belief in, republicanism as a necessary civic virtue in the design of the armed force's structure.

Second, the state of the military today is absent four required conditions considered essential in 1973 for the U.S. to have a viable volunteer force sufficient to meet its requirements as a global power. One, the AVF relied on an embedded sense of individual republicanism enabled by providing volunteers with a modest salary—in this way, more individuals could demonstrate their ingrained sense of republicanism by volunteering for military service because it would no longer be cost-prohibitive. Two, the military's demographics would remain representative of society, with the increased participation of women. Third, recruiting for the AVF would not affect representation, and if it did, this social compact would require redress outside the military. Fourth, the AVF would comprise an active force greater than 2 million servicemembers plus a ready reserve and a stand-by reserve (i.e., a stand-by draft) to be used in times of war. When the AVF was founded, the presence of these conditions was thought to ensure that the U.S. had a military representative of society, and in doing so, negated the most significant criticism of ending the draft—that the burden of national defense would not be shared. Since then, robust personnel compensation increases could not provide adequate accessions during the GWOT, and the national budget leaves little room for a significant increase. The lack of geographic and demographic representation in the New Warrior Caste does not represent society. By 2022, the DOD's end-strength had fallen to 1.3 million, and during the GWOT the ready reserve did not serve as the intended tripwire, and the stand-by reserve was not used.

The third finding, the lack of representation in the AVF, is not surprising given the violation of the four conditions noted above and the nature of professions and technology. The foremost imperative of the Army profession is subservience to civilian authority, but it inherently protects its jurisdiction in the course of compliance. This behavior causes the continued reliance on recruiting technology for the fulfillment of accession missions (i.e., providing enough recruits) at the expense of ensuring a representative force. The result over time is an increasingly disproportional number of military enlistments from the southeast United States, a pattern referred to as "the crooked smile." When considering a return to a volunteer military in 1973, three characteristics were regarded as metrics of representativeness: race, gender, and education. The analysis here illustrates that while education level was relatively constant and geographically represented in accessions, race and gender accessions became increasingly concentrated in the Southeast—despite having distinct geographic distribution patterns before 1990. In 1990 and 2022, the percentage of women and Black Army accessions was 15% and 5%, respectively. By 2022 the percentages had increased to 16% and 23%, respectively. In real numbers, the number of Blacks in the U.S. military has doubled, while the number of women has fallen almost in half. The 62% reduction in the size of the Army from 1990 to 2022 makes the "increased" participation of Blacks, women, and Black women less indicative of improved social equity. When considered in this context, the participation of Blacks and Black women may indicate either a bias in recruiting technology, a slower decline in civic virtue, or fewer opportunities in society.

Lastly, the creation of the AVF marked the first time the U.S. relied on a volunteer force since becoming a post-World War II superpower. This moved American civil-military relations into uncharted territory and, in doing so, allowed the American Paradoxical Trinity to more easily become unbalanced. While the U.S. had a long tradition of volunteer-based armed forces, it had not previously had one in a period of rapid technological advancement and high demand for the military. Under conscription, the U.S. Government, with the Selective Service System (SSS) as its agent, directed who from society could/would enter military service. This engagement process occurred via more than six thousand SSS draft boards that were resident in every U.S. County and, in doing so, provided a mechanism to connect the government to society regarding military matters. When the SSS ceased, the burden of communicating to society what the military needed fell solely to the military profession. While functionally committed to fulfilling this role, the military profession was not structurally or systematically equipped to replace the SSS relationship between the government and society regarding its need for personnel. In an environment with little political/governmental oversight and a high demand for forces, market-based recruiting technology flourished, resulting in a force that does not represent America and decreases citizen efficacy on military matters.

IMPLICATIONS

Knowing these four findings related to the AVF's growing recruiting problem builds on other scholarship on accessions and civil-military relations. These findings explain systemic problems with the AVF that, if left unchecked, will perpetuate a downward recruiting spiral and/or further reductions in end-strength. At the same time, chronic accession shortfalls also signal an imbalance of America's Paradoxical Trinity, which puts America at risk in future military operations. Some might argue that in the absence of an existential national crisis, a military that is too small is not a real problem because, when needed, the national system will self-correct to make necessary increases to the force structure and changes to the force design. This is a perilous argument as it relies on two assumptions. First, it assumes that when a crisis arises, there will be enough time for the correction to the military's size and structure. Second, the argument assumes that when confronted with a crisis, the nation's institutions will be sufficient to create a national consensus that compels necessary and rapid change to how it is designed. These assumptions are very tenuous, and the analysis and findings here contribute to a recognition of the current precarious condition of civil-military relations. Consider the following five implications of these four findings.

First, how large of a military does America require? The pattern of civil-military relations regarding the size of the U.S. armed forces since 1990 has been determined by exception. The end of the Cold War resulted in the Government calling for a "peace dividend" that included a reduction in the military end-strength. The strategic accuracy of this decision lies outside this discussion; what is germane is that the American Paradoxical Trinity was exercised based on a public discussion of the security environment. America's democracy, however imperfect, functioned as designed. Since then, national security has been assumed rather than measured or assessed. The arbitrator of military size has been the ability of the AVF to meet end-strength authorizations, not the result of public discourse. By 2022, the AVF was known to be insufficient for global operations short of war, limited war, and (arguably) for war. Failure of the military profession and civilian leaders to address this condition results in a national defense strategy characterized by the means (recent accessions) defining the ends (size of the military) rather than the logical reverse. Since 1990, there has not been an existential threat to compel a rebalancing of America's Paradoxical Trinity. While the security of the U.S. during this time may make the current approach to defense strategy seem plausible, it is not a safe refuge as it assumes that this laissez-faire approach will have sufficient time for the republic to respond to a crisis and that the resulting correction costs (in blood and treasure) are less in the aggregate. As a historical contrast, in 1939, the President pursued authorization from Congress to increase the size of the armed forces in the absence of an existential threat but in anticipation of what might be required in the future.

Second, should the military be required to be more representative of America in terms of geography, race, and gender? The burden of being prepared for war and the prosecution of war are costly in terms of monetary and human capital. The requisite payments come at the expense of other social priorities and liberties. When the military is representative of the society, it provides greater legitimacy to the costs and the military-related actions directed by the State, and it improves citizens' efficacy on such matters. Out of necessity, military forces have long relied on those generally young and healthy to fill their ranks, with special exclusions and exceptions based on social norms and necessity. In the U.S. Army today, Soldiers are young, healthy, and smart. Beyond this, there is little to indicate that the Army is representative. Thus, it is not surprising that there is a great separation of society from military matters such as resourcing and utilization. The separation is not differences of opinion regarding the suitability of costs and appropriateness of deployments, which would indicate that the vortexes of the Trinity were being exercised. Instead, the division is a cancerous indifference—hidden from view and debilitating—of society on military matters. While recruiting failures have led to a smaller military, thereby decreasing the depth of its connectedness with society, recruiting technology has decreased the breadth of society's connection with the military. Now more than ever, large segments of civil society have "no skin in the game" and little connection to those that do. The presence of an Army that has devolved into a warrior caste is not the sole cause of the current political divide, but in this state, the Army as an institution with truncated (non-representative) connections to society cannot be the structural mechanism to reduce the civil-military divide.

Third, what are the appropriate metrics for successful recruiting? The metric of successful recruiting requires modification to meet *societal expectations*. Since 1990, recruiting success has been defined by efficiently meeting volume targets that fulfill demand. On the occasions when the accessions provided select social representation (i.e., participation rate of Blacks) or met quality requirements (i.e., percentage with a high school diploma), the military profession was lauded. However, the attainment of such goals did not drive a change in the profession's use of recruiting technology to be more effectively representative rather than efficient. Inversely, the lack of meeting other accession goals (i.e., geographic dispersion, Asian minorities) is seen as a shortcoming but has not changed the profession's application of recruiting technology to be more efficient.

Most servicemembers today are one to four years from becoming a veteran—the greatest influence on a youth's likelihood of committing to an enlistment once aware of the opportunity. Gaps in accession geography or demographics result in subsequent gaps in the veteran population. This condition enables false perceptions of the armed forces and what constitutes selfless service to the country to perpetuate. Over time, these regionally unbalanced inductions have a multiplicative effect on declining civil-military relations. First, the absence of association with a veteran allows the public to disassociate from military operations. Second, the absence of first-hand connections to veterans means they cannot be the influencers of youth to consider the merits of military service and civic duty. This trend will only worsen as the number of recruits dwindles, and they become increasingly less representative and geographically concentrated. In this way, the New Warrior Caste becomes even more homogeneous and insular, while social cohesion—the foundation of a democracy—is reduced. When large sections of the country are absent from military accessions then the social artifacts and veteran population that legitimizes a tradition of republicanism as a civic virtue are removed. To thwart this, the metric of successful recruiting requires modification. Beyond being merely efficient in meeting personnel requirements, recruiting must also be assessed against its effectiveness in providing a representative force. The desired result is a new *cultural horizon* that values republicanism, which is shared across society and government.

Fourth, what is the role and responsibility of the government in defining what and who constitutes effective accessions? From 1939 through 1973, the government engaged society on the needs of the military through the SSS. With the advent of the AVF, that duty fell upon the respective services. While this was the method employed during other periods when the U.S. had a volunteer military, those times were marked by a small force that was not heavily committed to operations. While the Army has leveraged recruiting technology—coupled with declining end-strength—to fulfill accession requirements such that recruiting is now a commodity, the military profession's role in the stewardship of the institution through this change has proven insufficient to bolster the republican tradition. Because recruiting is now a commodity that meets the accession requirement, civic duty has devolved into an expression of "virtual support" as the new cultural horizon.

Missing today is the Government's connection to society on military matters, such as participation. The result is a military profession that, on matters of recruiting, takes a path of least resistance by assuming increased responsibility for accessions. By virtue of its ethos and structure, the military profession was never intended to be, and cannot, arbitrate its needs between oppositional positions within society and the government. In this manner, the military profession portrays itself as politically neutral by offering politically neutral recommendations (non-principled) in order to avoid being seen as partisan. The profession's answer to a problem is often the one that does not take a side, thus shirking its best military advice. The Constitutional authority of the civilian leadership in government is purposefully bifurcated between the executive and the legislative branches to provide the means to both command the military and synchronize the military's requirements with society. In the AVF's fifty years post-SSS, no replacement mechanism has emerged to connect the government with society; the military profession cannot do so and remain true to its central warfighting requirements. The problems identified here with military accessions that are inadequate and not representative of society indicate a breakdown of the American Paradoxical Trinity.

Fifth, where is the limit of the military institution's social responsibilities when they conflict with the effectiveness of the military as an armed force? While the logic that democracy is best protected by a representative military goes back to ancient Greece, the application of this logic has changed in modern times. The prestige, influence, and benefits of serving in the military have incentivized select social groups to pursue mechanisms to force greater inclusion of select groups in the armed forces. Advocates call this social equality; opponents refer to forced inclusions as a means of social engineering at the expense of warfighting competency. At the same time, the military profession has used its position of increased autonomy to make arguments based on efficiency (i.e., low attrition during initial training, greater retention to the end of enlistment) as to who should be allowed to serve, at the expense of having more people eligible to serve. Absent a directed purposeful discussion that defines "who" shoulders the burden of a shared civic duty to the State, one must question whether the Army has the force it wants or the force it needs to defend America in the future.

RECOMMENDATIONS

The findings identified in this research do not negate other previously referenced causes of the AVF's recruiting problem, such as a youth pool with a declining propensity to serve while being increasingly overweight and with a record of misconduct. Nor do these findings change the positive or negative consequences on recruiting from the state of the economy, implementation of social programs through the institution, and service member compensation on recruiting. In the near term, these conditions will require additional recruiters and increased compensation. However, only reacting to these temporal explanations and causes while failing to address the above four findings and five implications risks perpetuating the larger decline with only brief respites. Responding with solely a "near-term solution" has been the pattern since 1990, where the primary means of resolving the accession problem has been the dysfunctional reduction of the military's end-strength and increasing servicemembers' compensation without regard to operational requirements. The result is an AVF as a New Warrior Caste. In pursuit of solutions to the systemic problems associated with the AVF accession, one could consider the following four recommendations.

First, restructure and resource the current Selective Service System HQs to serve as the government's principal office for accessions that operate in each state and, to some degree, within communities. In this capacity, it would: a) reconcile the personnel requirements of the National Defense Strategy and the National Military Strategy within the government (Congressional and Executive branches) with the DOD's accession requirements for all components of the force design, b) communicate and coordinate with society the DOD's personnel requirements, and c) ensures accessions reflect national values for effectiveness and efficiency and opportunity. In this way, the *g-s vertex* remains, but the *g-m* and *g-s vertices* are strengthened to restore balance to America's Paradoxical Trinity. In this way America gets the force it needs, not the force the military wants when only the *m-s vertex* is exercised.

Second, establish criteria of effectiveness in providing a representative force as more important than pure cost efficiency when evaluating Army recruiting. The U.S. needs a representative force that is adequate in size to meet operational requirements; the two criteria are not mutually exclusive. Lauding the attainment of one criterion while ignoring the absence of the other only masks an unbalanced American Paradoxical Trinity. To effect change will require the military and the government to recognize that recruiting will cost different amounts per recruit in different areas. With representative effectiveness as a first-order principle, the military profession can apply recruiting technology differently to yield a new, representative force that improves citizen efficacy and attachment to the military.

Third, the Army's "Total Force Policy" should be revised, beginning with the integration of active and reserve components' recruiting enterprise. Rather than the Army having separate recruiting enterprises in the active component, Reserves, and National Guard, they should be combined under a single recruiting command. Each recruiter would function with the authority, requirements, and incentives to place a recruit in any of the three components. Such integration would double the geographical points of outreach for all concerned and link the active component to the resident communities of the other two components. With necessary changes to Federal statutes and regulations, a life cycle approach to servicemembers' participation in the armed forces could begin. For example, an applicant could be pursued for service in one component initially (i.e., active duty), with the purposeful intention that she would subsequently transfer the learned skills to the local National Guard unit after the initial enlistment, and maybe even return to active duty later. Monetary incentives (i.e., enlistment bonuses) could be offered to the recruit to encourage them to pursue an active-duty occupational specialty that was in demand at the local guard or reserve unit. In this way, when the Soldier was discharged from active duty, they could transition to the local reserve unit without requiring additional expenditure of money for training in a different career field. While such hometown occupation incentives under a Total Force Policy would cost more on a case-by-case basis, the total cost would be less than that incurred from retraining unqualified formerly active-duty Soldiers for service in the local reserve unit, and it would increase readiness by filling reserve personnel billets faster.

Fourth, the Army should seek ways to connect or embed local veterans with its recruiting efforts to increase the legitimacy of military service in the eyes of the youth. A revised Total Force Policy on recruiting would better disperse veterans across the U.S., as would geographically representative accessions. Additional new actions should seek to put veterans in contact with a greater array of parents and youth. For example, one method would be to increase Army sponsorship of Junior Reserve Officer Training Corps (JROTC) detachments in high schools. Those students who participate in this voluntary civics-based class with physical education activities show higher rates of attendance and graduation than nonparticipants, especially in innercity schools. The waiting list for such programs in high schools is long and slow-moving. Recruiting benefits aside, these youth outcomes are simply good for society at large and raise the question of whether other civics-based education is needed in schools. Additionally, increased hiring of veterans for local, state, and federal positions would increase veteran exposure.

These four recommendations are not simple, but in some form are necessary. Without large, deliberate actions to balance the American Paradoxical Trinity and reinforce republican virtue, the problems with military accessions that have been growing since 1990 will increasingly threaten the AVF. The default alternative to the AVF need not be a return to conscription but could instead be a recognition that a large adjustment to the AVF is needed, to create *AVF 4.0*. This change would provide both effective armed forces for near-term security requirements and, in the long term, preserve a foundation of virtue—republicanism—in the national consciousness. The proposed changes require two actions.

As a start, additional scholarship on military accessions now and going forward is more than prudent, starting with the areas identified at the end of each chapter. Further research should verify the amount of accession covariance found in the other services and potentially in other democracies. Regarding the restoration of republicanism, while accession reforms will help, a large portion of the population will be incapable of serving. To instill republicanism in this group, research should pursue identifying and modeling non-martial forms of civic duty that enable and incentivize personal sacrifice for the state across society. Second, when the military institution's responsibilities go unmet, military professionals and civilian leaders must confront this on the national stage for the benefit of engaging society, thus exercising all three vertices of the Trinity. Recall the actions of GEN Myer's display of personal courage to state publicly to Congress what many suspected, that the U.S. had a hollow Army. Similarly, President Roosevelt's leadership in the face of strong political isolationism propelled the passage of the Selective Service Act almost two years before the Japanese attacked Pearl Harbor. Without strong moral character and national leadership, loud minority groups can continue to wield outsized influence over military requirements for their own gain.

GLOSSARY

100k: 100,000
AC : Active Component
AEF: Allied Expeditionary Force
APT: American Paradoxical Trinity
AVF: All-Volunteer Force
B: Billions (of dollars)
BG : Brigadier General (1-star)
BRAC: Base Realignment and Closing
CBO: Congressional Budget Office
CCC: Civilian Conservation Corps
CDC: Civilian Defense Corps
CSA: Chief of Staff of the Army
CY : Calendar Year
DA : Department of the Army
DAA: Defense Appropriations Act
DEP: Delayed Entry Program
DOD: Department of Defense
FDR: Franklin Delano Roosevelt
FOIA: Freedom of Information Act

FY: Fiscal year
GAO: Government Accountability Office
GEN: General (4-star)
GTM: Grounded Theory Method
GWOT : Global War on Terrorism
HAC: House Appropriations Committee
HASC: House Armed Services Committee
HS : High School
IED: Improvised Explosive Device
KP : Kitchen Patrol
LTG: Lieutenant General (3-star)
M: Millions (of dollars)
MIC: Military Industrial Complex
MG: Major General (2-star)
NDAA: National Defense Authorization Act
NPS: Non-Prior Service
OAD: Office of Army Demographics
OEF: Operation Enduring Freedom (Afghanistan)
OIF: Operation Iraqi Freedom
OPTEMPO : Operational Tempo
PMC: Private Military Company
PME: Professional Military Education
PMSC: Private Military Security Company
PSC: Private Security Company
Q-I: Quadrant 1 (lower left)
Q-II: Quadrant 2 (upper left)
Q-III: Quadrant 3 (upper right)
Q-IV: Quadrant 4 (lower right)
RC : Reserve Component
ROTC: Reserve Officer Training Corps
SA: Secretary of the Army
SAC: Senate Appropriations Committee
SASC: Senate Armed Services Committee
SES: Socio-Economic Status
SSS: Selective Service System
TRADOC: Training and Doctrine Command

UMT: Universal Military Training
USAREC: United States Army Recruiting Command
WAC: Women's Army (Auxiliary) Corps
WAVES: Women Accepted for Voluntary Emergency Service
WPA: Works Progress Administration

BIBLIOGRAPHY

Abbott, Andrew. *The System of Professions: An Essay on the Division of Expert Labor.* Chicago, IL: University of Chicago Press, 1988.

Amara, Jomana. "Revisiting the Justification for an All-Volunteer Force." *Defense & Security Analysis* 35, no. 3 (July 3, 2019): 326–42. https://doi.org/10.1080/14751798.2019.1640425.

Ambrose, Stephen E., and James Alden Barber, Jr., eds. *The Military and American Society - Essays and Readings.* 1st edition. New York, NY: Free Press, 1973.

Asch, Beth. *Navigating Current and Emerging Army Recruiting Challenges: What Can Research Tell Us?* Santa Monica, CA: RAND Corporation, 2019. https://doi.org/10.7249/RR3107.

Askew, Andrew. "Conscription Is Resurging across Europe." *Euronews*, September 1, 2023. https://www.euronews.com/2023/09/01/conscription-is-seeing-a-revival-across-europe-is-that-a-good-thing.

Asoni, Andrea, Andrea Gilli, Mauro Gilli, and Tino Sanandaji. "A Mercenary Army of the Poor? Technological Change and the Demographic Composition of the Post-9/11 U.S. Military." *Journal of Strategic Studies* 45, no. 4 (August 2022): 568–614. https://doi.org/10.1080/01402390.2019.1692660.

Assistant Secretary of the Army (Financial Management and Comptroller. "FY 2023 President's Budget Highlights." Washington, DC: Department of the Army, April 2022.

Atkins, Will. "Who Lost Afghanistan? Samuel Huntington and the Decline of Strategic Thinking." *Armed Forces & Society (0095327X)* 49, no. 4 (October 2023): 965–81. https://doi.org/10.1177/0095327X221116129.

Avant, Deborah. "Losing Control of the Profession Through Outsourcing?" In *The Future of the Army Profession, Revised and Expanded Second Edition*, edited by Don Snider and Lloyd Matthews, 2nd ed., 271–90. Boston, MA: McGraw Hill-Education, 2005.

———. "The Mobilization of Private Forces after 9/11: Ad Hoc Response to Inadequate Planning." In *How 9/11 Changed Our Ways of War*, edited by James Burk, 209–31. Palo Alto, CA: Stanford University Press, 2013.

Bacevich, Andrew J. "Tradition Abandoned: America's Military in a New Era." *National Interest*, no. 48 (July 15, 1997): 16–25. https://ez-salve.idm.oclc.org/login?url=https://search.ebscohost.com/login.aspx?direct=true&db=ssf&AN=510839364&site=ehost-live.

———. "Who Will Serve?" *Wilson Quarterly* 22, no. 3 (Summer 1998): 80–92. https://web-s-ebscohost-com.ez-salve.idm.oclc.org/ehost/detail/detail?vid=9&sid=e39e8a18-7d6c-457c-a2ba-4d530f7c8696%40redis&bdata=JnNpdGU9ZWhvc3Qtb Gl2ZQ%3d%3d#AN=2887466&db=lfh.

Bailey, Beth. *America's Army: Making the All-Volunteer Force.* 1st edition. Cambridge, MA: Belknap Press: An Imprint of Harvard University Press, 2009.

Baldor, Lolita. "Army Sees Safety, Not 'Wokeness,' as Top Recruiting Obstacle." *Army

Times, February 12, 2023, sec. Your Army. https://www.armytimes.com/news/your-army/2023/02/12/army-sees-safety-not-wokeness-as-top-recruiting-obstacle/.

———. "Army Misses Recruiting Goal by 15,000 Soldiers." *Army Times*, October 2, 2022. https://www.armytimes.com/news/your-army/2022/10/02/army-misses-recruiting-goal-by-15000-soldiers/.

———. "Army to Meet 2025 Recruiting Goals in Dramatic Turnaround, Denies 'Wokeness' Is Factor." PBS News, January 17, 2025. https://www.pbs.org/newshour/politics/army-to-meet-2025-recruiting-goals-in-dramatic-turnaround-denies-wokeness-is-factor.

———. "US Army Misses Recruiting Goal; Other Services Squeak By." *U.S. News and World Report*, October 1, 2022. https://www.usnews.com/news/politics/articles/2022-10-01/us-army-misses-recruiting-goal-other-services-squeak-by.

Barber, Benjamin R. *A Passion for Democracy*. Princeton University Press, 1998. https://doi.org/10.2307/j.ctv1ddczkb.

Barber, James Allen. "The Draft and Alternatives to the Draft." In *The Military and American Society - Essays and Readings*, edited by Stephen E. Ambrose and James Alden Barber, Jr., 1st edition., 205–18. New York, NY: Free Press, 1973.

———. "The Social Effects of Military Service." In *The Military and American Society - Essays and Readings*, edited by Stephen E. Ambrose and James Alden Barber, Jr., 1st edition., 151–65. New York, NY: Free Press, 1973.

Barndollar, Gil, and Matthew C. Mai. "America's Army Is Shrinking. Its Missions Aren't." *The Hill*, August 11, 2023. https://thehill.com/opinion/national-security/4148419-americas-army-is-shrinking-its-missions-arent/.

Barno, David W., and Nora Bensahel. "Addressing the U.S. Military Recruiting Crisis." War on the Rocks, March 10, 2023. https://warontherocks.com/2023/03/addressing-the-u-s-military-recruiting-crisis/.

———. "The Deepest Obligation of Citizenship: Looking Beyond the Warrior Caste." War on the Rocks, May 15, 2018. https://warontherocks.com/2018/05/the-deepest-obligation-of-citizenship-looking-beyond-the-warrior-caste/.

Barsuhn, Adam. "'We Don't Negotiate with Terrorists'—Afghanistan, Bargaining, and American Civil–Military Relations." *Armed Forces & Society (0095327X)* 49, no. 4 (October 2023): 953–64. https://doi.org/10.1177/0095327X221077299.

Battalion Commander - Cleveland. "3rd Recruiting Brigade 2QFY22 Operational Update Brief." Quarterly Report, Fort Knox, KY, February 28, 2021.

BBC. "Denmark to Start Conscripting Women for Military Service." March 13, 2024, sec. World-Europe. 68557038. https://www.bbc.com/news/world-europe-68557038.

Beehner, Lionel, Risa Brooks, and Daniel Maurer, eds. *Reconsidering American Civil-Military Relations: The Military, Society, Politics, and Modern War*. New York: Oxford University Press, 2020.

Ben-Ari, Eyal, Eitan Shamir, and Elisheva Rosman. "Neither Conscript Army nor an All-Volunteer Force: Emerging Recruiting Models." *Armed Forces and Society* 49, no. 1 (January 2023): 138–59. https://journals.sagepub.com/doi/10.1177/0095327X211048216.

Bergan, Daniel E. "The Draft Lottery and Attitudes Towards the Vietnam War." *Public Opinion Quarterly* 73, no. 2 (July 15, 2009): 379–84. https://doi.org/10.1093/poq/nfp024.

Berger, David H. "Recruiting Requires Bold Changes." *Proceedings* 148, no. 11 (November 2022): 1437–45. https://www.usni.org/magazines/proceedings/2022/november/recruiting-requires-bold-changes.

Beynon, Steve. "Army Sees Sharp Decline in White Recruits." *Military Times*, January 10, 2024, sec. Daily News. https://www.military.com/daily-news/2024/01/10/army-sees-sharp-decline-white-recruits.html.

———. "Military Focusing on JROTC Programs as Chances to Paint Picture of Service to Gen Z Dwindle." *Military.Com*, December 20, 2023, sec. Daily News. https://www.military.com/daily-news/2023/12/19/military-focusing-jrotc-programs-chances-paint-picture-of-service-gen-z-dwindle.html.

———. "Soldiers Are Getting Burned Out. Army Leadership Knows It's a Problem." *Military.Com*, October 16, 2023, sec. Daily News. https://www.military.com/daily-news/2023/10/16/senior-army-leaders-agree-soldiers-need-more-time-home-theres-no-plan-make-it-happen.html.

Beynon, Steve, and Kelsey Baker. "The Army's Recruiting Problem Is Male." *Military Times*, June 17, 2024. https://www.military.com/daily-news/2024/06/14/armys-recruiting-problem-male.html?utm_campaign=dfn-ebb&utm_medium=email&utm_source=sailthru.

Blankshain, Jessica D. "Who Has 'Skin in the Game'?" In *Reconsidering American Civil-Military Relations: The Military, Society, Politics, and Modern War*, edited by Lionel Beehner, Risa Brooks, and Daniel Maurer, 97–114. New York: Oxford University Press, 2020.

Blount, Jeb. *Fanatical Military Recruiting: The Ultimate Guide to Leveraging High-Impact Prospecting to Engage Qualified Applicants, Win the War for Talent, and Make Mission Fast*. 1st edition. Hoboken, New Jersey: Wiley, 2019.

Board, Editorial. "Opinion | A Big Navy Is Vital. A More Lethal One Would Be Even Better." *Washington Post*, January 4, 2024. https://www.washingtonpost.com/opinions/2024/01/04/navy-houthis-ships-shipyards-sailors/.

Borgmann, Albert. "Focal Things and Practices." In *Readings in the Philosophy of Technology*, edited by David M. Kaplan, 2nd edition., 56–75. Lanham: Rowman & Littlefield Publishers, 2009.

———. *Technology and the Character of Contemporary Life: A Philosophical Inquiry*. Chicago: The University of Chicago Press, 1987.

Bornstein, Daniel B., Ryan S. Sacko, Sybil Prince Nelson, George Grieve, Michael Beets, Lanna Forrest, Keith Hauret, Laurie Whitsel, and Bruce Jones. "A State-by-State and Regional Analysis of the Direct Medical Costs of Treating Musculoskeletal Injuries among US Army Trainees." *Progress in Cardiovascular Diseases* 74 (September 1, 2022): 53–59. https://doi.org/10.1016/j.pcad.2022.10.008.

Brady, Richard. "Recruiting the All-Volunteer Force: New Approaches for a New Era." Nonprofit. The Heritage Foundation, October 18, 2022. https://www.heritage.org/military-strength/topical-essays/recruiting-the-all-volunteer-force-new-approaches.

Brett, Derek, Angelos Nikolopoulos, Esa Noresvuo, Maike Rof, Istvan Rytkonen, Semih Sapmaz, and Alexia Tsouni. "Conscientious Objection to Military Service in Europe 2020." Annual Report. Brussels, Belgium: European Bureau for Conscientious Objection, February 15, 2021. https://wri-irg.org/sites/default/files/public_files/2021-02/2021-02-15-ebco_annual_report_2020.pdf.

Briscoe, Detrick L. "The Black Community Perspective: Recruiting Blacks into Combat Arms:" Carlisle, PA: Army War College, March 1, 2013. Defense Technical Information Center. https://doi.org/10.21236/ADA589048.

Brito, Gary. "Professionalism Is the Foundation of the Army and We Will Strengthen It." *War on the Rocks*, March 18, 2024. https://warontherocks.com/2024/03/professionalism-is-the-foundation-of-the-army-and-we-will-strengthen-it/.

Brooks, Risa. "The Best They Could Do? Assessing U.S. Military Effectiveness in the Afghanistan War." *Armed Forces & Society (0095327X)* 49, no. 4 (October 2023): 913–22. https://doi.org/10.1177/0095327X221116876.

Brooks, Rosa. "Civil Military Paradoxes." In *Warriors and Citizens: American Views of Our Military*, edited by Jim Mattis and Kori N. Schake, 21–68. Stanford, California: Hoover Institution Press, 2016.

———. "Civil-Military Paradoxes." In *Warriors and Citizens: American Views of Our Military*, edited by Kori N. Schake and Jim Mattis, 21–68. Stanford, California: Hoover Institution Press, 2016.

Brown, Ethan. "The Ghost of GWOT Haunting the Military Recruiting Crisis." West Point, NY: Modern War Institute, December 28, 2023. https://mwi.westpoint.edu/the-ghost-of-gwot-haunting-the-military-recruiting-crisis/.

Bryant, Antony, and Kathy Charmaz, eds. *The SAGE Handbook of Current Developments in Grounded Theory*. Second edition. Thousand Oaks, CA: SAGE Publications Ltd, 2019.

Bureau of Labor Statistics. "Unemployment Rate 1947-2022." XLSX. Washington, DC: United States Department of Labor. Accessed August 30, 2023. https://data.bls.gov/timeseries/LNU04023554&series_id=LNU04000000&series_id=LNU03023554&series_id=LNU03000000&years_option=all_years&periods_option=specific_periods&periods=Annual+Data.

Burk, James. "Expertise, Jurisdiction, and the Legitimacy of the Military Profession." In *The Future of the Army Profession, Revised and Expanded 2d Edition*, edited by Don Snider and Lloyd Matthews, 2nd ed., 39–60. Boston, MA: Learning Solutions, 2005. My Book.

———. "Patriotism and the All-Volunteer Force." *Journal of Political & Military Sociology* 12, no. 2 (1984): 229–41. https://www.jstor.org/stable/45293434.

———. "Theories of Democratic Civil-Military Relations." *Armed Forces & Society* 29, no. 1 (October 2002): 7–29. https://doi.org/10.1177/0095327X0202900102.

———. "Thinking Through the End of the Cold War." In *The Adaptive Military: Armed Forces in a Turbulent World*, edited by James Burk, 2nd ed., 25–48. New Brunswick, NJ: Transaction Publishers, 1998.

Buscha, Connie A. "Overturning the 'Risk Rule' of 1988, Opting for New Risks: U.S. Women Servicemembers and the War in Afghanistan." *Armed Forces & Society (0095327X)* 49, no. 4 (October 2023): 1035–47. https://doi.org/10.1177/0095327X221103295.

Camarillo, Gabe. "Army FY 23 Budget Overview." Presented at the Under Secretary of the Army Budget Briefing, Washington, DC, March 28, 2022. https://www.asafm.army.mil/Portals/72/Documents/BudgetMaterial/2023/pbr/Army%20FY%202023%20Budget%20Overview.pdf.

Camp, Theodore. "The Military Depends on Virtues That Are Fading." *Public Discourse*, March 23, 2023. https://www.thepublicdiscourse.com/2023/03/87979/.

Carter, Phillip, Amy Kuzminski, Amy Shafer, and Andrew Swick. "AVF 4.0: The Future of the All-Volunteer Force." Washington, DC: Center for a New American Security, March 28, 2017. https://www.cnas.org/publications/reports/avf-4-0-the-future-of-the-all-volunteer-force.

Castells, Manuel. *The Rise of the Network Society (The Information Age: Economy, Society and Culture)*. 2nd ed. Vol. 1. Oxford, UK: Blackwell Publishers, Inc., 2000.

CFR Editors. "Demographics of the U.S. Military." *Council on Foreign Relations*, Backgrounder, July 13, 2020. https://www.cfr.org/backgrounder/demographics-us-military.

Chesterman, Simon, and Chia Lehnardt, eds. *From Mercenaries to Market: The Rise and Regulation of Private Military Companies*. 1st edition. Oxford; New York: Oxford University Press, 2007.

Choi, Min Jae, Seung Wook Yoo, and Zack Bowersox. "Conscription and Political Participation: How Conscription Policies Affect Voter Turnout." *Armed Forces & Society (0095327X)* 50, no. 1 (January 2024): 315–36. https://doi.org/10.1177/0095327X221112028.

Clausewitz, Carl von. *On War*. Translated by Michael Eliot Howard and Peter Paret. Reprint. Princeton, NJ: Princeton University Press, 1984.

Cocke, Karl E., ed. *Department of the Army Historical Summary: FY 1974*. Washington, DC: Center of Military History, 1978. https://history.army.mil/books/DAHSUM/1974/ch02.htm.

Cohen, Eliot A. *Supreme Command: Soldiers, Statesmen, and Leadership in Wartime*. New York, NY: Free Press, 2002.

———. "A Revolution in Warfare." *Foreign Affairs* 75, no. 2 (April 1996): 37–54. http://www.jstor.org/stable/20047487.

———. *Citizens and Soldiers: The Dilemmas of Military Service*. 1st Edition. Cornell Studies in Security Affairs. Ithaca, NY: Cornell University Press, 1985. https://doi.org/10.7591/9781501733772.

———. "Why the Gap Matters." *The National Interest*, no. No. 61 (Fall 2000): 38–48.

Cohen, Rachel. "Air Force Recruiting Rebounds While Army, Navy Still Struggle." *Military Times*, February 17, 2024, sec. Your Military. https://www.militarytimes.com/news/your-air-force/2024/02/17/air-force-recruiting-rebounds-while-army-navy-still-struggle/.

Coleman, David. "U.S. Military Personnel 1954-2014: The Numbers." Research, July 24, 2014. https://historyinpieces.com/research/us-military-personnel-1954-2014.

Commissioners, et al. "Inspired to Serve, Executive Summary to the Final Report of the National Commission on the Military, National, and Public Service." Washington, DC, March 2020. www.inspire2serve.gov.

Connor, Richard. "Germany Outlines Plans for 'new' Model of Military Service." *DW News*, June 12, 2024. https://link.defensenews.com/.

Correll, Diana. "Navy Misses Active Duty, Reserve Recruiting Goals for 2023." *Navy Times*, October 10, 2023, sec. Your Navy. https://www.navytimes.com/news/your-navy/2023/10/10/navy-misses-active-duty-reserve-recruiting-goals-for-2023/.

Creveld, Martin L. Van. *Training of Officers: From Military Professionalism to Irrelevance*. New York, NY: Free Press, 1990.

Dandecker, Christopher. "A Farewell to Arms? The Military and the Nation-State in a

Changing World." In *The Adaptive Military: Armed Forces in a Turbulent World*, edited by James Burk, 2nd ed., 139–62. New Brunswick, NJ: Transaction Publishers, 1998.

Dempsey, Jason K. *Our Army: Soldiers, Politics, and American Civil-Military Relations*. Princeton, NJ: Princeton University Press, 2010. http://www.degruyter.com/isbn/9781400832170.

Department of Defense. "Defense Casualty Analysis System." Defense Manpower Data Center, 2022. Accessed December 5, 2024. https://dcas.dmdc.osd.mil/dcas/app/conflictCasualties.

———. "Defense Casualty Analysis System." Defense Manpower Data Center. Accessed October 19, 2023. https://dcas.dmdc.osd.mil/dcas/app/conflictCasualties/oif/byMonth.

———. "Defense Manpower Data Center." DoD Personnel, Workforce Reports & Publications. Accessed May 16, 2023. https://dwp.dmdc.osd.mil/dwp/app/dod-data-reports/workforce-reports.

———. "Portrait of Women in the Services," 2022. https://diversity.defense.gov/Portals/51/Images/Women%20Infographic_2022.pdf?ver=uhaWt04gv3bdYGQo3RMJIg%3d%3d.

———. "U.S. Army Accessions Command. 2/15/2002-01/192012." National Archives NextGen Catalog. Accessed May 12, 2023. https://catalog.archives.gov/id/10532571.

———. "U.S. Army Recruiting Command History." Government. National Archives NextGen Catalog. Accessed May 12, 2023. https://catalog.archives.gov/id/10677594.

"Department of Defense Personnel Reform and Strengthening the All-Volunteer Force." Washington, DC: U.S. Government Publishing Office, December 2, 2015. https://www.govinfo.gov/content/pkg/CHRG-114shrg20957/pdf/CHRG-114shrg20957.pdf.

Department of Labor. "Black Veterans Research." Black Veterans Research, October 2024. Accessed December 5, 2024. https://www.dol.gov/agencies/vets/resources/black-veterans-research.

———. "Labor Force Participation Rate by Sex, Race and Hispanic Ethnicity." DOL, 2022. http://www.dol.gov/agencies/wb/data/latest-annual-data/working-women/Labor-Force-Participation-Rate-by-Sex-Race-Hispanic-Ethnicity.

DeVore, Chuck. "States That Defend Us—Where Do Our Military Volunteers Call Home?" *Forbes*, February 20, 2020. https://www.forbes.com/sites/chuckdevore/2020/02/19/states-that-defend-uswhere-do-our-military-volunteers-call-home/.

Dickstein, Corey. "Republicans Blame 'Woke' Policies for Recruiting Sag; Military Claims It's More Complicated than That." *Stars and Stripes*, December 13, 2023. https://www.stripes.com/theaters/us/2023-12-13/military-recruiting-diversity-pentagon-republicans-12350995.html.

DOD Public Affairs. "Department of Defense Announces Recruiting and Retention Numbers for Fiscal Year." Department of Defense, October 15, 2022. https://prhome.defense.gov/Portals/52/Documents/MRA_Docs/MPP/pressreleases/2022/Press%20Release%20September%202022%20-%20FY%202022.pdf?ver=WCikMkd8oW6lYt0PBb3VTA%3d%3d.

Downing, Brian. *The Military Revolution and Political Change*. Princeton University Press, 1992.

Dubik, James M., and Martin Dempsey. *Just War Reconsidered: Strategy, Ethics, and Theory.* Kindle. Lexington, Kentucky: The University Press of Kentucky, 2016.

Efflandt, Scott L. "Military Professionalism & Private Military Contractors." *Parameters: U.S. Army War College* 44, no. 2 (Summer 2014): 49–60. https://doi.org/10.55540/0031-1723.2884.

Eikenberry, Karl W. "Reassessing the All-Volunteer Force." *Washington Quarterly* 36, no. 1 (Winter -2013 2012): 7–24. https://doi.org/10.1080/0163660X.2013.751647.

Ender, Morten. *Army Spouses: Military Families during the Global War on Terror.* Charlottesville, VA: University of Virginia Press, 2023. https://www.upress.virginia.edu/title/5923/.

Epictetus. *Discourses and Selected Writings.* Edited by Robert Dobbin. 1st edition. London: Penguin Classics, 2008.

Farley, Tom. "The Cell-Phone Revolution." *American Heritage*, December 2011. https://www.americanheritage.com/content/cell-phone-revolution.

Farrell, Brenda S. "Military Personnel: Military and Civilian Pay Comparisons Present Challenges and Are One of Many Tools in Assessing Compensation." Washington, DC: Government Accountability Office, 4/1/2010 2010. https://ez-salve.idm.oclc.org/login?url=https://search.ebscohost.com/login.aspx?direct=true&db=bth&AN=49049242&site=ehost-live.

Feaver, Peter D. "Foreword." In *Reconsidering American Civil-Military Relations: The Military, Society, Politics, and Modern War*, edited by Lionel Beehner, Risa Brooks, and Daniel Maurer, vii–x. New York: Oxford University Press, 2020.

———. *Armed Servants: Agency, Oversight, and Civil-Military Relations.* Revised edition. Cambridge, MA: Harvard University Press, 2005.

———. "Foreword." In *Reconsidering American Civil-Military Relations: The Military, Society, Politics, and Modern War*, edited by Lionel Beehner, Risa Brooks, and Daniel Maurer, vii–x. New York: Oxford University Press, 2020.

———. *Thanks for Your Service: The Causes and Consequences of Public Confidence in the US Military.* New York, NY: Oxford University Press, 2023.

Feenberg, Andrew. "Democratic Rationalization: Technology, Power, and Freedom." In *Readings in the Philosophy of Technology*, edited by David M. Kaplan, 2nd Edition., 139–55. Lanham, MD: Rowman & Littlefield Publishers, 2009.

———. "The Ambivalence of Technology." *Sociological Perspectives* 33, no. 1 (Spring 1990): 35–50. https://doi.org/10.2307/1388976.

Field, Kelly. "After Repeal of 'Don't Ask,' Elite Colleges Reconsider ROTC." *Chronicle of Higher Education* 57, no. 19 (January 14, 2011): A1–18.

Finney, Nathan, and Tyrell Mayfield, eds. *Redefining the Modern Military: The Intersection of Profession and Ethics.* Annapolis, MD: Naval Institute Press, 2021.

Firmin, Titus. "Socioeconomics." In *The All-Volunteer Force: Fifty Years of Service*, edited by William A. Taylor, 138–63. Lawrence, Kansas: University Press of Kansas, 2023.

Fitzgerald, David, David Ryan, and John M. Thompson. *Not Even Past: How the United States Ends Wars.* New York, NY: Berghahn, 2020. https://public.ebookcentral.proquest.com/choice/publicfullrecord.aspx?p=6111189.

Friedman, Leon. "Conscription and the Constitution: The Original Understanding." *Michigan Law Review* 67 (1969): 1493–1552. https://scholarlycommons.law.hofstra.edu/faculty_scholarship/19.

Gallup. "Conservatives Greatly Outnumber Liberals in 19 U.S. States," February 22, 2019. https://news.gallup.com/poll/247016/conservatives-greatly-outnumber-liberals-states.aspx.

Gambone, Michael D. *The New Praetorians: American Veterans, Society, and Service from Vietnam to the Forever War*. Veterans. Amherst, MA: University of Massachusetts Press, 2021. https://search.ebscohost.com/login.aspx?direct=true&scope=site&db=nlebk&db=nlabk&AN=3100606.

Garamone, Jim. "After Tough Year, Military Recruiting Is Looking Up." U.S. Department of Defense. DOD News, December 22, 2023. https://www.defense.gov/News/News-Stories/Article/Article/3625464/after-tough-year-military-recruiting-is-looking-up/https%3A%2F%2Fwww.defense.gov%2FNews%2FNews-Stories%2FArticle%2FArticle%2F3625464%2Fafter-tough-year-military-recruiting-is-looking-up%2F.

Golby, James, Lindsay P. Cohn, and Peter D. Feaver. "Thanks for Your Service: Civilian and Veteran Attitudes after Fifteen Years of War." In *Warriors and Citizens: American Views of Our Military*, edited by Kori N. Schake and Jim Mattis, 97–142. Stanford, California: Hoover Institution Press, 2016.

Goldberg, Matthew S., Karen Cheng, Nancy M. Huff, Dennis D. Kimko, and Alexandra Saizan. "Geographic Diversity in Military Recruiting." Alexandria, VA: Institute for Defense Analyses, November 2018. https://apps.dtic.mil/sti/pdfs/AD1122506.pdf.

Golding, Heidi, and Adebayo Adedeji. "The All-Volunteer Military: Issues and Performance." Washington, DC: Congressional Budget Office, July 2007. https://www.cbo.gov/sites/default/files/110th-congress-2007-2008/reports/07-19-militaryvol_0.pdf.

Government Accountability Office. "Military Personnel: Reporting Additional Servicemember Demographics Could Enhance Congressional Oversight." Report to Congressional Requesters. Washington, DC: Government Accountability Office, September 2005. https://www.gao.gov/assets/gao-05-952.pdf.

Griffin, Jr, Robert K., and John W. Mountcastle. *The U.S. Army's Transition to the All-Volunteer Force, 1968-1974*. London, England: Military Bookshop Company, 2011.

Gunderson, Gordon W. "The National School Lunch Program: Background and Development." Washington, DC: Department of Agriculture, 1971. https://www.fns.usda.gov/nslp/program-history.

Hajjar, Remi, and Morten Ender. "The McDonaldization in the U.S. Army: A Threat to the Profession." In *The Future of the Army Profession*, by Don Snider and Lloyd J. Matthews, 215–30, 2nd Edition. Boston, MA: McGraw-Hill Education, 2005. My Book.

Heidegger, Martin. "The Question Concerning Technology." In *Readings in the Philosophy of Technology*, edited by David M. Kaplan, Second Edition., 9–25. Lanham, MD: Rowman & Littlefield Publishers, 2009.

Heinlein, Robert A. *Starship Troopers*. New York, NY: Ace Books, 1997.

Helfgott, Roy B. "America's Third Industrial Revolution." *Challenge* 29, no. 5 (December 1986): 41–46.

Hlad, Jennifer. "Military Must Recruit More Women, Immigrants for the Future Force, Experts Say." Defense One, January 27, 2023. https://www.defenseone.com/policy/2023/01/military-must-recruit-more-women-immigrants-future-force-experts-say/382317/.

Hobbes, Thomas. *Hobbes: Leviathan*. Cambridge University Press, 1993.

Holman, Barry W. "Military Base Closures: Observations on Prior and Current BRAC

Rounds." Washington, DC: Government Accountability Office, May 3, 2005. https://ez-salve.idm.oclc.org/login?url=https://search.ebscohost.com/login.aspx?direct=true&db=bth&AN=18179970&site=ehost-live.

Huntington, Samuel P. *The Soldier and the State: The Theory and Politics of Civil-Military Relations*. Cambridge, MA: Belknap Press, 1957.

Inbody, Donald S., and Patricia M. Shields. "Perspectives on the Afghanistan War: Commentaries on a Misadventure." *Armed Forces and Society* 49, no. 4 (October 2023): 883–92. https://doi.org/10.1177/0095327X231155220.

Ingesson, Tony. "When the Military Profession Isn't." In *Redefining the Modern Military: The Intersection of Profession and Ethics*, edited by Nathan Finney and Tyrell Mayfield, 70–85. Annapolis, MD: Naval Institute Press, 2021.

Isenburg, David. "A Government in Search of Cover: Private Military Companies in Iraq." In *From Mercenaries to Market: The Rise and Regulation of Private Military Companies*, edited by Simon Chesterman and Chia Lehnardt, 1st edition., 82–93. Oxford; New York: Oxford University Press, 2007.

Janowitz, Morris. "Characteristics of the Military Environment." In *The Military and American Society - Essays and Readings*, edited by Stephen E. Ambrose and James Alden Barber, Jr., 1st edition., 166–76. New York, NY: Free Press, 1973.

———. *On Social Organization and Social Control*. Edited by James Burk. 1st edition. Chicago: University of Chicago Press, 1991.

———. *The Professional Soldier*. Glencoe, IL: Free Press, 1960.

Janowitz, Morris, and Charles C. Moskos. "Five Years of the All-Volunteer Force: 1973-1978." *Armed Forces & Society* 5, no. 2 (January 1, 1979): 171–218. https://doi.org/10.1177/0095327X7900500201.

Jehn, Christopher, and Zachary Selden. "The End of Conscription in Europe?: Contemporary Economic Policy." *Contemporary Economic Policy* 20, no. 2 (April 2002): 93–100. https://doi.org/10.1093/cep/20.2.93.

Johnson, Allan G. *The Blackwell Dictionary of Sociology: A User's Guide to Sociological Language*. 1st ed. Cambridge, MA: Wiley-Blackwell, 1995.

Johnson, Daniel. "Op-Ed: Military Could Help Recruitment by Doing More to Resolve Disparities." *Chicago Tribune*, January 4, 2023. https://www.chicagotribune.com/opinion/commentary/ct-opinion-military-recruiting-crisis-systemic-issues-black-members-20230104-w2t7zslsufbmtjomtkawyucbne-story.html?utm_campaign=dfn-ebb&utm_medium=email&utm_source=sailthru&SToverlay=2002c2d9-c344-4bbb-8610-e5794efcfa7d.

Judson, Jen. "Here Are the Winners and Losers in US Army's Force Structure Change." *Defense News*, February 27, 2024, sec. Land. https://www.defensenews.com/land/2024/02/27/here-are-the-winners-and-losers-in-us-armys-force-structure-change/.

Kamarck, Kristy N. "Diversity, Inclusion, and Equal Opportunity in the Armed Services: Background and Issues for Congress." Washington, DC: Congressional Research Service, October 24, 2017. https://crsreports.congress.gov/product/pdf/R/R44321/12.

Kanellos, Michael. "PCs: More than 1 Billion Served." CNET, March 18, 2009. https://www.cnet.com/culture/pcs-more-than-1-billion-served/.

Kapp, Lawrence. "Recruiting and Retention: An Overview of FY2011 and FY2012 Results for Active and Reserve Component Enlisted Personnel." Government. Washington,

DC: Congressional Research Service, May 13, 2013. https://catalog.archives.gov/id/203762594.

———. "Recruiting and Retention in the Active Component Military: Are There Problems?" Government. Washington, DC: Congressional Research Service, February 25, 2002. https://crsreports.congress.gov/product/pdf/RL/RL31297.

Kapp, Lawrence, and Charles A. Henning. "Recruiting and Retention: An Overview of FY2006 and FY2007 Results for Active and Reserve Component Enlisted Personnel." Washington, DC: Congressional Research Service, February 7, 2008. Defense Technical Information Center. https://apps.dtic.mil/sti/pdfs/ADA480780.pdf.

Kieran, David. "The Patriot Penalty: National Guard and Reserve Troops, Neoliberalism, and Manufactured Precarity in the Era of Perpetual Conflict." In *Service Denied: Marginalized Veterans in Modern American History*, by John M. Kinder and Jason A. Higgins, 181–202. Veterans. Amherst, MA: University of Massachusetts Press, 2022. https://muse.jhu.edu/book/102909/.

Kieran, David, and Edwin A. Martini. *At War: The Military and American Culture in the Twentieth Century and Beyond*. War Culture. New Brunswick, NJ: Rutgers University Press, 2018. https://www.degruyter.com/isbn/9780813584331.

Kim, Choongsoo, Gilbert Nestel, Robert Philips, and Michael E. Borus. "The All-Volunteer Force: A 1979 Profile and Some Issues." Youth Knowledge Development Report. Washington, DC: U.S. Department of Labor, Employment and Training Administration, Office of Youth Programs, 1980. WorldCat.org. https://permanent.fdlp.gov/gpo61400/ED203059.pdf.

Kinder, John M., and Jason A. Higgins. *Service Denied: Marginalized Veterans in Modern American History*. Veterans. Amherst, MA: University of Massachusetts Press, 2022. https://muse.jhu.edu/book/102909/.

King, William R. "The All-Volunteer Armed Forces." *MILITARY REVIEW* LIX--September 9 (1977): 85–94. https://www.armyupress.army.mil/Portals/7/PDF-UA-docs/King-UA.pdf.

Kipling, Rudyard. "The Choice." In *World War One British Poets: Brooke, Owen, Sassoon, Rosenberg and Others*, edited by Candace Ward, 1 edition. New York, NY: Dover Publications, 1997.

Kleykamp, Meredith, Daniel Schwam, and Gilad Wenig. "What Americans Think About Veterans and Military Service: Findings from a Nationally Representative Survey." Research Reports. Santa Monica, CA: RAND Corporation, 2023. https://doi.org/10.7249/RRA1363-7.

Kohn, Richard H. "The Erosion of Civilian Control of the Military in the United States Today." *Naval War College Review* 55, no. 3 (Summer 2002): 9–59. https://ez-salve.idm.oclc.org/login?url=https://search.ebscohost.com/login.aspx?direct=true&db=a9h&AN=7498206&site=ehost-live.

Koch, Alexandra. "US Army Recruiting Shatters Record After Trump Election Win." News. New York Post, February 5, 2025. https://www.foxnews.com/us/army-recruiting-shatters-records-after-president-trump-election-win-inauguration.

Krebs, Ronald R. *Fighting for Rights: Military Service and the Politics of Citizenship*. 1st edition. Ithaca, NY: Cornell University Press, 2006.

Krebs, Ronald R., and Robert Ralston. "Patriotism or Paychecks: Who Believes What About Why Soldiers Serve." *Armed Forces & Society* 48, no. 1 (January 2022): 25–48.

https://doi.org/10.1177/0095327X20917166.

Kube, Courtney, and Molly Boigon. "Every Branch of the Military Is Struggling to Make Its 2022 Recruiting Goals." NBC News, June 22, 2022. https://www.nbcnews.com/news/military/every-branch-us-military-struggling-meet-2022-recruiting-goals-offi cia-rcna35078.

Kuhn, Thomas S. *The Structure of Scientific Revolutions*. 1st ed. University Of Chicago Press, 1996.

Landru, Kasey. "Evolution of Defining the Army Profession." In *Redefining the Modern Military: The Intersection of Profession and Ethics*, edited by Nathan Finney and Tyrell Mayfield, 36–52. Annapolis, MD: Naval Institute Press, 2021.

Leal, David L. "American Public Opinion toward the Military: Differences by Race, Gender, and Class?" *Armed Forces & Society* 32, no. 1 (October 1, 2005): 123–38. https://doi.org/10.1177/0095327X05278168.

Leander, Anna. "Regulating the Role of Private Military Companies in Shaping Security and Politics." In *From Mercenaries to Market: The Rise and Regulation of Private Military Companies*, edited by Simon Chesterman and Chia Lehnardt, 1st edition., 49–64. Oxford; New York: Oxford University Press, 2007.

Lehrfeld, Jonathan. "Poll Says Confidence in US Military Lowest in 25 Years." *Military Times*, July 31, 2023, sec. Your Military. https://www.militarytimes.com/news/your-military/2023/07/31/poll-says-confidence-in-us-military-lowest-in-25-years/.

Lewis, Adrian. "Military Culture." In *The All-Volunteer Force: Fifty Years of Service*, edited by William A. Taylor, 233–54. Lawrence, Kansas: University Press of Kansas, 2023.

Lindberg, Todd. "The 'Very Liberal' View of the US Military." In *Warriors and Citizens: American Views of Our Military*, edited by Kori N. Schake and Jim Mattis, 219–44. Stanford, California: Hoover Institution Press, 2016.

Lyall, Jason. *Divided Armies: Inequality and Battlefield Performance in Modern War*. Illustrated edition. Princeton, NJ: Princeton University Press, 2020.

Machiavelli, Niccolo. *The Prince*. 2nd ed. Chicago, IL: University of Chicago Press, 1998.

Mackinnon, Amy. "What Is Russia's Wagner Group?" Foreign Policy, July 6, 2021. https://foreignpolicy.com/2021/07/06/what-is-wagner-group-russia-mercenaries-military-contractor/.

Mai, Michael. "The All-Volunteer Army at 50 – Does Milton Friedman's Case Still Make Sense?" Real Clear Defense, July 1, 2023. https://www.realcleardefense.com/articles/2023/07/01/the_all-volunteer_army_at_50__does_milton_friedmans_case_still_make_sense_963429.html.

McKitrick, Jeffrey, James Blackwell, Fred Littlepage, George Kraus, Richard Blanchfield, and Dale Hill. "Chapter 3: Revolution in Military Affairs." In *Battlefield of the Future*. Selma, Alabama: Air War College, Maxwell AF Base, 1995. http://www.airpower.maxwell.af.mil/airchronicles/battle/chp3.html.

Military Extraterritorial Jurisdiction Act, Pub. L. No. 18 USC Sec 3261, § 3261, Part II Title 18 (2012). http://uscode.house.gov/download/pls/18C212.txt.

Mittelstadt, Jennifer. "Military Demographics: Who Serves When Not All Serve?" In *At War: The Military and American Culture in the Twentieth Century and Beyond*, edited by David Kieran and Edwin A. Martini, 87–107. War Culture. New Brunswick, NJ: Rutgers University Press, 2018. https://www.degruyter.com/isbn/9780813584331.

Moore, Brenda L. "African-American Women in the U.S. Military." *Armed Forces &*

Society (0095-327X) 17, no. 3 (March 1, 1991): 363–84. https://doi.org/10.1177/0095327X9101700303.

Moskos, Charles, and John Sibley Butler. *All That We Can Be: Black Leadership and Racial Integration the Army Way*. New York, NY: Basic Books, 1997.

Moskos, Charles C., and James Burk. "The Postmodern Military." In *The Adaptive Military: Armed Forces in a Turbulent World*, edited by James Burk, 2nd ed., 14–31. New Brunswick, NJ: Transaction Publishers, 1998.

Moskos, Charles C., John Allen Williams, and David R. Segal, eds. *The Postmodern Military: Armed Forces after the Cold War*. 1st edition. New York, NY: Oxford University Press, 1999.

Muhammad, Askia. "Rangel: The Iraq War Is a 'Death Tax' on the Poor." *Final Call News* (blog), April 29, 2004. https://new.finalcall.com/?p=4757.

Myers, Meghann. "Army, Navy and Air Force Predict Recruiting Shortfalls This Year." *Military Times*, April 19, 2023, sec. Your Military. https://www.militarytimes.com/news/your-military/2023/04/19/army-navy-and-air-force-predict-recruiting-shortfalls-this-year/.

———. "Experts, Data Point to Women as Best Military Recruiting Pool." *Military Times*, January 26, 2023, sec. Your Military. https://www.militarytimes.com/news/your-military/2023/01/26/experts-data-point-to-women-as-best-military-recruiting-pool/.

———. "Military Services Grappling with Filling Their Ranks in Budget Request." *Military Times*, March 13, 2023, sec. Your Military. https://www.militarytimes.com/news/your-military/2023/03/13/military-services-grappling-with-filling-their-ranks-in-budget-request/.

Nieberg, Patty. "Army Debuts New Recruiting Ads Aimed at High-Tech Civilians Rather than Soldiers." *Task & Purpose*, May 9, 2024. https://taskandpurpose.com/military-life/army-commercial-open-civilian-jobs/.

Novelly, Thomas, Steve Beynon, Drew F. Lawrence, and Konstantin Toropin. "Big Bonuses, Relaxed Policies, New Slogan: None of It Saved the Military from a Recruiting Crisis in 2023 | Military.Com." *Military Times*, October 17, 2023. https://www.military.com/daily-news/2023/10/13/big-bonuses-relaxed-policies-new-slogan-none-of-it-saved-military-recruiting-crisis-2023.html?utm_campaign=dfn-ebb&utm_medium=email&utm_source=sailthru&SToverlay=2002c2d9-c344-4bbb-8610-e5794efcfa7d.

Office of People Analytics. "Fall 2021 Propensity Update." Washington, DC: Department of Defense, August 9, 2022.

———. "Official DOD Quality of Military Availability (QMA) Study (2022)." Official. Washington, DC: Department of Defense, June 22, 2022.

———. "State of the Recruiting Market Joint Advertising, Market Research & Studies." Washington, DC: Department of Defense, June 2022.

Office of the Assistant Secretary of Defense (Force Management Policy). "The Department of Defense Report on Social Representation in U.S. Military Services." Population Representation in the Military Services. Washington, DC: Department of Defense, 2000. https://prhome.defense.gov/portals/52/Documents/POPREP/poprep99/html/chapter2/c2_recruiting.html.

Office of the Deputy Assistant Secretary of Defense for Military Community and Family

Policy. "2017 Demographics: Profile of the Military Community." Washington, DC: Department of Defense, n.d.

Office of the Secretary of Defense. "Accession Demographics of Active Component Services in the DOD from 1990-2022." XLSX, FOIA Request. Washington, DC: Department of Defense, May 24, 2023.

———. "Military Personnel Policy." Government. Office of the Secretary for Personnel and Readiness. Accessed May 16, 2023. https://prhome.defense.gov/M-RA/Inside-M-RA/MPP/Reports/.

Office of the Under Secretary for Personnel and Readiness. "Military Personnel Policy." Department of Defense, 2022. https://prhome.defense.gov/M-RA/Inside-M-RA/MPP/.

Orvis, Bruce R., Steven Garber, Philip Hall-Partyka, and Tiffany Tsai. *Recruiting Strategies to Support the Army's All-Volunteer Force*. Santa Monica, Calif: RAND Corporation, 2016.

Owens, Mackubin Thomas. "Is Civilian Control of the Military Still an Issue?" In *Warriors and Citizens: American Views of Our Military*, edited by Kori N. Schake and Jim Mattis, 69–96. Stanford, California: Hoover Institution Press, 2016.

———. "Military Officers: Political without Partisanship." *Strategic Studies Quarterly* 9, no. 3 (Fall 2015): 88–101.

———. "The Bush Doctrine: The Foreign Policy of Republican Empire." *Orbis* 53, no. 1 (January 2009): 23–40. https://doi.org/10.1016/j.orbis.2008.10.010.

———. "What Military Officers Need to Know About Civil-Military Relations." *Naval War College Review* 65, no. 2 (Spring 2012): 67–87.

Parker, Christopher. "Lack of Will: How the All-Volunteer Force Conditioned the American Public." *Military Review*, October 2023, 44–56. https://www.armyupress.army.mil/Journals/Military-Review/English-Edition-Archives/September-October-2023/.

Perez, Zamone. "Poor Fitness among Recruits Is Costing the Army Millions, Study Says." *Army Times*, April 3, 2023, sec. Your Army. https://www.armytimes.com/news/your-military/2023/04/03/poor-fitness-among-recruits-is-costing-the-army-millions-study-says/.

Perri, Timothy. "The Evolution of Military Conscription in the United States." *The Independent Review* 17, no. 3 (Winter 2013): 429–39. https://web-s-ebscohost-com.ez-salve.idm.oclc.org/ehost/detail/detail?vid=5&sid=e39e8a18-7d6c-457c-a2ba-4d530f7c8696%40redis&bdata=JnNpdGU9ZWhvc3QtbGl2ZQ%3d%3d#AN=84548197&db=bft.

Philipps, Dave. "U.S. Army, Navy and Air Force Struggle for Recruits. The Marines Have Plenty." *The New York Times*, October 17, 2023, sec. U.S. https://www.nytimes.com/2023/10/17/us/marines-army-recruits.html.

Philips, Jeffrey E. "Reserve Components." In *The All-Volunteer Force: Fifty Years of Service*, edited by William A. Taylor. Lawrence, Kansas: University Press of Kansas, 2023.

Press Release. "The Final Report of the National Commission on Military, National, and Public Service." Washington, DC: Selective Service System, March 25, 2020. https://docs.house.gov/meetings/AS/AS00/20210519/112680/HHRG-117-AS00-Wstate-HeckJ-20210519-SD001.pdf.

Quester, Aline O., and Robert F. Lockman. "The All-Volunteer Force: Outlook for the

Eighties and Nineties." Alexandria, VA: Center for Naval Analysis, March 1984. https://apps.dtic.mil/sti/pdfs/ADA153703.pdf.

Rapp, William E. "Crisis in the Civil-Military Triangle?" In *Reconsidering American Civil-Military Relations: The Military, Society, Politics, and Modern War*, edited by Lionel Beehner, Risa Brooks, and Daniel Maurer, 191–206. New York: Oxford University Press, 2020.

Rempfer, Kyle. "Army 'Ahead of Schedule' in Integrating Women in Combat Arms, Outgoing SMA Says as He Departs." *Army Times*, August 18, 2019, sec. Your Army. https://www.armytimes.com/news/your-army/2019/08/16/army-ahead-of-schedule-in-integrating-women-in-combat-arms-outgoing-sma-says-as-he-departs/.

"Report of the President's Commission on an All-Volunteer Armed Force." Washington, DC, February 1970. Nixon Foundation. https://www.nixonfoundation.org/wp-content/uploads/2012/01/The-Report-Of-The-Presidents-Commission-On-An-All-Volunteer-Armed-Force.pdf.

Roland, Alex. *War and Technology: A Very Short Introduction*. Illustrated edition. New York, NY: Oxford University Press, 2016.

Roque, Ashley. "Army's Wormuth: Congress Will Soon Hear Plans to Revamp Force Structure, Trim SOF." *Breaking Defense* (blog), October 3, 2023. https://breakingdefense.sites.breakingmedia.com/2023/10/armys-wormuth-congress-will-soon-hear-plans-to-revamp-force-structure-trim-sof/.

Rostker, Bernard D. *I Want You!: The Evolution of the All-Volunteer Force*. 1st ed. Santa Monica, CA: RAND Corporation, 2006. http://www.jstor.org/stable/10.7249/mg265rc.

———. "The Evolution of the All-Volunteer Force." Santa Monica, CA: RAND Corporation, August 28, 2006. https://www.rand.org/pubs/research_briefs/RB9195.html.

Rousseau, Jean-Jacques. *The Social Contract*. Modern Reprint. New York, NY: Penguin Classics, 1968.

Ryan, Michael. "Military Readiness, Operations Tempo (OPTEMPO) and Personnel Tempo (PERSTEMPO): Are U.S. Forces Doing Too Much?" Congressional Research Service. Washington, DC: The Library of Congress, January 14, 1998. http://www.congressionalresearch.com/98-41/document.php.

Saballa, Joe. "US Army Recruitment Surges to 15-Year High: Hegseth." The Defense Post, February 7, 2025. https://thedefensepost.com/2025/02/07/us-army-recruitment-surges/.

Sands, Leo. "U.K. Conservatives Want Mandatory National Service. Gen Z Is Cringing." *Washington Post*, May 27, 2024. https://www.washingtonpost.com/world/2024/05/27/national-service-rishi-sunak-memes-election/.

Saucier, Jeremy K. "Mobilizing the Imagination: Army Advertising and the Politics of Culture in Post-Vietnam America." University of Rochester, 2010. https://www.google.com/url?sa=t&rct=j&q=&esrc=s&source=web&cd=&ved=2ahUKEwiun MKgh7H8AhWRPewKHfIxDFM4HhAWegQICBAB&url=https%3A%2F%2Furre search.rochester.edu%2FfileDownloadForInstitutionalItem.action%3FitemId% 3D12084%26itemFileId%3D27546&usg=AOvVaw2dETA27h3nmMxFZp8IYpg7.

Sawers, John. "Technology, Security, Freedom." *Vital Speeches of the Day* 82, no. 2 (February 2016): 43–47. https://ez-salve.idm.oclc.org/login?url=https://search.ebscohost.com/login.aspx?direct=true&db=mth&AN=112697772&site=ehost-live.

Schafer, Amy. "Generations of War: The Rise of the Warrior Caste & the All-Volunteer Force." Washington, DC: Center for a New American Security, 2017. https://www.jstor.org/stable/resrep06443.

Schake, Kori N., and Jim Mattis. "A Great Divergence?" In *Warriors and Citizens: American Views of Our Military*, edited by Kori N. Schake and Jim Mattis, 1–20. Stanford, California: Hoover Institution Press, 2016.

———. "Ensuring a Civil-Military Connection." In *Warriors and Citizens: American Views of Our Military*, edited by Kori N. Schake and Jim Mattis, 287–326. Stanford, California: Hoover Institution Press, 2016.

Schapp, Jason. "ESports Team Ready for Today's CODE Bowl." Press Release. Fort Knox, KY: U.S. Army, December 11, 2020. https://recruiting.army.mil/News/Article/2443775/esports-team-ready-for-todays-code-bowl/.

Scott, Wilbur J., Karin Modesto De Angelis, and David R. Segal. *Military Sociology: A Guided Introduction*. New York, NY: Routledge, 2022. https://www.routledge.com/Military-Sociology-A-Guided-Introduction/Scott-Angelis-Segal/p/book/9781032252919.

Seck, Hope Hodge. "Marines Move Some Recruiting Centers to Urban Hubs in Massive Realignment." *Marine Corps Times*, June 17, 2024. https://www.marinecorpstimes.com/news/recruiting/2024/06/17/marines-move-some-recruiting-centers-to-urban-hubs-in-massive-realignment/?utm_campaign=dfn-ebb&utm_medium=email&utm_source=sailthru.

Segal, David R. *Recruiting for Uncle Sam: Citizenship and Military Manpower Policy*. 1st edition. Lawrence, KS: University Press of Kansas, 1989.

Segal, Mady Wechsler, and Chris Bourg. "Professional Leadership and Diversity in the Army." In *The Future of the Army Profession, Revised and Expanded Second Edition*, edited by Don Snider and Lloyd Matthews, 2nd ed., 705–22. Boston, MA: McGraw Hill-Education, 2005.

Segal, Mady Wechsler, David G. Smith, David R. Segal, and Amy A. Canuso. "The Role of Leadership and Peer Behaviors in the Performance and Well-Being of Women in Combat: Historical Perspectives, Unit Integration, and Family Issues." *Military Medicine* 181, no. Supplement (January 2016): 28–39.

Selective Service System. "Historical Timeline." Selective Service System. Accessed October 17, 2023. https://www.sss.gov/history-and-records/timeline/.

———. "Order to Report for Induction," February 13, 1943.

———. "Selective Service System Annual Report to the Congress of the United States." Government. Arlington, VA: Selective Service System, 2022. https://www.sss.gov/reports/annual-reports-to-congress/.

———. "Women." Government. Selective Service System. Accessed November 6, 2023. https://www.sss.gov/register/women/.

Senate Committee on Armed Services. "Summary of the Fiscal Year 2023 National Defense Authorization Act." Washington, DC, December 27, 202AD.

Serbu, Jared. "Army Stands Up Chicago-Based Marketing Operations to Help Bolster Recruitment." Federal News Network, August 22, 2019. https://federalnewsnetwork.com/army/2019/08/army-stands-up-chicago-based-marketing-operation-to-help-bolster-recruitment/.

Shane III, Leo. "Political Fights Aren't Discouraging Recruits, Military Recruiters Say."

Military Times, December 6, 2023, sec. Pentagon & Congress. https://www.militarytimes.com/news/pentagon-congress/2023/12/06/political-fights-arent-discouraging-recruits-military-recruiters-say/.

Shanks-Kaurin, Pauline. "Questioning Military Professionalism." In *Redefining the Modern Military: The Intersection of Profession and Ethics*, edited by Nathan Finney and Tyrell Mayfield, 9–21. Annapolis, MD: Naval Institute Press, 2021.

Smith, Monroe. "Lecture at Columbia University-1916." In *Citizens and Soldiers: The Dilemmas of Military Service*, by Eliot A. Cohen, 1st Edition. Cornell Studies in Security Affairs. Ithaca, NY: Cornell University Press, 1985. https://doi.org/10.7591/9781501733772.

Snider, Don. *Once Again, the Challenge to the U.S. Army During a Defense Reduction: To Remain a Military Profession*. Enlarged Edition. Carlisle, PA: Strategic Studies Institute, 2013. https://a.co/d/gKNiiEp.

———. "The U.S. Army as Profession." In *The Future of the Army Profession*, by Don Snider and Lloyd J. Matthews, 3–38, 2nd Edition. Boston, MA: McGraw-Hill Education, 2002. My Book.

Snider, Don, and Lloyd Matthews, eds. *The Future of the Army Profession, Revised and Expanded Second Edition*. 2nd ed. Boston, MA: McGraw Hill-Education, 2005.

Snow, Donald M. "The Shifting Threat and American National Strategy: Sources and Consequences of Change." In *The Adaptive Military: Armed Forces in a Turbulent World, Second Edition*, edited by James Burk, 2nd ed., 115–38. New Jersey: Transaction Publishers, 1998.

Snyder, Claire R. *Citizen-Soldiers and Manly Warriors: Military Service and Gender in the Civic Republican Tradition*. Lanham, MD: Rowman & Littlefield Publishers, 1999. My Book.

South, Todd. "The Army Keeps Getting Smaller." *Army Times*, March 13, 2023, sec. Your Army. https://www.armytimes.com/news/your-army/2023/03/13/the-army-keeps-getting-smaller/.

Spearin, Christopher. *Private Military and Security Companies and States: Force Divided*. 1st ed. 2017 edition. New York, NY: Palgrave Macmillan, 2017.

Spoehr, Thomas. "The Incredible Shrinking Army: NDAA End-Strength Levels Are a Mistake." *Breaking Defense* (blog), December 20, 2022. https://breakingdefense.sites.breakingmedia.com/2022/12/the-incredible-shrinking-army-ndaa-end-strength-levels-are-a-mistake/.

Statista. "Mobile Phone Users United States 2012-2020," February 23, 2017. https://www-statista-com.ez-salve.idm.oclc.org/statistics/222306/forecast-of-smartphone-users-in-the-us/.

Stilwell, Blake. "The Top 5 Reasons Americans Were Unfit for Military Service During World War I." Military.com, April 10, 2023. https://www.military.com/history/top-5-reasons-americans-were-unfit-military-service-during-world-war-i.html.

Swed, Ori. "The Afghanistan War's Legacy: The Reimagining of the Outsourcing of War and Security." *Armed Forces & Society (0095327X)* 49, no. 4 (October 2023): 1027–34. https://doi.org/10.1177/0095327X221101340.

Taibl, Paul. "U.S. Base Closures Bring Post-Cold War Jitters." *Forum for Applied Research & Public Policy* 10 (January 15, 1995): 24–28. https://ez-salve.idm.oclc.org/login?url=

https://search.ebscohost.com/login.aspx?direct=true&db=ssf&AN=510120141&site=ehost-live.

Taylor, William A. *Military Service and American Democracy: From World War II to the Iraq and Afghanistan Wars.* Illustrated edition. Lawrence, KS: University Press of Kansas, 2020.

———. *The Advent of the All-Volunteer Force.* 1st edition. New York, NY: Routledge, 2023.

———, ed. *The All-Volunteer Force: Fifty Years of Service.* Lawrence, Kansas: University Press of Kansas, 2023.

"The Evolution of the All-Volunteer Force." Research Brief. Santa Monica, CA: RAND Corporation, 2006. www.rand.org.

The Philadelphia Tribune. "Minorities Continue to Pay a High Price for Iraq." March 24, 2013. https://www.phillytrib.com/news/minorities-continue-to-pay-a-high-price-for-iraq/article_80d3ee27-ef47-56c9-926a-c2c613cbdd72.html.

Thompson, Mark. "An Army Apart: The Widening Military-Civilian Gap." *TIME Magazine,* October 23, 2011. https://nation.time.com/2011/11/10/an-army-apart-the-widening-military-civilian-gap/. Time.com.

Thucydides. *The Landmark Thucydides: A Comprehensive Guide to the Peloponnesian War.* Edited by Robert B. Strassler. Translated by Richard Crawley. 1st ed. Free Press, 1998.

Tirpak, John. "Military Growing More Distant from Most Americans, Hicks Says." *Air & Space Forces Magazine,* November 7, 2023. https://www.airandspaceforces.com/hicks-military-growing-distant-americans/.

Tompkins, Erin. "Obesity in the United States and Effects on Military Recruiting." Government. In Focus. Washington, DC: Congressional Research Service, December 22, 2020. https://crsreports.congress.gov/product/pdf/IF/IF11708.

Travis, Donald S. "Why the U.S. Military Lost Afghanistan." *Armed Forces & Society* (0095327X) 49, no. 4 (October 2023): 939–52. https://doi.org/10.1177/0095327X221100584.

Ulrich, Marybeth P. "Civil-Military Relations Norms and Democracy: What Every Citizen Should Know." In *Reconsidering American Civil-Military Relations: The Military, Society, Politics, and Modern War,* edited by Lionel Beehner, Risa Brooks, and Daniel Maurer, 41–62. New York: Oxford University Press, 2020.

———. "The Civil-Military Gap." In *The All-Volunteer Force: Fifty Years of Service,* edited by William A. Taylor, 279–302. Lawrence, Kansas: University Press of Kansas, 2023.

Under Secretary of Defense for Personnel and Readiness. "Department of Defense Instruction on Qualitative Distribution of Military Manpower, with Change 2." Department of Defense, May 4, 2020.

Unger, Debi, Irwin Unger, and Stanley Hirshson. *George Marshall: A Biography.* 1st edition. New York, NY: Harper, 2014.

United States Army. "The Army and Diversity." U.S. Army Center of Military History. Accessed October 11, 2023. https://history.army.mil/faq/diversity.html.

United States Army Recruiting Command. "Army Recruiting 1974-2021." XLSX. Fort Eustis, VA: U.S. Army Training and Doctrine Command, January 15, 2022.

———. "U.S. Army Recruiting Command -- About." Government. U.S. Army Recruiting Command: Official Website, 2022. https://recruiting.army.mil/aboutUSAREC/.

———. "USAREC Brigades and Battalions." United States Army, 2024. https://recruiting.army.mil/bde_bn/.

United States Census Bureau. "1990 Census of Population: General Population Characteristics." Washington, DC: United States Department of Commerce. Accessed November 30, 2023. https://www.census.gov/library/publications/1992/dec/cp-1.html.

———. "1990 State Population Estimates: Annual Time Series." ASCI. Washington, DC: United States Department of Commerce, December 29, 1999. https://www2.census.gov/programs-surveys/popest/tables/1990-2000/state/totals/st-99-03.txt.

———. "2020-2022 State Population Totals and Components of Change." XLSX. Washington, DC: United States Department of Commerce, December 15, 2022. https://www.census.gov/data/datasets/time-series/demo/popest/2020s-state-total.html#v2022.

United States Census Bureau, and Michael Martin. "Computer and Internet Use in the United States, 2018." American Community Survey Reports. Washington, DC: United States Department of Commerce, April 2021. https://www.census.gov/library/publications/2021/acs/acs-49.html.

United States Congress. "An Act for Enrolling and Calling out the National Forces, and for Other Purposes." Congressional Record, March 3, 1863. Congressional Record. 37th Cong. 3d. Sess. Ch. 74, 75. 1863. https://glc.yale.edu/act-enrolling-and-calling-out-national-forces.

United States: Congress: House of Representatives: Office of the Law Revision Counsel. Enlistments: recruiting campaigns; compilation of directory information. Sec. 503, Subtitle A-General Military Law PART II-PERSONNEL CHAPTER 31-ENLISTMENTS Title X, Armed Forces § 503 (2011). https://www.govinfo.gov/app/details/USCODE-2011-title10/USCODE-2011-title10-subtitleA-partII-chap31-sec503.

U.S. Army. "Army Announces Transformation of Its Recruiting Enterprise." U.S. Army Public Affairs, October 3, 2023. https://www.army.mil/article/270458/army_announces_transformation_of_its_recruiting_enterprise.

———. "Army Demographics 2022." Office of Army Demographics, 2022. https://www.army.mil/article/219140/demographics.

———. "Army Pamphlet 601-208: Army Marketing." Department of the Army, November 10, 2021. https://armypubs.army.mil/epubs/DR_pubs/DR_a/ARN31147-PAM_601-208-000-WEB-1.pdf.

———. "Army Regulation 601-208: The Army Marketing Program." Department of the Army, November 10, 2021. https://armypubs.army.mil/epubs/DR_pubs/DR_a/ARN32229-AR_601-208-000-WEB-1.pdf.

———. "New Army Brand Redefines 'Be All You Can Be' for a New Generation." www.army.mil, March 8, 2023. https://www.army.mil/article/264594/new_army_brand_redefines_be_all_you_can_be_for_a_new_generation.

———. "USAREC Manuel 3-0: Recruiting Operations." United States Army Recruiting Command, September 18, 2019. https://recruiting.army.mil/Portals/15/Documents/Forms%20and%20Pubs/USAREC%20Manuals/USAREC%20MANUAL%203-0(On%20site%20w%20cover).pdf?ver=2019-12-17-092905-513.

U.S. Army Public Affairs. "Army Announces Creation of Future Soldier Preparatory

Course." United States Army, June 25, 2022. https://www.army.mil/article/258758/army_announces_creation_of_future_soldier_preparatory_course.

U.S. Army Training and Doctrine Command. "Army Capstone Concept." Department of Defense, December 19, 2012.

"U.S. Constitution | Constitution Annotated | Congress.Gov | Library of Congress." Accessed November 9, 2022. https://constitution.congress.gov/constitution/.

USAREC. "Station Listing." PDF, July 11, 2024.

Vasquez, Joseph Paul, III. "Shouldering the Soldiering: Democracy, Conscription, and Military Casualties." *Journal of Conflict Resolution* 49, no. 6 (December 2005): 849–73.

Vego, Milan. "Is the Conduct of War a Business?" *Joint Forces Quarterly*, no. 59 (2010): 57–65. ndupress.ndu.edu.

Vespa, Jonathan E. "Those Who Served: America's Veterans from World War II to the War on Terror." American Community Survey Report. Washington, DC: U.S. Department of Commerce, U.S. Census Bureau, 2020. WorldCat.org. https://purl.fdlp.gov/GPO/gpo140251.

Wankhede, Calvin. "The History of Cell Phones: A Decade-by-Decade Timeline." Android Authority, July 14, 2023. https://www.androidauthority.com/history-of-cell-phones-timeline-3264425/.

Warner, John T. "The Effect of the Civilian Economy on Recruiting and Retention." In *Report of the Eleventh Quadrennial Review of Military Compensation*, 71–91. Washington, DC: Department of Defense, June 23012. https://militarypay.defense.gov/Portals/3/Documents/Reports/SR05_Chapter_2.pdf.

Warner, John T, and Beth J Asch. "The Record and Prospects of the All-Volunteer Military in the United States." *Journal of Economic Perspectives* 15, no. 2 (May 1, 2001): 169–92. https://doi.org/10.1257/jep.15.2.169.

Weigley, Russell F. *The American Way of War: A History of United States Military Strategy and Policy*. Paperback Edition. Bloomington: Indiana University Press, 1977.

Wellman, Phillip Walter. "Perception of 'Wokeness' Isn't Major Driver of Recruitment Woes, Army Former Enlisted Leader Says." *Stars and Stripes*, June 23, 2023. https://www.stripes.com/branches/army/2023-06-23/sergeant-major-army-unawareness-recruitment-10526444.html.

Wilkerson, Lawrence B. "Efficiency." In *The All-Volunteer Force: Fifty Years of Service*, edited by William A. Taylor, 181–96. Lawrence, Kansas: University Press of Kansas, 2023.

Williams, John Allen, Stephen J. Cimbala, and Sam C. Sarkesian. *US National Security: Policymakers, Processes, and Politics*. 6th edition. Boulder: Lynne Rienner Publishers, Inc., 2022.

Williams, Lauren C. "More Money for Info Ops, Army Recruiting, Cyber In Omnibus." Defense One, December 22, 2022. https://www.defenseone.com/defense-systems/2022/12/more-money-info-ops-army-recruiting-cyber-omnibus/381278/.

Wilson, Woodrow. "Message Regarding Military Draft." Presidential Speeches. University of Virginia, May 19, 1917. https://millercenter.org/the-presidency/presidential-speeches/may-19-1917-message-regarding-military-draft.

Winkie, Davis. "Army Doubles Down on Retention for Fiscal 2023 Amid Recruiting Woes." *Army Times*, January 18, 2023, sec. Your Army. https://www.armytimes.com/

news/your-army/2023/01/18/army-doubles-down-on-retention-for-fiscal-2023-amid-recruiting-woes/.

———. "Army Recruiting Reforms Go 'Back to the Future' to Fix Ongoing Crisis." *Army Times*, November 8, 2023, sec. Army Recruiting. https://www.armytimes.com/news/recruiting/2023/11/08/army-recruiting-reforms-go-back-to-the-future-to-fix-ongoing-crisis/.

———. "Can the Army Fill Its Ranks?" *Military Times*, December 26, 2022, sec. Your Military. https://www.militarytimes.com/news/your-army/2022/12/26/can-the-army-fill-its-ranks/.

———. "Exclusive: Army Secretary Talks Force Structure Cuts, SOF 'Reform.'" *Army Times*, June 28, 2023, sec. Your Army. https://www.armytimes.com/news/your-army/2023/06/28/exclusive-army-secretary-talks-force-structure-cuts-sof-reform/.

———. "Exclusive: The Inside Story of How the Army Rethought Recruiting." *Army Times*, October 9, 2023, sec. Your Army. https://www.armytimes.com/news/your-army/2023/10/09/exclusive-the-inside-story-of-how-the-army-rethought-recruiting/.

———. "US Army to 'Overhaul' Recruiting School amid Personnel Shortage." *Defense News*, March 29, 2023. https://www.defensenews.com/global/the-americas/2023/03/29/us-army-to-overhaul-recruiting-school-amid-personnel-shortage/.

Wittes, Benjamin, and Cody Poplin. "Public Opinion, Military Justice, and the Fight against Terrorism Overseas." In *Warriors and Citizens: American Views of Our Military*, edited by Kori N. Schake and Jim Mattis, 143–60. Stanford, California: Hoover Institution Press, 2016.

Worsencroft, John. "The Wrong Man in Uniform: Antidraft Republicans and the Ideological Origins of the All-Volunteer Force, 1966-73." In *Service Denied: Marginalized Veterans in Modern American History*, by John M. Kinder and Jason A. Higgins, 159–78. Veterans. Amherst, MA: University of Massachusetts Press, 2022. https://muse.jhu.edu/book/102909/.

Yuengert, Louis G. "America's All-Volunteer Force: A Success?" *Parameters* 45, no. 4 (December 1, 2015): 53–64. https://doi.org/10.55540/0031-1723.2986.

INDEX

Abbott 27, 160, 161, 189, 242
Abrams 76, 182
Active Component AC 3, 17, 18, 75, 79, 91, 105, 142, 207, 213, 236, 239, 254, 258
active-duty 6, 63, 68, 101, 177, 236, 248
Adedeji 77, 117, 123, 129, 133, 251
Afghanistan 17, 18, 20, 24, 28, 29, 40, 76, 78, 85, 90, 95, 118, 124, 125, 130, 136, 149, 159, 162, 172, 173, 177, 180, 181, 183, 185, 188, 203, 240, 242, 244, 246, 252, 263, 264
African Americans 15
agent 26, 69, 112, 154, 160, 167, 228
Air Force 2, 12, 39, 42, 65, 75, 153, 248, 257, 258
Allied Expeditionary Force AEF 55, 239
Amara 79, 242
Ambrose 15, 31, 57, 134, 135, 242, 243, 253
America's Paradoxical Trinity 38, 42, 81, 93, 97, 112, 113, 117, 118, 125, 149, 150, 155, 163, 165, 170, 171, 176, 191, 196, 198, 202, 206, 221, 224, 228, 229, 233, 235, 237, 239
American Trinity 43, 57, 72, 86, 114, 184, 190, 192

Anderson 61
Armed Forces Qualification Test AFQT 133
armor 130
Army Training and Doctrine Command TRADOC 2, 187, 211, 264, 266
artificial horizon 218, 221
Arver v. United States 49
Asch 78, 85, 105, 242, 266
Askew 7, 242
Asoni 35, 122, 129, 213, 242
Assistant Secretary of the Army 13, 242
Athens 49
Atkins 159, 185, 242
attitudes 69, 120, 128, 131, 135, 176, 201
autonomy and demand 163, 164, 165, 188, 189, 191
Avant 177, 203, 242
AVF 1.0 13, 71, 97, 112, 116, 127, 139, 165, 189
AVF 2.0 16, 73, 97, 112, 115, 121, 128, 135, 165, 170, 171, 180, 187, 189, 205, 206, 209
AVF 3.0 17, 18, 76, 94, 106, 112, 116, 129, 136, 139, 165, 171, 172
AVF 4.0 4, 13, 18, 71, 78, 79, 93, 112, 118, 130, 138, 154, 165, 189, 205, 237, 247
Bacevich 19, 21, 22, 49, 93, 175, 185, 242
Bailey 4, 14, 15, 16, 17, 18, 20, 30, 31, 61, 72, 74, 76, 79, 80, 115, 121, 122, 128, 132, 133, 134, 136, 243
Baker 131, 244
Baldor 1, 2, 3, 9, 67, 124, 243
Barber 31, 57, 134, 135, 204, 242, 243, 253
Barndollar 91, 243
Barno 10, 18, 19, 23, 90, 243
Barsuhn 176, 177, 244
Base Realignment and Closure BRAC 73
BBC 7, 244
Beehner 19, 26, 34, 41, 103, 162, 182, 244, 245, 250, 259, 264
Beets 245
Ben-Ari 32, 244

Benshal 10, 18, 19, 23, 90, 243
Bergan 58, 86, 244
Berger 82, 83, 105, 244
Beynon 77, 122, 131, 244, 257
Black 37, 58, 111, 119, 120, 121, 122, 124, 125, 128, 139, 140, 141, 142, 143, 145, 146, 148, 151, 227, 245, 249, 256
Blacks 14, 37, 69, 117, 119, 120, 122, 123, 124, 125, 127, 140, 141, 142, 144, 145, 146, 147, 151, 152, 159, 227, 231, 245
Blankshain 182, 244
Blount 87, 205, 212, 245
Boigon 2, 255
Bonaparte 21, 47
Borgmann 198, 199, 200, 202, 207, 217, 245
Bornstein 102, 245
Borus 254
Bowersox 86, 247
Brady 78, 87, 245
Brett 245
Briscoe 125, 245
British 21, 52, 254
Brito 187, 245
Brooks 10, 19, 26, 34, 41, 162, 175, 181, 182, 244, 245, 246, 250, 259, 264
Brown 3, 246
Bryant 33, 246
budget 4, 12, 62, 84, 85, 115, 175, 181, 205, 210, 212, 227, 257
Bureau of Labor Statistics 246
bureaucracy 32, 203
Burk 16, 23, 30, 32, 45, 67, 73, 89, 90, 157, 171, 172, 177, 197, 203, 242, 246, 248, 253, 256, 262
Buscha 130, 246
Butler 120, 121, 124, 256
Camarillo 12, 85, 246
Camp 205, 247
Carter 4, 13, 18, 71, 78, 79, 93, 112, 129, 130, 154, 247
Castells 30, 197, 247

casualties 54, 56, 58, 113, 117
CDC 22, 239
Charmaz 33, 246
Chesterman 17, 183, 184, 247, 253, 255
Chief of Staff of the Army CSA 14, 92, 180, 182, 211, 239
children 10, 19, 37, 80, 147
Choi 86, 247
civic obligation 90, 114
Civil War 50, 53, 54, 92
Civilian Conservation Corps CCC 55, 239
civilian wages 40, 85
civil-military 3, 8, 11, 14, 20, 21, 22, 24, 25, 26, 29, 33, 34, 37, 40, 41, 42, 43, 45, 79, 80, 81, 84, 86, 88, 90, 91, 92, 96, 106, 107, 110, 111, 118, 123, 125, 149, 150, 153, 156, 157, 158, 159, 161, 163, 166, 170, 173, 183, 184, 186, 188, 198, 203, 205, 222, 223, 228, 229, 231, 232
civil-military relations 8, 11, 14, 20, 21, 22, 24, 25, 26, 33, 34, 37, 40, 41, 43, 45, 80, 84, 86, 88, 91, 92, 96, 107, 149, 150, 153, 156, 157, 158, 159, 161, 163, 166, 170, 173, 183, 184, 186, 188, 198, 203, 205, 222, 223, 228, 229, 232
Clausewitz 19, 21, 34, 36, 42, 43, 47, 48, 80, 150, 155, 162, 163, 191, 247
coach(es) 9, 86, 103, 151
Cocke 89, 247
Cohen 13, 20, 34, 48, 75, 153, 176, 197, 205, 247, 248, 262
Cold War 6, 23, 32, 73, 112, 121, 165, 187, 229, 246, 256, 263
Coleman 3, 16, 73, 248
Columbia 93, 153, 262
compensation 12, 17, 28, 40, 62, 66, 67, 75, 76, 77, 81, 82, 83, 84, 85, 89, 95, 104, 105, 106, 107, 110, 112, 114, 116, 205, 206, 223, 227, 234
Congress 4, 14, 15, 21, 28, 34, 40, 49, 53, 59, 72, 74, 75, 87, 90, 97, 103, 113, 118, 126, 127, 137, 149, 151, 152, 154, 163, 174, 177, 178, 183, 190, 212, 214, 217, 224, 230, 238, 253, 259, 260, 261, 265, 266
Connor 7, 248
conscription 2, 6, 7, 13, 14, 22, 32, 41, 44, 49, 50, 52, 53, 54, 55, 59, 61, 62, 64, 65, 67, 70, 72, 79, 80, 86, 104, 110, 111, 112, 117, 126, 127, 129, 223, 224, 226, 228, 237, 242
Constitution 15, 22, 49, 50, 52, 127, 251, 266
contractors 17, 18, 28, 76, 79, 155, 169, 177, 178, 179, 183, 192, 203

Correll 6, 248
cost-efficient 118, 152, 181, 182
Creveld 248
criminal behavior 8
Crooked Smile ii, 36, 82, 110
cultural divergence 93
cultural horizon 201, 232, 233
Dandecker 172, 248
Defense Appropriations Act DAA 4
Delayed Entry Program DEP 40, 239
democracy 8, 10, 25, 58, 106, 157, 159, 192, 200, 202, 204, 229, 232, 233
democratic 12, 44, 86, 104, 117, 159, 176, 198, 202
Dempsey 34, 87, 95, 96, 248, 249
Department of Defense DOD 2, 3, 12, 17, 39, 42, 69, 76, 82, 84, 85, 124, 133, 138, 154, 157, 178, 210, 211, 213, 220, 239, 248, 249, 251, 257, 258, 264, 266
Department of Labor 123, 125, 128, 246, 249, 254
Desert Storm 30, 172, 183
DeVore 3, 94, 249
Dickstein 154, 249
diploma 133, 136, 139, 144, 145, 146, 231
Downing 16, 74, 249
draft 7, 20, 22, 28, 41, 49, 50, 53, 54, 56, 58, 59, 60, 61, 63, 64, 65, 67, 68, 73, 77, 80, 88, 111, 112, 113, 121, 131, 135, 136, 154, 171, 182, 226, 228, 267
drug 8, 213
Dubik 34, 249
Dykstra 56
economic 12, 14, 33, 36, 40, 41, 54, 61, 62, 66, 81, 83, 84, 85, 88, 96, 101, 105, 110, 115, 122, 178, 215
educated 75, 110, 116, 121, 135, 213
education 8, 14, 15, 25, 37, 58, 68, 69, 88, 107, 112, 117, 119, 122, 130, 131, 133, 134, 135, 136, 137, 138, 139, 140, 144, 145, 147, 149, 151, 152, 158, 170, 181, 202, 224, 227, 237
Efflandt 28, 156, 182, 183, 185, 250
Eikenberry 181, 182, 184, 185, 250
Eisenhower 65

Ender 32, 126, 204, 250, 252
end-strength 4, 6, 40, 59, 64, 65, 66, 77, 83, 85, 88, 89, 90, 94, 122, 131, 147, 155, 177, 178, 180, 188, 192, 195, 206, 212, 219, 220,223, 227, 229, 232, 234, 262
Epictetus 223, 250
Equal Rights Amendment 15, 127
Europe 6, 7, 46, 47, 53, 55, 242, 244, 245, 253
European 6, 7, 21, 52, 53, 54, 188, 245
Executive Branch 28, 34
family business 10, 19, 101
Farley 209, 250
Farrell 40, 250
Feaver 10, 25, 26, 34, 41, 91, 103, 148, 149, 157, 158, 159, 160, 165, 167, 171, 174, 175, 185, 198, 250, 251
female 37, 111, 129, 130, 139, 143, 147, 148
Field 93, 250
field artillery 130
Finney 26, 31, 70, 156, 163, 180, 251, 253, 255, 261
Firmin 16, 74, 251
Fitzgerald 23, 24, 171, 172, 185, 251
focal practice 200, 201, 217, 218
force design 7, 51, 53, 59, 72, 80, 103, 112, 223, 224, 229, 235
Forrest 245
France52, 54, 55
free market principles 14, 62
Freedman 61
Freedom of Information Act Request 208
French 48
Friedman 22, 40, 41, 49, 50, 61, 251, 256
Gallup 99, 251
Gambone 128, 173, 177, 183, 251
Garamone 3, 251
Garber 258
Gates Commission 37, 38, 63, 64, 66, 69, 70, 72, 86, 94, 96, 102, 110, 111, 112, 118, 120, 122, 125, 139, 140, 147, 148, 157, 182, 187, 189, 195, 196, 206
Gates Report 13, 14, 36, 88, 91, 97, 102, 110

gender 37, 107, 112, 113, 117, 119, 129, 130, 131, 138, 140, 145, 147, 149, 150, 151, 170, 178, 190, 195, 215, 219, 222, 224, 227, 230
Gender 9, 37, 45, 109, 126, 139, 255, 262
geographic 36, 37, 53, 54, 68, 78, 83, 96, 98, 100, 101, 103, 110, 111, 126, 136, 138, 140, 142, 143, 144, 145, 146, 147, 149, 150, 178, 215, 218, 227, 231
geography 14, 54, 83, 88, 95, 103, 112, 131, 147, 149, 151, 170, 190, 195, 203, 224, 230, 231
Germany 7, 248
Gilli 242
Global War on Terrorism GWOT 4, 110, 203, 223, 240
g-m vertex 44, 71, 76, 164, 168, 188, 221
Golby 171, 174, 185, 251
Goldberg 10, 78, 79, 251
Golding 77, 117, 123, 129, 133, 251
Government Accountability Office GAO 17, 74, 75, 77, 112, 122, 124, 137, 239, 250, 252
Greenspan 61
Grieve 245
Griffin 15, 29, 63, 71, 88, 89, 210, 252
Grounded Theory 33, 240, 246
g-s vertex 44, 48, 50, 57, 112, 136, 138, 149, 151, 152, 168, 221, 235
guidance counselors 9
Gunderson 29, 252
Hajjar 252
Hall-Partyka 258
Hauret 245
Heidegger 220, 252
Heinlein 252
Helfgott 197, 252
Hershey 56, 58
Higgins 17, 22, 23, 61, 113, 179, 254, 267
high school HS 133, 136, 139, 144, 145, 146, 211, 213, 231
Hispanic 122, 128, 139, 249
Hlad 130, 252
Hobbes 46, 252
Holman 74, 252

homosexuals 15, 168
Huntington 25, 26, 45, 92, 101, 157, 158, 159, 163, 166, 176, 187, 242, 252
Inbody 20, 173, 252
individual liberty 13, 22, 48, 51, 62, 80, 221, 226
individual-ready reserve 17
Industrial Revolution 53, 196, 197, 203, 225, 252
infantry 119, 130
Ingesson 163, 253
institution 3, 9, 15, 19, 23, 35, 42, 48, 51, 55, 82, 93, 99, 109, 121, 135, 153, 155, 164, 167, 172, 187, 204, 231, 232, 233, 234, 238
Intel Corporation 197
Iraq 17, 18, 23, 28, 29, 40, 73, 76, 78, 85, 90, 95, 118, 123, 124, 125, 136, 149, 162, 172, 180, 183, 188, 203, 253, 257, 263
Isenburg 17, 76, 183, 253
Israel 32
Jae 86, 247
Janowitz 26, 32, 45, 72, 88, 91, 92, 101, 134, 157, 158, 159, 169, 179, 187, 253
Jehn 6, 253
Johnson 15, 25, 60, 115, 124, 139, 156, 253
Jones 245
Junior Reserve Officer Training Corps JROTC 237
jurisdictions 27, 160
Kanellos 209, 254
Kapp 75, 82, 105, 136, 177, 254
Kieran 17, 58, 76, 137, 254, 256
Kim 123, 129, 254
Kinder 17, 22, 23, 61, 113, 179, 254, 267
King 72, 254
Kipling 109, 254
Kleykamp10 24, 254
Kneedler v. Lane 49
Koch1 255
Kohn 176, 187, 188, 255
Korea 5, 22, 65
Korean War 22, 59

Krebs 15, 95, 114, 123, 137, 255
Kube 255
Kuhn 194, 255
Kuwait 16
Landru 180, 255
Leal 9, 255
Leander 184, 255
Lehnardt 17, 183, 184, 247, 253, 255
Lehrfeld 153, 154, 255
Lewis 19, 56, 103, 255
liberal society 44
Lindberg 174, 256
Lockman 73, 112, 259
Lyall 44, 113, 256
Machiavelli 45, 46, 183, 256
Mackinnon 170, 256
Mai 41, 91, 243, 256
male 113, 119, 125, 128, 131, 139, 148, 244
Marine Corps USMC 2, 12, 39, 42, 75, 82, 105, 166, 205, 208, 214, 258, 260
market-driven 11, 192
Marshal 55, 59, 65
Martini 58, 137, 254, 256
Mattis 10, 154, 171, 173, 174, 176, 177, 181, 246, 251, 256, 258, 260, 267
Maurer 19, 26, 34, 41, 103, 162, 182, 244, 245, 250, 259, 264
McKinley 176
McKitrick 197, 256
mental 8, 130, 132, 134, 137, 213
mercenary 46, 88
Military Extraterritorial Jurisdiction Act 256
Military Leadership Diversity Commission 118, 179
military-industrial complex 45
militia 45, 48, 51, 52, 56
minorities 18, 79, 111, 117, 118, 119, 121, 122, 125, 130, 152, 231, 263
Mittelstadt 58, 126, 256
Moore 128, 197, 219, 225, 256

Moskos 16, 23, 32, 72, 73, 120, 121, 124, 171, 172, 253, 256
m-s vertex 44, 47, 57, 75, 92, 111, 136, 164, 166, 169, 186, 221, 235
Muhammad 123, 257
Myer 14, 72, 238
Myers 2, 85, 130, 257
National Defense Authorization Act NDAA 4, 94, 118, 212, 240, 261
National Defense Strategy 178, 235
National Guard 4, 17, 236, 254
National School Lunch Program 29, 107, 252
national security 4, 29, 30, 40, 86, 94, 115, 197, 205, 223, 229
Navy 2, 5, 6, 12, 31, 39, 42, 65, 75, 126, 153, 194, 245, 248, 257, 258
Nelson 245
Nestel 254
New Warrior Caste ii, 11, 34, 36, 37, 38, 82, 84, 101, 102, 103, 107, 111, 118, 138, 147, 150, 155, 157, 162, 176, 192, 196, 207, 217, 218, 219, 221, 223, 224, 227, 232, 234
Nieberg 194, 257
Nikolopoulos 245
Nixon 12, 23, 60, 61, 70, 88, 178, 259
Noresvuo 245
Novelly 39, 257
obesity 8
Objective civilian control 45
objective control 25, 158, 159, 166, 176
Office of Army Demographics 119, 240, 265
Office of People Analytics
OPA 2, 8, 9, 214, 257
Office of the Under Secretary for Personnel and Readiness 213, 258
officer corps 91, 101, 125, 159
oligarchy 204
Operation Enduring Freedom OEF 123, 183, 240
Operation Iraqi Freedom OIF 123, 183, 240
operational tempo OPTEMPO 75, 164
Orvis 213, 258
Owens 27, 56, 175, 176, 185, 186, 187, 258
Paradoxical Trinity 34, 42, 43, 71, 80, 91, 92, 102, 104, 106, 107, 111, 147,

149, 150, 151, 155, 162, 179, 191, 192, 195, 206, 217, 218, 219, 223, 224, 225, 229, 230, 235
Parker 76, 77, 258
patriotic 66
patriotism 1, 5, 13, 24, 47, 66, 87, 95, 110, 123, 172, 205
Peace Dividend 94, 115
peacekeeping 6, 73, 112, 165
Perez 118, 258
Perri 53, 54, 56, 258
Philipps 39, 258
Philips 17, 76, 254, 259
philosophy 33, 34, 39, 42, 43, 91, 194, 219
physical 8, 74, 130, 132, 139, 199, 208, 213, 217, 220, 223, 224, 237
pig in the python 60
political science 33
President 12, 13, 15, 23, 29, 49, 51, 53, 55, 59, 61, 70, 88, 101, 103, 110, 115, 129, 169, 174, 176, 217, 230, 238, 242, 259
principal 26, 45, 95, 110, 154, 160, 167, 224, 235
Private Military Security Companies PMSC 28, 178
profession 16, 24, 25, 26, 27, 28, 31, 32, 33, 34, 38, 43, 45, 53, 55, 56, 70, 74, 77, 155, 156, 157, 158, 159, 160, 161, 162, 163, 164, 165, 166, 167, 168, 169, 170, 172, 174, 175, 176, 177, 179, 180, 181, 182, 183, 184, 186, 187, 188, 189, 190, 191, 192, 195, 198, 203, 204, 218, 219, 220, 224, 225, 227, 228, 230, 231, 232, 233, 234, 235, 252, 262
Project 100,000 15, 134, 136
propensity 3, 9, 19, 63, 67, 81, 83, 87, 95, 105, 127, 131, 137, 152, 234
Putin 170
Quester 73, 112, 259
race 9, 14, 20, 37, 68, 69, 79, 88, 107, 109, 112, 113, 119, 120, 123, 124, 125, 126, 128, 130, 131, 138, 139, 140, 143, 145, 146, 147, 149, 150, 151, 222, 227, 230, 249, 255
Racial 119, 120, 256
racism 122, 123, 124, 132
Ralston 95, 123, 137, 255
Rapp 34, 162, 259
Reagan 72

recruiters 9, 18, 68, 89, 132, 154, 206, 207, 209, 210, 213, 216, 218, 220, 221, 234, 261

Recruiting Command USAREC 2, 34, 40, 97, 186, 207, 208, 210, 211, 214, 217, 241, 249, 264, 265

Reimer 75

Rempfer 130, 259

republic 21, 109, 168, 180, 230

republican virtue 14, 21, 38, 47, 54, 109, 220, 224, 237

republicanism 5, 11, 21, 23, 32, 36, 41, 42, 45, 46, 47, 48, 50, 51, 56, 67, 80, 81, 83, 84, 86, 87, 88, 91, 92, 95, 102, 109, 110, 112, 114, 117, 118, 123, 125, 126, 132, 138, 147, 150, 151, 162, 168, 184, 192, 195, 203, 205, 206, 215, 221, 226, 232, 237

Reserve Officer Training Corps ROTC 93, 241, 250

Reserves 17, 167, 236

Revolution in Military Affairs 16, 74, 256

Revolutionary War 49

Rice 75

Risk Rule of 1988 130

Rof 245

Roland 30, 209, 259

Roosevelt FDR 55, 56, 238, 239

Roque 40, 259

Rosman 32, 244

Rostker 4, 14, 18, 23, 30, 31, 51, 61, 70, 79, 127, 129, 132, 133, 259

Rostker v. Goldberg 129

Rousseau 46, 259

Russia 5, 6, 170, 180, 256

Ryan 23, 24, 75, 89, 165, 171, 172, 185, 245, 251, 259

Rytkonen 245

Saballa 1, 260

Sacko 245

Sanandaji 242

Sands 7, 260

Sapmaz 245

Saucier 16, 30, 115, 210, 212, 260

Sawers 197, 260

Schafer 10, 260
Schake 10, 154, 171, 173, 174, 176, 177, 181, 246, 251, 256, 258, 260, 267
Schapp 212, 260
Schwam 10, 24, 254
Scott 15, 28, 121, 126, 127, 128, 183, 250, 260
scoutmaster 151
Seck 208, 260
Secretary of Defense 3, 18, 34, 61, 78, 88, 130, 133, 138, 153, 174, 257, 258, 264
Segal 15, 16, 32, 48, 73, 74, 78, 111, 113, 114, 115, 116, 117, 121, 127, 128, 129, 134, 183, 256, 260, 261
Selective Draft Law Cases 22, 49
Selective Service Act 49, 55, 59, 238
Selective Service System SSS 14, 29, 56, 57, 60, 62, 68, 72, 88, 92, 112, 129, 154, 224, 228, 235, 241, 259, 261
Serbu 205, 212, 261
Shamir 32, 244
Shane 154, 261
Shanks-Kaurin 180, 261
Shields 20, 173, 252
shirk 27, 160, 168
Smith 153, 261, 262
Snider 26, 32, 113, 156, 157, 161, 162, 180, 203, 242, 246, 252, 261, 262
Snow 197, 203, 206, 262
Snyder 45, 114, 124, 262
sociology 33
South 79, 95, 99, 118, 212, 262
Soviet 16, 30, 59, 64, 73, 89, 115, 170, 171
Sparta 49
Spearin 28, 183, 184, 262
Spoehr 178, 262
standards 15, 26, 31, 44, 82, 108, 117, 132, 134, 136, 137, 152, 159, 173, 213, 214
stand-by reserve 17, 226
Stilwell 263
strategy 51, 52, 59, 61, 128, 173, 185, 187, 194, 230

subjective civilian control 45
Swed 183, 263
Taibl 73, 263
Taylor 4, 9, 14, 15, 16, 17, 18, 19, 28, 29, 56, 57, 58, 59, 60, 62, 64, 65, 66, 68, 71, 76, 79, 88, 119, 127, 128, 135, 169, 182, 183, 251, 255, 259, 263, 264, 266
teacher 39, 151
technology 11, 16, 21, 26, 30, 31, 32, 33, 35, 38, 40, 41, 50, 74, 80, 89, 90, 116, 144, 157, 158, 166, 168, 169, 171, 173, 175, 179, 181, 187, 191, 192, 194, 196, 197, 198, 199, 200, 201, 202, 203, 204, 205, 206, 207, 208, 209, 211, 213, 214, 216, 217, 219, 220, 221, 225, 226, 227, 228, 231, 232, 235
The President's Commission on an All-Volunteer Force 51, 61
Thompson 10, 23, 24, 171, 172, 185, 251, 263
Thucydides 21, 82, 263
Tirpak 153, 263
Tompkins 8, 263
Total Force 17, 18, 76, 79, 235, 236
Total Force Policy 17, 235, 236
Travis 173, 264
true volunteers 66, 81, 96, 102, 110, 195, 205, 206
Truman 29, 59, 101, 169
Tsai 258
Tsouni 245
U.S. Army Public Affairs 40, 136, 265
U.S. v. O'Brien 50
Ukraine 6, 170
Ulrich 4, 9, 18, 29, 34, 79, 171, 264
unemployment 19, 105, 124, 154, 246
Unger 55, 58, 59, 264
United Kingdom 7
United States Census Bureau 3, 208, 210, 264
Universal Military Training
UMT 59, 241
USMC 39, 65
Vasquez 87, 266
Vego 180, 266

Vespa 128, 266
veteran 74, 86, 87, 96, 103, 110, 113, 124, 126, 129, 147, 150, 151, 162, 167, 169, 171, 179, 192, 218, 220, 224, 231, 237
Vietnam 7, 16, 22, 23, 30, 50, 58, 60, 64, 65, 70, 73, 80, 86, 87, 92, 112, 115, 117, 119, 124, 125, 128, 134, 165, 167, 171, 172, 176, 181, 226, 244, 251, 260
Vietnam War 22, 50, 58, 60, 65, 70, 80, 86, 119, 125, 134, 181, 226, 244
Women's Army Corps WAC 22, 241
Wagner Group 170, 256
Wankhede 209, 266
Warner 78, 85, 105, 266
warrior caste 10, 11, 19, 33, 35, 87, 97, 101, 107, 117, 191, 215, 231
Washington 2, 3, 4, 7, 8, 10, 12, 17, 29, 31, 48, 52, 74, 75, 77, 85, 87, 89, 94, 123, 128, 133, 136, 137, 181, 210, 212, 242, 245, 246, 247, 248, 249, 250, 251, 252, 253, 254, 257, 258, 259, 260, 261, 263, 264, 266
Women Accepted Voluntary Emergency Service WAVES 22, 58, 126, 241
Weigley 51, 59, 60, 266
welfare 15, 115, 132
Wellman 9, 18, 266
Wenig 10, 24, 254
Westmorland 180
Weyland 92
white 113, 122, 123, 129, 139, 143, 148, 244
Whitsel 245
Wilkerson14, 64, 266
Williams 20, 25, 32, 92, 93, 157, 158, 174, 175, 177, 197, 213, 256, 266, 267
Wilson 22, 53, 54, 243, 267
Winkie 4, 40, 136, 178, 186, 210, 267
Wittes 173, 174, 267
wokeness 1, 3, 123, 243
women 14, 18, 22, 37, 78, 111, 126, 127, 128, 129, 130, 131, 139, 142, 143, 145, 146, 148, 152, 226, 227, 249, 252, 257, 259, 261
Women's Army Corps WAC 58, 126
Work Project Administration WPA 55
workforce 122, 127, 128, 130, 178, 248
World War I 22, 50, 53, 54, 55, 56, 57, 113, 263

World War II 22, 25, 29, 56, 58, 64, 80, 87, 90, 93, 107, 119, 126, 128, 133, 137, 157, 159, 171, 226, 228, 263, 266
Worsencroft 22, 60, 70, 267
Yoo 86, 247
Yuengert 13, 163, 267

www.ingramcontent.com/pod-product-compliance
Lightning Source LLC
Chambersburg PA
CBHW041039050426
42337CB00059B/5060